Transformations of Post-Communist States

Transformations of Post-Communist States

Edited by

Wojciech Kostecki
Senior Research Fellow
Institute for Political Studies
Polish Academy of Sciences
Warsaw

Katarzyna Żukrowska
Professor
Institute of Development and Strategic Studies
Ministry of Economy
Warsaw

and

Bogdan J. Góralczyk
Counsellor for Press and Political Affairs
Polish Embassy
Budapest

First published in Great Britain 2000 by
MACMILLAN PRESS LTD
Houndmills, Basingstoke, Hampshire RG21 6XS and London
Companies and representatives throughout the world

A catalogue record for this book is available from the British Library.

ISBN 0–333–74876–X

 First published in the United States of America 2000 by
ST. MARTIN'S PRESS, INC.,
Scholarly and Reference Division,
175 Fifth Avenue, New York, N.Y. 10010

ISBN 0–312–23002–8

Library of Congress Cataloging-in-Publication Data
Transformations of post-communist states / edited by Wojciech Kostecki,
Katarzyna Zukrowska and Bogdan J. Góralczyk.
    p. cm.
Includes bibliographical references and index.
ISBN 0–312–23002–8 (cloth)
    1. Europe, Eastern—Politics and government—1989—Case studies.
2. Post-communism—Europe, Eastern—Case studies. 3. Democracy—Europe,
Eastern—Case studies. I. Kostecki, Wojciech. II. Zukrowska, Katarzyna.
III. Góralczyk, Bogdan

JN96.A58 A732   1999
320.947'09'049—dc21
                                                                99–050363

This book is printed on paper suitable for recycling and made from fully managed and sustained
forest sources.

10   9   8   7   6   5   4   3   2   1
09   08   07   06   05   04   03   02   01   00

Printed and bound in Great Britain by Antony Rowe Ltd, Chippenham, Wiltshire

Contents

PART III
Democratic victory and the legacy of communism

CONCLUSION

Acknowledgements

Work on this book began as a part of my responsibilities as guest scholar at the Copenhagen Peace Research Institute (COPRI, formerly Centre for Peace and Conflict Research) in 1993–94, and was continued at my home Institute for Political Studies of the Polish Academy of Sciences in Warsaw.

Among the many people to whom I am indebted for assistance in its preparation and publication I must single out Professor Håkan Wiberg, the director of COPRI, for his inspiration and advice, and my colleagues from the Research Team on Changes in Eastern Europe who took part in our workshops. Special thanks are due to my friends and co-editors, Katarzyna Zukrowska and Bogdan Goralczyk, for their help in working out the concept of the book and in the selection and editing of the texts. Andrew Caldwell performed the hard task of pruning and tidying the language of 15 different authors, and Tor Nonnegaard, Paul Roe and Mads Vöge contributed greatly to the final shape of the book.

Wojciech Kostecki

Notes on the contributors

Attila Agh is Professor of Political Science at the University of Economic Sciences, Budapest and research director of a major project on East-Central European Parliaments. Research interest: theoretical questions of political science and international relations. Editor of Budapest Papers on *Democratic Transition* (over 200 issues) and books: *The Emergence of East-Central European Parliaments: The First Steps* (Budapest 1994), *Democratization and Europeanization in Hungary: The First Parliament* (1990–1994) (Budapest 1995), *Parliaments and Organized Interests in Central Europe: The Second Steps* (Budapest 1996).

Leszek Balcerowicz is the leader of Union of Freedom in Poland. Ph.D. in economics. Deputy Prime Minister and Minister of Finance in two Polish governments (September 1989 – December 1991). The author of the economic plan for Poland known as the 'Balcerowicz Plan'. Since 1972 lecturer of the Warsaw School of Economics (SGH, previously known as SGPiS). The author of over 100 articles and books on economic issues. Recent publications: *Wolnosc i rozwoj: Ekonomia wolnego rynku* [Freedom and development: Free market economy] (Warsaw 1995) and *Socialism, Capitalism, Transformation* (Budapest–London 1995).

Jozsef Bayer is head of the Department of Political Science, University ELTE, Budapest. Studied in Hungary, Germany and the USA. Ph.D. since 1981, *habilitation* in Political Science in 1995. Guest professor for three years at Department of Political Science, University of Vienna. Major fields: political philosophy and political theory, comparative politics. Recently published 'Nationalismen in Ostmitteleuropa', in: *Krieg und gewaltfreie Konfliktlösung: Friedensbericht 1994* (Zürich 1994).

Sergei Bolshakov is senior research fellow, Institute of US and Canadian Studies, Russian Academy of Sciences, Moscow. Guest research fellow at the Institute for Political Studies, Polish

Academy of Sciences for several years. M.A., Moscow State Institute of International Relations, Modern History, 1968; Ph.D., American History, Institute of the US and Canadian Studies, 1972. Research field: history and historiography of US foreign policy. Books and publications on the history of East–West relations.

Evgenii Dainov is director of the Centre for Social Practices, New Bulgarian University, Sofia, editor of 'The Insider' magazine. B.A. in Modern History and Modern Languages, Corpus Christi College, Oxford 1979; Ph.D. in Modern Political History, Sofia 1985. Contributed to the numerous collective publications. Recently: *The Citizen and the Institution* [in Bulgarian] (Sofia 1996*), Coalitions and Local Elections* [in Bulgarian] (Sofia 1996), *Bulgaria in Transition. Three Viewpoints* [in English] (Sofia 1996).

Terence Duffy, Ph.D., teaches in the Division of Politics and International Studies of the University of Ulster, Magee College in Northern Ireland. He has written widely in the general field of human rights, peace and democracy and in 1995 organized UNESCO's International Expert Meeting on Education for Conflict Resolution in Dublin. He has a good deal of experience of the Balkans region having served with the UN, OSCE and other international organizations as a human rights and electoral observer in both the former Yugoslavia and Albania.

Ivan Gabal is private consultant and part-time lecturer at Charles University, Prague. Ph.D. in sociology. Participant in the Civic Forum Movement (1989–1990), head of the Analytical Department and adviser to President Vaclav Havel (1991). Publishes regularly in main Czech dailies on domestic and foreign policy. Monthly live TV programme. Recent studies and books: *Five Years After* (University of Essex 1995), *The 1990 Election to the Czechoslovak Federal Assembly* (editor, Berlin 1996), *Ethnic Minorities and Ethnic Conflicts in Europe* (editor, Prague 1997).

Tom Gallagher is Professor of Ethnic Conflict and Peace at the University of Bradford, Great Britain. Ph.D. in Government from the University of Manchester. His work focuses on how the politics of ethnicity shape the agenda of representative government and has published widely on the transition to democracy in both Southern and Eastern Europe. The most recent book: *Romania after Ceausescu: the Politics of Intolerance* (Edinburgh 1995). His study of the role played by nationalism in Romanian politics from 1989 till 1996 is due to be published in Bucharest in 1998.

Bogdan Goralczyk, Ph.D., is Counsellor for Press and Political Affairs of the Polish Embassy in Budapest. Political scientist and sinologist. Specialising in East-Central Europe and Asia-Pacific region. Recently published a volume of translations of George Konrád's essays from 1990 to 1994: *Wielkie wyzwanie: Europa Srodkowo-Wschodnia po komunizmie* [Great Challenge: East-Central Europe after Communism] (Warsaw 1994), and a study 'Polish Trade Relations with Major Asia-Pacific Region Countries', in: *The Path to Economic Development* (Budapest 1995).

Wojciech Kostecki, Ph.D., is senior research fellow at the Institute for Political Studies, Polish Academy of Sciences, Warsaw, and convener of the international Research Team on Changes in Eastern Europe. Graduated from the Institute of Political Science, Warsaw University. Fields of interest: theory of politics, international security, transformations in Eastern Europe. Recent publications: 'Poland', in: *European Integration and National Adaptations: A Theoretical Inquiry* (together with Håkan Wiberg, New York 1996) and *Europe after the Cold War: the Security Complex Theory* (Warsaw 1996).

Eugenijus Maldeikis, Ph.D. (econ.), is Chairman of the Board of the Property Bank, Partner at the Economic Research Centre, Vilnius. Graduate of Moscow State University. Fields of interest: economic policy, finance, economic security and industrial restructuring. Publishes regularly in Lithuanian and foreign press on economic issues. Recent publications: *Privatization in Lithuania: Expectations, Process and Consequences* (Edinburgh 1996) and *The National Security of Lithuania: Economic Threats* (Vilnius 1996).

Gediminas Rainys, Ph.D. (econ.), is Director of the Economic Research Centre in Vilnius. Graduated from Vilnius University.

Research interests: industrial policy, transformation of Lithuania's economy, integration issues. Recent publications: *Economic Reform and Defence Industry Conversion in Lithuania* (Bonn 1995), *Industrial Restructuring in Lithuania* (Vilnius 1996), *Enterprise Exit in Lithuania* (Vilnius 1996).

Janusz Stefanowicz, Ph.D., is Head of the Research Unit of European Political Relations at the Institute for Political Studies, Warsaw. Former Ambassador of Poland to France. Author of over twenty books and numerous essays on modern history, international relations and European security. Recently: *Rzeczypospolitej pole bezpieczenstwa* [Poland's Security Field] (Warsaw 1993), *Polityka europejska V Republiki* [The Fifth Republic European Policy] (Warsaw 1994), *Lad miedzynarodowy: doswiadczenie i przyszlosc* [International Order: Experience and Future] (Warsaw 1996).

Håkan Wiberg, has been director of the Copenhagen Peace Research Institute (formerly: Centre for Peace and Conflict Research) since 1988. Degrees in Mathematics and in Philosophy; Ph.D. and docent in Sociology at Lund University in 1977. Former research fellow and guest professor at the Inter-University Centre in Dubrovnik, International Peace Research Institute Oslo, Free University (Amsterdam) and Kyung Hee University (Seul). President of the European Peace Research Association (1989–1993). Recent books: *Changes, Chances and Challenges: Europe 2000* (co-editor, Budapest 1995), *European Integration and National Adaptations: a Theoretical Inquiry* (co-author, New York 1996), *Organized Anarchy in Europe* (co-editor, London–New York 1996).

Katarzyna Zukrowska is professor in the Institute of Development and Strategic Studies in the Ministry of Economy, Warsaw. Graduate of Warsaw School of Economics. Fields of interest: systemic transformation in East-Central Europe and defence economy. Recent publications: *Szerokie otwarcie: Polska gospodarka w aktywnym otoczeniu miedzynarodowym* [Wide Opening: Polish Economy in an Active International Environment] (Warsaw 1994), *International Institutions in the Transformation of East Central European Countries* (Warsaw 1995), *Conversion in*

Poland: The Defense Industry and Base Redevelopment (co-author, Bonn 1996).

INTRODUCTION

1

Ten years after

Wojciech Kostecki

Almost ten years have passed since the memorable 'Autumn of Nations'.[1] Such concepts as 'socialist camp', 'world revolutionary process' or 'directing force' (that is, the communist party) have faded into history. The Soviet Union no longer exists, the Cold War has ended. The former communist countries have embarked on a course of fundamental changes. The pace and nature of these, the features specific to each country and the more general patterns are undoubtedly subjects worth careful observation and analysis.

TURNING POINTS AND PARADOXES

Today, the post-communist transformation already has its own history, marked by three distinctive turning points. The so-called *peaceful change* of 1989 was the first of them. The collapse of communist governments was accompanied by no bloodshed, except for the overthrow and execution of Nicolae Ceausescu, the infamous Stalinist dictator of Romania, and fights mainly provoked by his secret police. In other countries, strikes and huge mass protests led by the democratic movements brought down communist leaderships by peaceful means. The Polish example of 'round table' negotiations offered to the Solidarity movement by the communist leadership, and ideas of non-violence held by the former is worthy of note.

The appearance of a *'nostalgia syndrome'* in the early 1990s constituted the next turning point. The syndrome was caused by the high social costs of transformation, but also by difficulties with

3

adaptation to the new market conditions and the immaturity of the new political class. It brought about a yearning for the 'good old days' and hopes that the former elites would do better. In effect, after a few years of rule by the former anti-communist opposition, the post-communist parties returned to power in free, multiparty elections in several East-Central European countries (Lithuania 1992, Poland 1993, Hungary and Bulgaria 1994); in several others the nationalists, former (communist) party activists and open communists still exercised power. At the end of 1995, the governments formed by former dissidents and anti-communists remained only in Latvia, the Czech Republic, Slovenia, Croatia and Bosnia-Hercegovina.

The third turning point was created by the *'second wave'* of revolutions that emerged in 1996. This concerned both states where communists had never lost power (the new Yugoslavia and, *de facto*, Romania) and where they were severely persecuted (Albania), as well as states where they won democratic elections (Lithuania and Bulgaria). That revolution, too, had mainly economic roots, apart from political, social and nationalistic aspects. However, this time it was not the costs of reforms – such as unemployment and decline in living conditions for some people, but rather the costs of lack of reforms – the overall ruin of the national economy, that resulted in social dissatisfaction. Its manifestations varied from country to country. In Lithuania (September 1996) and Romania (November 1996), the transfer of power occurred through 'normal' democratic procedure. In Serbia and Bulgaria (at the turn of 1996 and 1997), turmoil and mass protests took place. In the former they induced political concessions from the communist president; in the latter they forced the post-communist party to give in and agree to dissolution of the parliament and appointment of a prime minister from democratic opposition. In Albania (March 1997), the social explosion resulted in violence, civil war and chaos.

The developments in East-Central Europe (ECE) that have occurred up to the present, provide enough material for both empirically oriented and theoretical studies. Of particular interest are three interrelated paradoxes – or dilemmas. First, the old system has lost but it seems still too early to speak of the victory of new solutions. On the one hand, the logic of the historical process says that a reversal of course is impossible because the political, economic and social changes in progress are too deep and extensive. On the other hand, there is a mounting sense of how distant the goal remains. There are many reasons for this. The factor that once unified society – the exhilaration of victory – has disappeared, and the role of anti-communism as the binding agent of the old opposition elites has waned. The social costs of transformation are rising, among them widening inequalities which give rise to counter-claims by large social groups. The tasks of governments are becoming more complicated as they are forced to fill out the watchwords of parliamentary democracy and rule of law with programmes for developing civil society projected far into the future.

Second, politicians in the post-communist states discovered on coming to power that only a part of the problems facing them is the legacy of communism which will 'automatically' vanish in the process of transformation. The economic arrears are the result not only of centralization, planned economies, state ownership and inefficient management, but also of centuries of retardation in ECE. The acute deficiencies in political culture spring not only from authoritarian forms of government over the last half-century but also from the longer history of this part of Europe. The same applies to the ethnic disputes and conflicts; these were 'frozen' by the years of totalitarianism rather than precipitated by them. This applies to both major trouble-spots in ECE: the Balkan region with Serbs, Croats, and Muslims clashing in Bosnia, quarrels between Serbia and Croatia regarding Krajina, Eastern Slavonia and Western Serbia, disputes between Macedonia, Serbia, Bulgaria and Albania, and the question of Hungarian minorities in Ukraine, Slovakia, Romania and the new Yugoslavia. Lastly, it should be noted that inordinate expectations of welfare provision by the state is a characteristic which can also be found among some West European nations.

Contradictory impulses emanating from the international environment constitute the third of our paradoxes. Having helped to bring the era of bipolarity to an end and remove the risk of full-scale nuclear war, the post-communist states find themselves occupying a 'no-man's-land'. Adding to their sense of diminished security are the weakness of the existing 'European security architecture' and the huge number of internal instabilities in ECE. The indisputable contribution of the West to the fall of communism and the encouraging signals it sent out raised expectations of swift admission to Western integration structures. The long-lasting indecision exhibited after the demise of the old order has left those expectations unfulfilled. What is more, the debate in NATO over outreach to the East and advocacy at the European Union of 'multi-speeds', 'three circles' and the like, arouse fears in the post-communist nations of a perpetuation of the division of Europe into an advanced, comprehensively integrated and stable centre and lagging, loose-knit and conflict-racked peripheries.

SECURITY ARRANGEMENTS FOR EAST-CENTRAL EUROPE

The European post-Cold war development, especially the break-down of the Soviet Union, put on the agenda a question which had been 'unthinkable' for forty years: the entrance of East-Central European states into the North Atlantic Treaty Organization. This question has two aspects. The first is the assumption that NATO is the only existing institution in post-Cold War Europe which actually guarantees security and stability to its members. The second aspect consists of a kind of test of the real worth of the post-communist states' freedom of choice in foreign policy. Their intent to achieve, first, a rapprochement with NATO, and later to achieve membership, was confronted with efforts by Soviet Union/Russia to maintain a sphere of influence in ECE. On the other hand, signs of moderation in the approach of Western countries towards NATO enlargement were justified by reference to the danger of a new power politics in Europe and were understood as an assent by the

West to a limitation on the East-Central European states' subjectivity in international relations.

Although the very first ideas concerning contacts with NATO appeared soon after the 1989 changes, there were no public declarations by the East-Central European politicians about their will to gain access to NATO until after the unsuccessful Soviet coup and disintegration in 1991. Only Czechoslovakia's President Vaclav Havel, during his visit to NATO headquarters in March 1991 – the first visit by a head of state from a WTO country – expressed the hope that NATO would not be closed forever to neighbouring countries that were guided by the same ideals of freedom and democracy. But, at the same time, NATO Deputy Secretary General Henning Wegener stated: 'NATO has no way to enlarge' and would not 'give any external security guarantees'. He added that this would push the military frontiers to the east of Poland and would give an unfortunate signal to the USSR.[2]

Both East-Central European countries and NATO went through a great many changes from that point onwards. In the former, the association with, and ultimate membership of NATO, was perceived both as joining an organization capable of providing the necessary means of national defence and also as the final confirmation of the irreversible nature of their systemic transformations. In effect, NATO's membership became a priority of East-Central Europeans' security policy. The latter gradually eased forward the opening to the East. At the beginning, it offered membership and common activity within the framework of the North Atlantic Cooperation Council – open to all members of the (then) CSCE. In October 1993, the United States presented the 'Partnership for Peace' proposal aimed at the establishment of bilateral cooperation between NATO and particular countries and bringing them closer to NATO. It was explained that the new concept did not imply giving security guarantees to the states of ECE as described in Article 5 of the North Atlantic Treaty, but an 'Article Four-like protection' through which the Allies would undertake consultation amongst themselves should their territorial integrity come under threat.[3]

The following year, announcements about the relationship between the security of the Atlantic Alliance and the security of *all* European states, as well as opening up NATO to new countries, were included in the Brussels declaration. Then came Clinton's encouraging proclamation after meetings with the presidents of the states in the Visegrad Group: 'The question is no longer whether NATO will take on new members, but when and how.'[4] As a consequence, in 1995, a special document – *Study on NATO Enlargement* discussed during the NATO summit at the end of that year – elaborated the following issues: why NATO would enlarge; how to ensure that enlargement contributes to the stability and security of the entire Euro-Atlantic area as part of a broad European security architecture; how to ensure that enlargement strengthens the effectiveness of the Alliance; what are the implications of membership for new members, including their rights and obligations.

Since then, the principles of enlargement have become the subject of a great number of diplomatic manoeuvres and political bargains between NATO and Russia as well as continuous endeavours by the East-Central European states, especially Poland, Hungary, and the Czech Republic, to maintain and advance their interests. In 1996, such countries as Romania, Bulgaria and Lithuania made several efforts to join NATO as soon as possible. Finally, at the end of 1996, the foreign ministers of NATO announced their intent to invite to the next summit meeting (Madrid, 8–9 July 1997) 'one or more countries' from ECE, and 'to welcome the new member(s) by the time of NATO's 50th anniversary in 1999'.[5]

Taking into account the complex nature of the European architecture, it is obvious that pressure for admission to NATO is not the only imaginable or desirable dimension of security arrangements for ECE. Another possibility comprises expansion of the European Union, admission of new members, acceptance of large political functions and responsibilities by the EU, its material assistance to the processes of democratization, marketization and civil society building in the post-communist states. The declarations of the East-Central European politicians concerning their wish to oin the EU have been on offer from the very beginning of economic reforms. Partially met by positive response from the other side, they resulted in a series of association agreements defining the first steps and institutional ties. But the subsequent course of events was far from the expectations held in ECE. The decisions made by the Copenhagen Summit of the EU in 1993 raised serious doubts. The formulation of the conditions to be met by countries hoping for access, especially 'the capacity to cope with competitive pressure and market forces within the Union' and 'the ability to take on the obligations of membership, including adherence to the aims of political, economic and monetary union'[6] (Joint Statement 1993), offered a rather limited prospect of full membership in the near future.

During the next three years neither a detailed schedule nor even a clear concept for the furthering of the accession process was worked out. Despite the adoption of the document entitled *Strategy for Preparing the Associated Central and Eastern European Countries for Future Accession to the EU* by the Essen Summit in 1994, there were in fact no recommendations concerning a more precisely delineated path towards full membership. The first step in this direction was made at the meeting of the EU's members and its associated partners in December 1996. The associated states were informed that the Union obliged itself to start negotiations on accession six months after the conclusion of the Intergovernmental Conference that, since early 1996, has been working on the necessary reforms. However, by the beginning of 1997, it was still to be decided how the EU would arrange its decision-making procedures, and implement its common agriculture and regional policies, if it were to consist of not 15, as today, but some 25 members.

IN SEARCH OF A PARADIGM

The search for a paradigm of transformations occurring in ECE is both a difficult and an inspiring undertaking. Such a paradigm must encompass a unique and complex process 'on the move' and involve both destructive (elimination of the communist systems) and constructive (building a new society) elements.

Various theoretical models have been implemented to study the post-communist transformation. Among them both actor- and system-oriented theories, descriptive and explanatory orientations, institutional and processual approaches. None of them appears to be satisfactory. This is because, first, there is lack of historical precedents for transformations of such magnitude and scope. Second, there are severe cognitive limitations caused by the often transitional character of the phenomena analysed, difficulties with assuming a value-free attitude, complications with accumulation of knowledge – examining the reasons for the end of communism does not suffice to understand the issues involved in post-communist developments. Last, but not least, there is a specific cause for the frustration of researchers: no theory predicted what was to happen in 1989.

Divergent remedies were formulated to overcome the above problems. They ranged from proposal of a 'grand theory' that explains 'both the end of communism and the process whereby the post-communist order takes shape' and applies knowledge provided by the so-called ontology of communism together with elements of the theories of institutionalization, paradigms of rational choice and historical epistemology,[7] through to demands for 'the formulation of medium-range theories, constituting a combination of several paradigms' and referring to developments in several post-communist societies,[8] and yet further, for a concept of comparative studies taking into account extensive historical data, that is 'former waves of democratization (1918ff, 1945ff, 1970s)'.[9]

A more empirically oriented investigation suggests that three essential components should be included in the paradigm of post-communist transformation, irrespective of the content of its philosophical and theoretical assumptions: *interdependence*, *multiplicity* and *revolutionary character*.

The indispensable feature of the changes taking place in ECE in the 1990s may be called the stability triangle. The apexes of the triangle represent the political sphere, the economic sphere and the sphere of security. The arms of the triangle grasp interrelationships between the political objectives of the transformation: consolidating democracy and freedom; the economic objectives – establishing the market economy and achieving prosperity; and the objectives of security policy – ensuring sovereignty and protection of national identity. Introduction of economic reform in the post-communist states is a matter of political decision and requires political protection. The dissatisfaction of society caused by the costs of reforms can turn against the politicians who stand behind them and usually leads to changes of government. Democratization of the political system and the successful development of the economy facilitate resolution of internal conflicts. Achievement of the political and economic goals of transformation needs the assistance of a security policy that adds to the domestic capabilities of a given state. That is why only a balanced advancement in all spheres of the transformation can provide long-term stability for ECE.

However, the diversity of dimensions inside the framework of post-communist transformation is much greater and touches literally all domains of social life. One could point here to at least seven challenges facing the East-Central European states. These are: democratization, marketization, privatization, civil society building, change in mentalities, shaping of national identity, and reconstruction of the international environment.

When the responses to those challenges are examined, it appears that the relevant paths of development lead to changes in the very essence of a given phenomenon. Thus, democratization means 'jumping' from totalitarianism into parliamentary democracy and the rule of law. Marketization consists of replacement of the centralized planned economy by market mechanisms. Privatization involves transition from public (in fact, state) to private property. The building of a civil society is a movement from the 'state as an instrument in the hands of the ruling class' (that is, the old Marxist principle) to a society based on human rights, ethical considerations and identification with common interest. To make changes in mentalities, attempts to replace passive and self-centred attitudes by sharing of responsibility, tolerance towards dissimilarity and pro-ecological attitudes, are needed. Shaping of national identity leads from 'socialist internationalism' back to Europe, commitment to protection of national minorities' rights and – in some cases – establishment of new independent states (the decay of the Yugoslavian federation, the divorce of Czechs and Slovaks). And reconstruction of the international environment results in moving from Soviet-bloc dependencies and Cold War divisions to good-neighbourly relations and desire for membership in (West) European structures.

WHAT THIS VOLUME OFFERS

The intellectual challenge of the transformations of the post-communist states has also been taken up by an international Research Team on Changes in Eastern Europe affiliated both to the International Peace Research Association and the European Peace Research Association. In 1990–96, the Team organized six annual workshops with the following topics: 'Eastern Europe in Transition',[10] 'Evolution in Eastern Europe', 'Recent Developments in What Used To Be the Soviet Union', 'Post-Communist States and Unifying Europe', 'Re-emergence of the Left' and 'Transformations of Post-Communist States'. Some of the best papers were, in the meantime, published in the collection *In pursuit of Europe*.[11]

Drawing on the proceedings of the above-mentioned meetings, the editors of this volume selected the most rewarding contributions which were then revised by their authors to fit the design of the whole. The editors also invited scholars of international renown to write special essays for this publication. The materials published earlier were carefully rewritten and extensively updated. The book is divided into three parts. The first discusses introductory questions related to East-Central European developments; the second contains 'progress reports' from various countries; and the third consists of overviews and stock-taking.

The first part begins with an erudite essay by *Håkan Wiberg*. He asks what is Eastern Europe and discusses notions of 'East' and 'West' in European history. Then, he considers the risks and chances of replacing the former 'Pax Sovietica' in the East-Central part of the continent: the CSCE/OSCE process, the predominantly peaceful character of the East-Central European transformations, the specific magnetism of West European institutions, and finally the democratization in post-communist countries. The effects of economic interdependencies and changes in normative systems are also taken into consideration. It is worth noting that this essay was originally written in the early 1990s – proving that much of the subsequent development was, in fact, quite predictable.

Sergei Bolshakov, in his chapter on the Russian approach to ECE, goes back to the changes which started within Mikhail Gorbachev's *perestroika* and *glasnost.* The argument that changes advocated by Gorbachev and his team as a long-range modernization program for the Soviet society included, as a crucial element, the reform of economic and political life in the East-Central European countries, is elaborated. Next, Bolshakov analyses the impact of the Soviet Union's dissolution, and the emergence (or rather re-emergence) of Russia and its foreign policy. In his conclusion, he expresses some doubts as to whether 'Yeltsinism', as a definite political category, is capable of negatively influencing the events in ECE or limiting the pace of its reform in different directions. As a whole, this chapter presents the Russian perspective on the subject, a viewpoint which is often neglected.

In the foreseeable future, the extension of NATO as a collective defence structure, interlocking with cooperative security arrangements of the OSCE type, supported by special relations with Russia, seems to be the only reasonable way to secure East-Central European countries, not only against real or potential threats, but also to put an end to the centuries-long division of the continent, argues *Janusz Stefanowicz.* He refers to investigations indicating that the following threats are perceived as the most serious in ECE: internal threats caused by a lack of stability, external threats of a political and economic nature, internal military threats of civil war or strife of a similar nature, threats connected with minority issues, organized crime transcending national borders or rackets undertaken by undisciplined and badly nourished neighbouring forces, and classic external military threats – conventional rather than nuclear in nature.

The social explosion in Albania in early 1997 made the task of *Terence Duffy* especially difficult. In his extensively documented chapter on Albania he shows that it is the country with the longest route to travel – from rigid Stalinism to democracy, effective economy and ethnic peace. He looks, too, at the problem of Kosovo, the autonomous Serbian province with a 90 per cent ethnic Albanian population and the questions of Albania's Greeks. Duffy points to the pessimistic assessment of Albania's political and economic performance in the first half of the 1990s and analyses the tendencies that have led to the return of authoritarian politics. Finally, he carefully traces the events which started with the failure of the 'pyramid banking schemes' and resulted in armed conflicts, loosening of governmental control over southern Albania and massive flows of refugees.

The transformations in Bulgaria are presented by *Evgenii Dainov*. From the start, they have attracted less attention than, for instance, the bloody events that accompanied the overthrow of the Ceausescu regime in Romania. The author analyses developments in the Bulgarian political system and division of power, progress in civil society building, evolution of public opinion, international challenges, achievements of ethnic policy and the dramatic economic regress. The chapter also covers the turmoil and events of 1996–97 that have led to the stepping down of the post-communist government. Judged by the standards of post-communist states most advanced in introducing reforms, Bulgaria's efforts must be assessed as a failure so far. But judged by the standards of neighbouring countries – Dainov concludes – it has been, at least, a partial success.

The chapter by *Ivan Gabal* focuses on the most dramatic events of the post-1989 history of the Czechs and Slovaks: the split of Czechoslovakia into two states: the Czech Republic and Slovakia. His account is based on a wealth of empirical data culled from public opinion surveys. Gabal begins with a summary of the 1990–92 period, which supplies the necessary background for the processes behind the break-up of Czechoslovakia, and a discussion of the negotiations of the 'divorce'. He apparently believes that, despite the nominally equal status of the 'divorcees', there is an asymmetry between them: the effective successor of Czechoslovakia is the Czech Republic. He contrasts the processes taking place in both countries in the domain of public opinion, building state institutions, arranging international affiliations, and economic development.

Eugenijus Maldeikis and *Gediminas Rainys* begin with examining the question whether the three Baltic states – Lithuania, Latvia and Estonia – constitute a geographical area or a zone of common interests. They then describe the new international environment of the Baltic states, processes of democratization, economic transformation, nation-building and moral and psychological revolution. The problem of national minorities is highlighted, since Estonians comprise 64.1 per cent of the populace in their country, Latvians 53.5 per cent, Lithuanians 81.1 per cent. The authors optimistically conclude that tendencies for political stability, democratic consolidation and economic advancement in the Baltic states enhance the formation of civil society and strengthen the moral foundations of the new elite. They also deepen the requirement for better representation of people's needs.

Among the former communist states, indicates *Attila Agh* in the next chapter, Hungary led the way in socio-economic development and political reform in the late 1980s but lost this position at the beginning of the 1990s. Agh has elaborated his own conceptual framework for analysis of the post-communist transformation: this distinguishes between structural, transitional and situational problems. He then applies this framework to the political, economic and social transformations in Hungary. His conclusion is that they have come at too high a price, though he is hopeful that after overcoming the 'infantile disorder' of the transition period, Hungary will move towards effective socio-economic and political progress within the context of the Europeanization process. The democratic institutionalization, which seems well-rooted, provides some basis for a cautious optimism.

In a chapter on Poland, *Katarzyna Zukrowska* shows that, despite a worse position at the start (market shortages, hyperinflation, external debt) than Czechoslovakia and Hungary, it took the lead within the Visegrad Group in many areas. It owed these successes to a government policy which was the locomotive of change, the efficacy of the strategy known as 'Balcerowicz's big bang', and the external support – both from international economic and financial institutions and Western governments. Zukrowska also considers some more general issues relating to the political divisions inside Polish society and the reversibility or irreversibility of the economic reforms. In her opinion, in Poland's case, the combination of economic shock therapy and gradual political change has worked. We can expect that after a temporary slow-down of the reforms, Poland will again undergo a period of acceleration.

Of all the post-communist states, the greatest degree of continuity in the sphere of politics and the filling of state and government posts was, according to *Tom Gallagher*, to be found in Romania. He examines the challenges which Romania will have to tackle if transformation is to move ahead: democratizing political life and implementing market reforms, activating the process of post-communist nation building, reinforcing a position as a stabilizing factor in an area of chronic insecurity stretching from the Balkans to former Soviet republics, carrying out a moral and psychological revolution in society. The incident-free election campaign in 1996 and the peaceful hand-over of power suggest that normalization of Romanian politics may be under way. But, the fate of the process of reform, concludes Gallagher, depends on the ability of the new regime to narrow the gulf between state and society deeply rooted in Romanian history.

The parties in Yugoslavia's conflicts, stresses *Håkan Wiberg* in the next chapter, had long been looking for pretexts to lay blame at others' doors, and the propaganda battles of 1990–91 between the Serbian and Croatian mass media played a serious part in provoking the actual explosion. This 'blame game' later spread to the outside world and was closely related to religious boundaries:

where one sees the main pretexts depends mainly on whether one lives in a Catholic, Orthodox or Islamic country. But the situation in former Yugoslavia was so complex and explosive, and the conflicts had so many sources, that to seek the basic cause of the war in some conspiracy-theory explanation is essentially fruitless. Thus, transformations in this state, Wiberg concludes, have been very heavily affected by the primacy of ethnonational and regional cleavages.

In his contribution, *Leszek Balcerowicz* compares the transition from communism in ECE with other major shifts: classical transition, meaning the extension of democracy in advanced capitalist countries; neo-classical transition, referring to democratization in basically capitalist countries after the Second World War; market oriented reform in non-communist countries; and Asian post-communist transition. Then he analyses the post-communist democratization process and describes special features of post-communist economic transition, the timing of reform, and the need for a short period of 'extraordinary politics'. Balcerowicz's conclusion is that a country will perform better in the medium-to-long run if it adopts a radical and comprehensive economic reform programme as quickly as possible and then stays on the course of reform by implementing far-reaching institutional changes.

Jozsef Bayer discusses four hypotheses that have been put forward to account for the rise of nationalism in post-communist Europe: the refrigerator hypothesis – 'freezing' of earlier conflicts by communist rule; the final step hypothesis – a situation in which 'natural' strivings for self-assertion were disrupted by hegemonic power; the vacuum hypothesis which postulates a crisis of identity; and the credibility gap hypothesis – a crisis of legitimacy. In the final section of his chapter, Bayer ponders the future of nationalism in Eastern Europe and lists the grounds for expecting that it will wane. He warns that Western policy towards the East, with its lack of creative imagination for reintegration of the Eastern part of Europe may, however, result in serious repercussions for the future of the European Union.

The next chapter, by *Katarzyna Zukrowska*, aims at answering the following questions: Why do the Visegrad countries form a separate group and is it a closed formation? Was the collapse of mutual trade unavoidable? Are the contacts recovering, what has stimulated them and what can be considered as a barrier? Is it possible to bring back the mutual relations to their former level? She describes the specifics of these countries and phases of their mutual relations. According to the conclusion, though, integration of the Visegrad countries is both possible and desirable. However, economic cooperation within CEFTA is a small segment of wider processes of subregional, regional and world-wide character. They are accompanied by huge costs, but in the long-run their effects will override today's burdens and inconveniences.

In the last chapter, *Bogdan Goralczyk* attempts a summing-up of the whole field of post-communist transformations, after first explaining why 'transformation' is the term which best captures the essence of the processes in question. He distinguishes five dimensions of transformation – grasped in a scheme of 'quintuple revolution': democratization – meaning creation of a parliamentary democracy, establishment of the rule of law and development of civil society; marketization, together with modernization and opening to the world; nation-building – construction of a modern open society; the new international environment – leading to reorientation of foreign policy and attachment of the highest priority to integration with Western structures; a mentality revolution – adaptation of social behaviours and attitudes to the requirements of the modernization which is now under way in the post-communist states.

Note: In the interest of reader-friendliness, accents and diacriticals have been omitted from East European names.

NOTES

1. One might consider this a rather inadequate expression, even if well established in the political jargon. The very term 'Autumn' suggests rather

the incipient decline, fall and not revival, of the East-Central European nations.

2. *Atlantic News*, no. 2311 (04.04.1991) p. 3.

3. *Atlantic News*, no. 2565 (27.10.1993) p. 1.

4. *International Herald Tribune*, 13.01.1994.

5. *Ministerial Meeting of the North Atlantic Council held at NATO Headquarters* (1996), Brussels, 10 December, Final Communiqué, retrieved electronically, NATO Gopher.

6. 'Joint Statement of the Royal Danish Embassy and the Delegation of the Commission of the European Communities on the Results of the Copenhagen Summit on Central and Eastern Europe' (1993), Warsaw, 25 June, duplicated material.

7. J. Staniszkis, 'In Search of a Paradigm of Transformation', in E. Wnuk-Lipinski (ed.), *After Communism: a Multidisciplinary Approach to Radical Social Change* (Warsaw: Institute for Political Studies, 1995) pp. 19-55, quotation from p. 53.

8. E. Wnuk-Lipinski, 'Is a Theory of Post-Communist Transformation Possible?', as above, pp. 5-18, quotation from p. 15.

9. K. von Beyme, *Transition to Democracy in Eastern Europe* (London: Macmillan, 1996), quotation from p. 164.

10. W. Kostecki (ed.), *Eastern Europe in Transition: A Chance or Threat to Peace: Proceedings of a seminar, Warsaw, October 1-3, 1990* (Warsaw: Polish Institute of International Affairs, 1991).

11. B. Goralczyk, W. Kostecki, K. Zukrowska (eds), *In Pursuit of Europe: Transformations of Post-Communist States 1989–1994* (Warsaw: Institute of Political Studies, 1995).

PART I

East-Central Europe:

a chance or threat to peace?

2

East-Central Europe – where and how?

Håkan Wiberg

A decade ago, few would have been in doubt as to what area to expect covered in a text on 'Eastern Europe'. The author's name would often have permitted a good guess concerning its contents. Neither is true today.

After the dramatic changes, the future is only partly predictable. Some possibilities are irrevocably discarded, some future scenarios paint a bright picture and others point up several possible crises. This will be the main topic of the present chapter.

Many new terms denote all, or different parts of, what was recently termed 'Eastern Europe'. Let us therefore begin by briefly discussing 'mental geography'.

WHAT IS EASTERN EUROPE?

I heard the same joke from several elderly Polish scholars: 'It is strange – when I went to school we were taught that Poland belonged to Central Europe; since then, they have moved all of Poland westwards, and now it is called Eastern Europe'.

From 1945 through 1989, the predominant feature of Europe was what was popularly called the 'East/West' conflict. The underlying *meaning* of 'East/West', however, was a fairly new one, at least on the surface. It centred on ideological and military matters, making *that* East/West division the most recent and ephemeral one in the complex set of East/West dimensions in European politics. With its fading away, older ones – most of which had also been more or less hidden connotations in discourses on 'East and West' – achieved renewed prominence. The common Polish, Czech, and so on aversion to being referred to as 'Eastern Europe' is probably based on *more* than a dislike of being lumped together as 'former Communist' countries, also reacting to these older connotations of 'Eastern'.

What are the strongest implications of the disappearance of the 'modern' East/West division for Europe as a whole and Eastern Europe in particular? What may we believe about the prospects of all the other East/West divisions and their probable effects? How do they affect different patterns of interdependence in Europe and their regional and local effects?

To penetrate these issues, we must study several types of premises: the millennial pattern of East/West divisions and relationships in Europe; the dynamics of ethnonational movements; and what theoretical and empirical research indicates about the relationships between interdependence, peace and war.

EAST AND WEST IN EUROPEAN HISTORY

Whereas the *physical* geography of Europe is largely constant, the *economic* geography has changed considerably, and the *social* and *political* geography even more. Two millennia ago, the overarching unit was the Mediterranean world, for a while united in the Roman empire; north of it resided a multiplicity of – in its eyes – barbarian tribes, Celtic, Teutonic and, later, Slavic. The invention of 'Europe' as some kind of unit came later, with the Age of Crusades and was reinforced in the Renaissance period. What set 'Europe' off from its hostile surroundings and provided the ideological fundament for various unification plans from Dante and onwards, was fundamentally *Christianity*. 'Europe' was largely tantamount to 'the Christian world', and the point of the propaganda was that it should avoid internecine conflict and unite against the Moslem menace from the South.

Some components of the 'East/West cleavage' are even older than the notion of 'Europe' itself. Let me highlight the *religious dimension* by selecting certain years (to be taken *cum grano salis*, as they substitute dramatic events for turning periods related to long-term processes):

- 395: Definite division of the Roman Empire into a Western part, kept together by Latin, and an Eastern part with Greek. (The dividing line went through Tito's Yugoslavia!)
- 864: Religious schism, and an ensuing Catholic-Orthodox 'mission race' (So did this dividing line.)
- 1054: Definite schism and mutual excommunication, only revoked in 1964.
- 1240: Orthodox Alexander Nevski defeated the Catholic Swedes close to (present) Saint Petersburg, largely ending the 'mission race'. The Orthodox/Catholic geography of Europe has then remained fairly unchanged. Two main details were later added: the Catholic/ Protestant division on one side of the boundary, and centuries of Moslem domination over Orthodox Southeastern Europe (with little religious effect, however, Albanians and Bosniacs being exceptions).
- 1453: The end of the Byzantine Empire and its 'special position' in Orthodox Christianity.
- 1570: Moscow took that position up as the 'Third Rome'.
- 1774: Malka Kainardja peace treaty, Turkey recognizing Russia as protector of its Christian minorities, predominantly Orthodox; Catholic Ragusa/Dubrovnik, *de jure* but not *de facto* a Turkish vassal, protested in Saint Petersburg.

This very old East/West cleavage in Europe goes far beyond theology. The relationships between state, people, church and legitimacy strongly tend to be *thought* differently on different sides of this boundary, probably due to the difference between autocephalic Orthodoxy and Papal Catholicism and the long experience of most Orthodox peoples of living under (religiously) foreign overlords. This is more rare in the Catholic(/Protestant) West, the main recent exception being Poland. While the religious geography has remained fairly constant, the political geography has often changed. After World War II, this East/West boundary sometimes roughly followed state boundaries (USSR to Finland, Poland and Hungary, Hungary to Romania), and sometimes cut through states (USSR: Estonia, Latvia, Lithuania and parts of Ukraine being 'Western' in this sense – and Yugoslavia: Slovenia, Croatia and minor parts of Serbia and Bosnia/Herzegovina). The clear changes of regimes in Europe started in the 'Western' part. By mid-1990, the dividing line between where they *had* and had not yet taken place practically coincided with the age-old religious dividing line, also *inside* states.

Other dividing lines or relations in Europe also have an 'East/West' axis, either entirely or predominantly. The *economic centre-periphery dimension* is about as old as the religious one. No matter what were the patterns of *political-military* domination, the Eastern part of Europe was always *economically* dominated by Western metropoles: the Hanseatic League, Venice and other Italian republics, the Netherlands, England, France, Germany, and so on. These metropoles were sometimes regional powers, sometimes powers on a European scale. Some eras and regions saw regional monopolies, others two or more competing metropoles. In some periods, the economic dominance was linked to a political one; in others, it was exerted over regional political great powers, like Russia, who could then also serve as military guarantors. The main pattern was always imperialist, Eastern Europe exporting raw labour (slaves, later *Gastarbeiter)*, agricultural products and raw materials and importing manufactured and luxury goods.

Who was on *what* side of this relationship varied somewhat over the centuries. The post-1945 boundary did not coincide with the political systems boundary (Bohemia and Slovenia were among the exceptions; Southern Italy and other parts of Southwestern Europe remain in a marked satellite position). Yet this dimension was important throughout; as the Soviet political dominance limiting *this* type of economic dependence disappeared, a renewed economic dominance by Western Europe in all or most of Europe followed quickly. Anxiety over such a development could be found over the entire political spectrum, from remaining Marxists to Premier Mazowiecki in Poland.

This is related to another economic dimension with an East–West (and North–South) axis: *feudalism/capitalism/socialism.* Capitalism is also a Western invention, although exactly when and where in Europe to locate its roots depends on the theoretical definition employed. We find a pattern of gradual diffusion from West to East over the centuries, but usually not in any simple process: versions of feudal patterns in the East were sometimes rather *preserved* by the dependence on the capitalist West.

The exact combination of feudalism and capitalism in Eastern Europe before 1945 is again a matter of debate (easily getting Byzantine), but two general points can be made. Gramsci saw one main reason why capitalism was so comparatively easily toppled in the East in its still being too weak to have become truly *hegemonical.* Kicinski and other Polish sociologists pointed out that the 'real socialism' with its *nomenklatura* had some strongly feudal features ('rewards to loyalty' tending to have priority before the more capitalist 'reward to achievements').

This relates to a *political* dimension: liberalism, parliamentarism and democracy (gradually travelling eastwards) *versus* authoritarianism or despotism; terms vary among analytical traditions and political orientations. It has constituted a political East/West dimension over the centuries, even if careful historians note exceptions to the rule about 'despotic reign in the East', such as the 'Golden Age' and the 1791 Constitution in Poland.

Apart from *social reality,* it also matters that this 'rule', whatever its historical merits, established itself strongly in *popular perception* in (Western) Europe – with *political* effects for East–West relations.

The West also entertains a widespread, albeit controversial, notion that the economic and political dimensions are strongly related. Most liberal theorists see a strong relationship between the diffusion of capitalism and that of democracy; the shifting political geography of Europe, however, adds some question marks here. There are solid historical arguments for parliamentary democracy only really thriving in capitalism; yet the European history of our century indicates that fascism and other dictatorships are equally able to thrive there. There is thus no *automatic* relationship; it may even be antagonistic, where the crucial third variable seems to be of centre–periphery character.

In earlier centuries, the self-reproducing centre–periphery relationships in Europe also conditioned continued despotism in the peripheral parts. In our century, one of the slogans of World War I was to 'make the world safe for democracy'; several new parliamentary democracies actually emerged in Europe after this war. By 1936, however, Czechoslovakia and Finland were the only surviving democracies. Democracy – such as it was – had lost out in Albania, Armenia, Austria, Bulgaria, Estonia, Georgia, Germany, Greece, Hungary, Latvia, Lithuania, Poland, Romania, Russia, Ukraine and Yugoslavia – and in Italy, Portugal and Spain in the West.

A great variety of dictatorships arose in several different ways. The immediate cause was sometimes external: the Soviet incorporation of short-lived sovereign states. In most cases, however, the immediate causes lay in the domestic dynamics, which permitted coups d'état, rule by decrees, military defeat in civil wars – or even dictators voted into power. To the extent we can find common denominators, one appears to be (very diverse) reactions in more peripheral capitalism to dominance from the centre in Britain and France.

Returning to popular perceptions and intellectual expressions, another 'thought figure' with an East–West dimension is 'the bastion of civilization *vis-à-vis* the primitive East'. It is found all over Europe, but with many bids as to *where* that bastion is. The most Eastern proposal (Solzhenitsyn belongs to an old tradition) is Russia, blocking or eventually evicting Mongol and Turkish invasions. A widespread Polish perception is that Poland constitutes it, as against Russians, Turks, and so on. Some Czech perceptions (Kundera) add Poles and Slovaks to the other side for good measure. Germans traditionally see themselves in that role, equating 'the East' with 'Slavs' (Rhineland Germany often counts

Prussia to 'the East'); the French traditionally add Teutons to the menaces to a bastion with France as ultimate core.

Ethno-national movements and chauvinist forms of nationalism provide new nourishment for these images and add new significance to several other East/West dimensions, and will now be discussed.

THE REVIVAL OF NATIONALISM – AND SOME ANTIDOTES

The liberal French revolution and conservative German romanticism were parents of another Western invention travelling eastwards: the notion of 'nation' with its corollary that nations should have states ('national self-determination').

As religious and dynastic legitimization were increasingly followed by democratic legitimization, this notion grew stronger and affected Europe in waves. In the mid-19th century, it was politically victorious in Germany, Italy, Hungary and parts of the Balkans, but was also the ideology of the political losers in Poland and elsewhere. Lenin and President Wilson propagated versions of it, with at least some effects on the redrawn map of Europe after World War I. The inter-war period also saw a growth in both 'state nationalism' and ethno-national movements *within* or *across* state boundaries.

During a long period after 1945, however, ethno-nationalism in Europe kept a very low profile for various reasons (another version triumphed elsewhere as decolonization). First, most of these movements were strongly delegitimized by their cooperation with Hitler, a master at playing Serbs against Croats, Hungarians against Romanians, Czechs against Slovaks, Poles against Ukrainians, Flemish against Walloons, Germans against everybody and everybody against Gypsies and Jews. Second, ethno-national movements were seen as dangerous by the nervous post-1945 states (separatism, irredentism) and therefore suppressed by various methods. In the 1960s, Marxist and liberal authors tended to proclaim that the era of ethno-nationalism had been succeeded by one of class struggle or integration (depending on the author). They were soon proven wrong.

There was a crucial difference between Western and Eastern Europe. The West was a region of inter-state integration (less 'state nationalism') and parliamentary democracy. State boundaries were losing their significance and ethno-national movements were decreasingly seen as threatening. They had legitimate channels for voicing complaints and could mobilize behind demands, form organizations and parties, protest, vote, bargain and haggle in democratic systems, with eventual results that all parties could somehow live with: Great Britain, France, Belgium, Switzerland, Italy, Spain, Denmark, and so on. Political violence was a weapon of *minority* factions in *a few* ethno-national movements, such as ETA and the IRA.

In the Eastern part of Europe, traditional ethno-national conflicts were put in the freezer after 1945. 'Pax Sovietica' prevented their expression between states; within states they constituted criminalized 'bourgeois nationalism'. (This probably contributed to the frequent nationalist language in the growing revolt against Soviet dominance.) When the freezer was opened, conditions differed from Western Europe in two important respects. First, there was little *integration* between states eagerly competing for entry into Western Europe (rather than seeking a common bargaining platform). Second, the surviving or emerging ethno-national conflicts had had little or no previous experience of expression in democratic forms. 'Pax Sovietica' disappearing, many conflicts (re)emerged in a region where most state boundaries moved at least once during the twentieth century and often correspond badly to ethnic boundaries. In 24 cases, boundaries between neighbouring countries in Central/Eastern Europe *were* moved at least once in the twentieth century. It is simpler to list the exceptions: Latvia with Estonia and Lithuania, Yugoslavia with Romania, Switzerland with Austria and Italy. Macedonia is extreme: in 1913, Serbia got most of it from Turkey, Bulgaria a minor part; during World War I, most was occupied by Bulgaria and reconquered by Serbia, which brought it into the Kingdom of

Serbs, Croats and Slovenes in 1919. In 1941, Bulgaria got most, (Italian) Albania a slice; in 1945, it rejoined Yugoslavia – leaving it in 1991.

Historically, the development of ethno-national movements contains processes with a considerable *potential* for violence within and between states, but there is no natural law linking them inevitably to violence. In particular, the problem of the *dynamics* of ethno-national conflicts is different from that of their *origins*. Most ethno-national conflicts seem to have important parts of their origins elsewhere – in class cleavages, competition for political power, and so on. Once they are manifest, however, they tend to grow and take priority before, for example class conflicts, in affecting how people identify, polarize and fight.

In some areas, regional identities are *nested in* (state) national identities as subidentities, rather than *conflicting* with them. Switzerland, Finland and *some* of the states in the list above have overcome previous tensions and clashes, making their bi- or multinationality an *asset* rather than a *problem.*

There are still many *potential* conflicts within or between states in Central and Eastern Europe. Let us therefore inspect possible *substitutes* for *pax Sovietica,* an institution which was known, both inside and outside the USSR, to *freeze* and sometimes *exploit* such conflicts rather than *resolve* them.

1. *The CSCE process* contributed important factors in this respect. It created the firm norm that *existing state boundaries can only be changed by peaceful means,* which contributed to the unified Germany seeking no changes. It arranged several *confidence and security-building measures* that, while originally constructed for the East–West conflict, are also valuable in a regional context and should be further extended. In the *human rights* basket, member states committed themselves to some important aspects of minority protection. *The process itself* provided valuable training for all in all-European negotiations. It may be extended and institutionalized to carry more responsibility for security in Europe, for example, by some kind of European Security Council, although it is uncertain how much institution-building the OSCE framework permits

without drastically altering its character. One weakness of the UN system is likely to be reproduced in Europe: it will probably be weak at handling ethnic conflicts *within* states.

2. The predominantly, often impressively, *peaceful character of the transformations* taking place in Europe was a hopeful sign. Considering the very fundamental issues for which the peaceful struggle was fought, it is something of a historical miracle that in all states except Romania the revolutions managed to remain peaceful enough to deprive the authorities of any pretext for massive violent repression. This indicates a vast fund of pragmatism and a sense of realities direly needed also in the complexities arising in inter-ethnic relations.

3. There is *the lure of (Western) Europe*. Several governments wanted to join the existing institutions (EC, Council of Europe, and so on) as much and as quickly as possible. The record of some of these institutions for screening membership candidates by domestic political behaviour (Spain, Portugal, Greece, Turkey) may have contributed to keeping conflicts within and between the present and potential applicants on a non-violent level.

4. *The process of democratization* provides more room than before for the *legitimate expression* of conflict, but also *legitimate channels* for them and apparent barriers – or at least thresholds – against their turning violent. Modern history seems to indicate that two parliamentary democracies always manage somehow to handle conflicts *between* them without military force. The recent history of Western Europe indicates that they mostly also manage *internal* conflict by peaceful means.

Yet modern European history also contains a *Mene tekel*. Most of the post-1918 democracies were too frail to cope with economic hardships and the breeding grounds they provided for populist xenophobia (with domestic or external targets). Several states are now experiencing great economic hardships in transition to capitalism. Western Europe largely had *capitalism before democracy*; Eastern Europe faces the more difficult problem of building capitalism while already having democracy, or building them simultaneously. The *birth pains* of capitalism and their lasting much longer than optimistically expected will severely test the new-born democracies, carrying considerable risks of *Latin-Americanization*, with Western Europe, or just Germany, in the role of the USA.

SYSTEMIC PROBLEMS

Interdependence in Europe has *static* and *dynamic* forms. There is a *security interdependence* both in the narrow and wider senses of 'security', treated by the theory of 'security complexes'.[1] One major East–West dimension *presumes* interdependence, 'centre' and 'periphery' only being definable in terms of (asymmetric!) economic interdependence.

The relations between other East–West dimensions and interdependence are more *accidental*, depending on the amount of interaction over the boundary of that dimension. East–West cleavages *inside* states (for example, Czech/Slovak, Serb/Croat, Hungarian/Romanian) tend to make the corresponding groups see themselves in ethno-national terms. Where an ethno-national group resides in two or more states, that type of interdependence *between states* is added to the interdependence it defines *within* each state. The degree of interdependence inside states depends on whether ethno-national groups are closely intertwined by a strongly centralist state or can arrange their own affairs in (con)federal structures. The historical experience of bi- or multinational states is that centralist states can only deal with ethno-national conflict by ruthless suppression, establishing a regime that *proclaims itself* (without credibility) trans-ethnic or amounts to a power monopoly for a single ethno-national group.

How is interdependence related to peace and war? No *general* answer can be given; it depends too much on the *historical period* studied and what *kind* of interdependence we refer to: military, economic or normative.

THE NEW MILITARY SCENE

The over-arching interdependence in the *maximal* security complex, that between the superpowers, was i.a. defined by their ability to *commit mutual suicide by nuclear weapons*. This will remain so, independent of changes in Europe, until somebody manages to *disinvent* nuclear weapons, or until the two main nuclear powers form a security community. Even the most optimistic assessment of either possibility must count with a *long-term* perspective.

Views differ strongly on the implications of the nuclear predicament. It *may* have increased the risk of war, thus far avoided by sheer luck. It *may* have been irrelevant, European dynamics being determined by other factors. And it *may* have made for stability in Europe, as a partial substitute for a conventional arms race (with even greater risks of war) and by providing mutual deterrence.

The important aspect of deterrence was *existential deterrence*. Notwithstanding the rhetorical exercises of the superpowers, the mere existence of enormous stockpiles of nuclear weapons made them tread extremely carefully *vis-à-vis* each other, whatever versions of nuclear metaphysics (called 'theories of deterrence') were *en vogue* at the time. The price for this caution was the *magnitude* of the potential destruction multiplied by the *risk* of an inadvertent nuclear war.

Conventional armaments also affect interdependence and its encompassing problems, as Europe well exemplifies. The *security dilemma* consists in A's attempts to safeguard his security being seen by B as threatening his and *vice versa*: a spiral. The *defence dilemma* for a state is that its means of defence may destroy more of its values than they defend. How much these dilemmas are exacerbated depends on several factors. The more *overarching security arrangements* there are, the more can the severity of this interdependence be reduced. Security arrangements range from *none* ('pure anarchy'), via *confidence-building measures* (to improve crisis stability), *arms control regimes* and general *security regimes* to *security communities* where war is unthinkable. The important thing about *regimes* (by explicit treaties or tacit understandings) is their imposing mutual self-restraint based on self-interest, when long-term gains of the norms surviving are seen to exceed short-term gains from unilateral violations. There is, however, no consensus on the optimal mix of tacit and explicit norms, unilaterally proclaimed and treaty-defined restrictions, and so on.

In the specific case of Europe in its bipolar period, there were two aspects. There was peace, or at least non-war, *between* the blocs, as well as *within* the blocs. The *pax Americana* managed to keep all conflicts peaceful, between Iceland and Great Britain (the 'Cold War' was not a war) as well as between Greece and Turkey (whose aggression against Cyprus was outside the bloc). The *pax Sovietica* was there *between* the satellites, but did not prevent the USSR itself from military interventions (1953, 1956, 1968). The effects of receding bipolarity are tendentially different in the Eastern and Western parts of Europe. In Western Europe, regional institution-building made the *pax Americana* largely superfluous a long time ago, except, perhaps, in the most pessimistic multipolar scenarios. In Eastern Europe, virtually all institution-building was based on, and disappeared with, *pax Sovietica;* much thinking in Eastern Europe sees (largely) *pan-European* rather than *regional* institutions as primary candidates for peace-building. The present lack of integration makes the possibility of security sub-complexes, threat perceptions between neighbours and local arms races more ominous than in Western Europe. How is it possible to counteract this?

One road parallels the development of Europe as a whole. Further work with Confidence and Security Building Measures must take these new needs into consideration; the same is true for the arms control and disarmament measures in the CFE negotiations. The last few decades have brought us a long way towards building a general security regime in Europe, perhaps also adaptable to treat new types of conflicts between neighbours in Central and Eastern Europe. Some optimism is permissible: the most serious East–West problems being drastically reduced, this should allow more attention and energy for these new problems (which are not *solved* yet).

Ideally, Europe might move beyond a *security regime* towards a *security community* – a much higher ambition. Whether it is possible within the foreseeable future must remain an open-ended question for an optimist (a pessimist would exclude it forever). The classical cases, like the Nordic area and Benelux, took a long time to build; if the entire EU is already a security community, this is true here, too.

Creating a security community takes far more than grandiose treaties, being *primarily* a matter of long experience of cooperation, warranted trust, institution-building and converging expectations. One specific problem: should the building of a Pan-European security community be a *substitute* for a Central–Eastern European one, or should these be parallel enterprises? The logic of decisions seems to favour the second alternative: if the Pan-European option succeeds, regional attempts will have done no harm and may have contributed to improving the success; if it does *not*, the latter will be positively useful.

The *character of the defence systems* of the actors in Europe are important. The more these are capable of offensives, the more severe is the military interdependence. This is so, whether that capability is doctrinally based on a version of deterrence by denial where counteroffensive (and hence dual capability) is essential, or on deterrence by punishment where offensive capability is indispensable. Conversely, the more the actors solve their defence problems by military structures with low offensive (but high defensive) capability, the more can the security dilemma inherent in this type of interdependence be ameliorated.[2] This *systemic* view, not mere *quantities* of armaments, should be the primary concern of arms control and disarmament negotiations – and the past decade has done better than the preceding ones. Making the military capability of the united Germany much less than the sums of the two previous Germanies may have prevented arms buildups among its Eastern neighbours that in turn might have spawned secondary arms races among them.

THE EFFECTS OF ECONOMIC INTERDEPENDENCE

Classical theories differ much on how economic interdependence is related to peace and war. Classical (Manchester) liberal theory sees economic interdependence as peace-promoting, i.a. by creating common interests that would be damaged by war. (There was a considerable overlap between the early peace movement and the free-trade movement.) This assumption is also incorporated in early theory-building on peace and war. In his classical arms-race model, Richardson[3] lets the volume of trade between the Entente and Central alliances measure a force decelerating arms races, concluding that *if* his model is correct and that trade had been slightly greater in 1907–8, the arms race and World War I would have been avoided. Classical liberal theory sees imperialist monopoly (in *its* sense) as a main danger: everybody should have equal access to every market in order for economic interdependence to be truly peace-building.

The classical theory on imperialism by Lenin and other Marxists views trade differently: competition over the control of, and access to, markets is one cause of wars *between imperialist powers*. The asymmetric dependence is seen as harmful to the colonized peoples, leading to *liberation wars*.

The term 'imperialist' is ambiguous. The liberal tradition defines it as *political* dominance and its harmful intervention in economic relations, whereas the Leninist tradition stresses *economic* dominance and exploitation in whatever constitutional forms. Modern imperialism theory, such as the *dependencia* tradition or Galtung's, see the composition of trade (raw materials or semi-processed goods in one direction, industrial or high technology goods and services in the other) as the crucial source of damage to the peripheral countries, i.a. because it tends to be *self-reproducing*. The success of *some* countries, for example in East Asia, calls for this generalization to be qualified, for example, by their general economic policies.

Classical Realism takes a third position. Trade, belonging to the 'soft' parts of international relations, is seen as irrelevant, or at least quite secondary, in relation to the 'hard' realities of armaments and alliances.

When contradicting theoretical positions are apparently convincingly argued, empirical research becomes indispensable. Wallensteen[4] clarifies some issues. Greatly simplified, his empirical conclusions are: *(a)* the bigger a power is, the more it engages in war; *(b)* major powers with the same socio-political system do not fight each other; *(c)* major powers are the only ones to fight non-neighbours; and *(d)* a major power fights non-major powers within its economic sphere of influence much more frequently than those outside it.

By the first conclusion, absolute levels of trade may not help much to avoid war; the second and third ones specify that point; the fourth conclusion states an important qualification: in major–minor relationships, interdependence is statistically associated with *war* rather than *peace*.

Before moving to the implications for Europe *today*, we must make necessary reservations to the last conclusion. First, since major–minor relations are normally asymmetric, *asymmetry*, rather than interdependence in itself, may be the belligenous feature. Second, Wallensteen does not factor out *contiguity*, leaving it open how much of his fourth finding is due to precisely economic interdependence and how much to the old observation (reproduced repeatedly since Richardson) that neighbouring pairs of states are more likely than other pairs to fight each other. Third, it is debatable how much to extrapolate from Wallensteen's period (1920–68) to the present situation in Europe.

Some lessons may still be drawn from the theoretical arguments being confronted by empirical studies. Increased economic interdependence apparently tends to be a pacificatory factor; it ought to be increased and political hindrances (like the former COCOM) lifted. The most important reservation and warning concerns *asymmetry*, underlined by the millennial European pattern of East–West asymmetric economic interdependence. A new architecture of Europe should include conscious and forceful efforts to *reduce* the degree of asymmetry otherwise automatically built into an increasing Pan-European economic interaction. If not, a low degree of interdependence may be preferable to a high degree of interdependence that is strongly asymmetric – at least from the point of view of peace.

This leads us to the more general question about *who* should decide *how much* about *what* in building a European normative system. I will limit myself to what seems optimal from the point of view of building and preserving peace.

THE NORMATIVE SYSTEM

To minimize the harmful effects of military interdependence and maximize the beneficial ones of economic interdependence, we need a *system of norms* regulating them – with implications for who can control whose *legitimacy*. International law defines the basic benchmark. To what extent should this least common denominator be supplemented by a particularly European normative system? How can such a system avoid becoming so Eurocentric that it increases the areas of conflict with other parts of the world?

Opinions differ on *how* such a normative system should be developed. The West obviously expects it to mean that the normative system developed in Western institutions becomes Pan-European. Other parts of Europe – North, East and South – may see themselves better served by compromises between existing normative systems when creating Pan-European norms. EU countries contain half the European *population* only; a simple extension of their normative system might well freeze great parts of the rest into 'hewers of wood and drawers of water' as indicated above – contrary to peace-building.

Yet, several studies shows that parties with weak bargaining positions tend to prefer a normative system favouring the stronger parties to *no normative system at all* – and no restraints on the strong. The odds will therefore be heavily stacked in favour of the core of the West and EU. It will call for statesmanship to let long-term interests dictate some self-restraint in negotiating the architecture of Europe, where short-term self-interests press for squeezing – under pious pretexts – all concessions possible out of the weaker states.

The theoretical alternative had bleak prospects within a foreseeable future: the *majority Europeans*, previously in EFTA and CMEA, finding common ground for a collective bargaining platform *vis-à-vis* the EU. There were several obstacles: no previous experience of any common forum for this wide group; much aversion against the USSR/Russia in its former satellites; competition between these satellites about relations to the West. Still, if it *could* be created, it might provide better chances for an equitable and peaceful Europe than relying on a Western statesmanship that was sometimes there, sometimes sadly lacking.

The price of a lack of such statesmanship may be high. Most emerging democracies in Europe are brittle. Free elections and parliamentary procedures do not immediately create democratic habits and traditions which are seen as the *only* legitimate methods for resolving conflicts; that takes a long time. The economic hardships accompanying the system transformation are of a magnitude that by historical experience risks going beyond toppling governments in elections to threatening the democratic regimes whether by coup d'états, civil wars or dictators voted into power. And the more this happens, the bleaker are the prospects of peace *within* as well as *among* the states that have recently recovered their sovereignty.

NOTES

1. The theory is presented in Barry Buzan, Ole Wæver & Jaap de Wilde, *Security: A Framework for Analysis* (Boulder, CO: Lynne Rienner, 1997).

2. Bjørn Møller, *Common Security and Non-offensive Defense: A Neorealist Perspective* (Boulder, CO: Lynne Rienner and London: UCL Press, 1992).

3. Posthumously published in Lewis Fry Richardson, *Arms and Insecurity* (Chicago: Quadrangle Books, 1960).

4. Peter Wallensteen, *Structure and War: On International Relations, 1920–1968* (Stockholm: Rabén & Sjögren, 1973).

3

Russia and East-Central Europe: changes and blessings

Sergei Bolshakov

In the middle of the 1980s, the dramatic changes in the political life of Soviet society initiated by the style and policies of Mikhail Gorbachev began to engender social and political unrest in the countries of East-Central Europe (ECE). A feeling of discomfort and uneasiness started spreading among the party leaders and political elites, many of whom had not expected any fundamental changes in the Kremlin's behaviour toward their domains. According to the recollections of William H. Luers, the former US Ambassador to Czechoslovakia (1983–86), published in *Foreign Affairs*:

> a well-informed contact in Prague recently told me that Gorbachev had said to his fellow East European general secretary at a spring 1985 meeting in Sofia: 'Socialism is a leaky ship. I do not want any of you jumping ship and going for the life boats. You must stay on board and help us patch up this mighty vessel'. Even if apocryphal, these words evoke the state of mind that Gorbachev's criticisms of the socialist system have brought about among the party officials of Eastern Europe.[1]

Thus, the first signs of unease in the East European 'corridors of power' meant that a message had been received. This was Gorbachev's proclaimed attempt to initiate a much-needed process of change in the repressed satellite states, intending to channel it in the right direction so that it would not damage or even doom his domestic reform programme whilst simultaneously aiding his efforts at a true reconciliation with the West. Gorbachev's words and promises to his own people, therefore, became both threats and incentives to the party leaders in ECE.

A reaction in the region quickly surfaced and spread, with all social strata of the societies cautiously observing a palpable spirit of change, this time coming from the East. People again began to court the idea of political liberalization as an attainable goal.

THE FIRST REFLECTIONS OF CHANGE

It has long been the accepted wisdom that real political and economic reform in ECE could come only when Moscow proposed it. That belief was dramatically underscored by the crushing of such home-grown liberalization attempts as the 1956 Hungarian uprising, the 1968 Prague Spring, and the 1980–81 Solidarity movement in Poland.

This time, the impetus for change came from the Kremlin, and it began to create the tantalizing prospect of a more open political system and a loosening of Moscow's grip over its allies. For all his proselytizing zeal, Gorbachev, however, had been rather careful not to impose a blueprint for reform in the countries of the region. During his visit to Czechoslovakia in April 1986, he declared that each country had 'a sovereign right to solve the questions of [its own] development'. He pointedly added that the 'successes of the socialist community are not possible without the concerns of each party and each state not only for its own, but also for common, interests'.

The translation of that statement implicitly proclaimed: 'Go about reform in your own way and at your own pace – but do it'. Nevertheless, the proposals advanced by Gorbachev in respect of Soviet society had not been planned to eliminate the principal foundations of the single party-system; but they did carry the implication that there should be a meaningful, and not delayed, modernization of the archaic and bureaucratic doctrine of central planning which was continuing to hamper any further economic development. That, in turn, demanded a thorough reversal, or at least a gradual discarding of totalitarian political rule.

Therefore, the changes advocated by Gorbachev and his team as a long-range modernization programme, *perestroika*, for Soviet society, included as a crucial element reform of economic and political life in the allied countries, though without undermining the credibility of the old alliance-system as such.

Gorbachev and his think-tanks had encouraged reforms in the region, whilst simultaneously making it clear that 'sovereign solutions' there had to be understood in the context of the bloc's 'common interests', warning against any overall resort to market mechanisms in place of direct planning. From the very outset, Gorbachev adopted a logic of half-measures, conjoined with much rhetoric which, in the final analysis, brought misunderstanding in his own society and was finally overshadowed by the dynamic of events in ECE – a process of complete political liberalization which he had never intended to concede and which, by the end of the 1980s, had already slipped beyond his grasp and control.

The majority of ageing Communist leaders in ECE – from dictatorial and self-aggrandizing Nicolae Ceausescu, presiding over the bloc's most repressive regime in impoverished Romania, to Erich Honnecker, once the Soviet Union's most reliable ideological ally – either feared or simply rejected Gorbachev's invitation to reform. Their own power had heavily depended upon their ability to resist change. Moreover, East Germany's leaders, who rightfully considered their country's economy the strongest and the most efficient, believed they could keep functioning without weakening centralized planning or introducing capitalist innovations. Together with the Gustav Husak regime in Czechoslovakia, which historically enjoyed the highest standard of living in Eastern Europe, or Thodor Zhivkov in Bulgaria, who ran one of the region's most repressive regimes, the bureaucratic *nomenklatura* in ECE demonstrated no appetite for economic experimentation or democratization in political life.

Nothing would have helped Gorbachev diffuse the reformist spirit through ECE more than a transfer of power to a new generation of like-minded leaders, those who would feel thoroughly enthusiastic about Soviet-style *perestroika*. The task was difficult, but crucially important, because the Gorbachev team saw ECE as the decisive laboratory, the test bed for reforms before they started being implemented in the huge and outdated economy of the Soviet Union.

Up to 1989, the bulk of the reforming venture had taken place in Hungary and Poland – in the former it was rather a continuation of the experiment which Janos Kadar's leadership had begun in 1968 by introducing some free-market levers into the country's economy, thus installing so-called 'goulash Communism'; in the latter, it was rather a native version of *glasnost*, tolerated by General Wojciech Jaruzelski to win more popular support. This strategy resulted in the release of virtually all political prisoners long before Gorbachev decided to release his own most notorious dissident, Andrei Sakharov, from internal exile, followed by the liberation of dozens of other jailed dissidents.

Gorbachev well understood that the reforms he urged ECE to undertake could certainly affect the two organizations that formally linked the countries and the Soviet Union, COMECON and the Warsaw Pact. COMECON had already functioned as a sort of reverse mercantile system, with the Soviet Union providing such raw materials as oil and mineral ores to its allies and receiving manufactured goods in return. Since COMECON's pricing system, based upon an artificial transferable ruble, had proved unworkable, almost all intra-bloc trade was done through barter deals.

The work proposed was enormous in scope, including fundamental changes necessary to make the system function with desirable results: the introduction of convertible currencies, the relaxation of obligatory trade agreements among COMECON partners, and an end to investments and trade restrictions on Western companies dealing with the East European countries. Gorbachev also tried to improve COMECON's performance by demanding better-quality goods and refusing to accept deliveries of inferior products from his trading partners.

His programme, apart from economics, boldly embraced the problems of military détente. Gorbachev had pushed for East–West negotiations on the removal of medium- and short-range nuclear weapons from Europe, as well as conducting discussions in Vienna on eventual conventional-force reductions by NATO and the Warsaw Pact. By so doing, he unleashed reform in the Soviet bloc's military institutions and their domain.

The great scope of the activities which the Gorbachev team had sanctioned for ECE brought about results far more extensive in nature than had ever been planned by their authors in the Kremlin, who had never wanted them to be beyond their reach and influence. Many students of Gorbachev's actions, in their earlier stages, had predicted, as did Charles Gati, that the risk of instability associated with *glasnost* and even *perestroika* was 'much higher in Eastern Europe than in the Soviet Union'. He wisely wrote that 'any reform in Eastern Europe carries with it the risk of being, and being seen as, too little and too late – fuelling spontaneous demands for fundamental change. [And] any change introduced by the region's authorities would generate demands for more – more democracy, more independence, more consumer goods, higher living standards'.[2]

That is why the regimes had often been so reluctant to set free the winds of change, fearing they would be blown away: and that is precisely what happened. The societies in ECE, from top to bottom, finally reposed a modicum of trust in Gorbachev's efforts to bring more freedom to the area, and they did bring it, far more of it than Gorbachev and his team had ever dreamed of.

Thus was the climate for change developed, although Gorbachev, even up to the end of 1990, had not quite grasped the nature of the changes he had set in train. He still publicly envisaged a strong Soviet Union, presiding over a strong socialist community in Europe and elsewhere.

INTERNATIONAL REPERCUSSIONS

Gorbachev, inspired by his pragmatically thinking experts, had embarked upon a virtual revolution in Soviet foreign policy that was destined to impress a profound effect not only on the Soviet Union's political relations with the countries of ECE but to revitalize international diplomacy, bringing an atmosphere of greater mutual confidence and dramatically changing the essence of the country's relationships with the United States, Germany and the whole international community.

The Cold War had begun in ECE, and Gorbachev felt that that was where détente with the West, and accommodation with the East European populace, should reveal their substance. The new Kremlin leadership had made up its mind to show the world a willingness to discard all cold war dogmas, bring an end to the infamous Brezhnev Doctrine and withdraw Soviet troops from the region.

In his December 1988 UN speech, Gorbachev proclaimed 'freedom of choice' which was bound to unleash those forces in the countries of ECE that had been striving, over the years, for greater autonomy. The unilateral withdrawal of 50,000 soldiers from the region, announced in the same speech, gave credibility to Gorbachev's renunciation of the Brezhnev Doctrine. Soviet military power no longer guaranteed the continued monopoly of power of communist parties in the region. Moreover, after the Gorbachev team demonstratively accepted the results of Poland's first free elections in 1989, which produced a government headed by Solidarity activist Tadeusz Mazowiecki, it was only a matter of time until opposition forces in the other countries of the dissolving bloc would also challenge the system.

The German question turned out to be the most striking example of the international dissemination of the Gorbachev revolution in foreign policy. Although, in early 1989, Soviet policy toward Germany still seemed to be on a traditional track (and nothing during West German Chancellor Helmut Kohl's visit to Moscow, in October 1988, indicated any hint of a change in the Soviet approach toward the GDR or the problem of German unification), by June

1989, however, the potential for such change was already implicit. It found its expression in the joint declaration signed by both governments on the occasion of Gorbachev's visit to Bonn after six months of negotiations. That declaration not only mentioned 'the right of all peoples and states to determine freely their destiny', but also the 'unqualified recognition of the integrity and security of every state and its right to choose freely its own political and social system as well as unqualified adherence to the norms and principles of international law, especially respect for the right of peoples to self-determination'.[3]

The declaration had actually referred to the possibility of German self-determination through free elections. It also constituted, as Karl Kaiser of the Research Institute of the Deutsche Gesellschaft für Auswärtige Politik in Bonn put it, 'an affront to the East German regime and thus heightened the insecurity of the state's political class', questioning the further existence of the GDR.[4] A paradox had appeared: the East German elite either did not believe in any coming changes or merely rejected the very thought of them, but on a grass-roots level, the odour of change was already hanging in the air.

Late in the summer of 1989, the flight of the GDR's citizens turned into a mass exodus. When Gorbachev attended the GDR's 40th anniversary celebration in early October, the collapse of the East German state was just around the corner. Finally, in November 1989, with thousands of East Germans fleeing from East to West and a rising groundswell of opinion favouring unification, the Honnecker regime fell, thus making German unification a sudden political reality, not just a political phantom.

There had been, though, some diplomatic battles behind the unification idea, because Gorbachev wanted a new Germany as a neutral state, but by February 1990 the Soviet Union came to agree with German unity according to the principles of the 1975 Helsinki Final Act, giving, therefore, Germany a right to choose its alliance and to direct the process.

For the Gorbachev team, it was not an easy solution: a vision of a united Germany as a NATO member, seen in a geopolitical perspective, meant the virtual abandonment of a long-held dogma of Soviet foreign policy. By betraying his most credible ally in favour of contributing to the credibility of East–West détente, Gorbachev had certainly set the whole generation of political and military conservatives in the Soviet Union and many countries of ECE against him, although NATO had done its best to make German membership look more acceptable to the Soviet Union, re-defining its role in a post-Cold War order. This had become evident in NATO's 'Message from Turnberry', announced at the North Atlantic Council meeting on 7–8 June 1990, in which the Alliance stressed its determination to build a European order based upon freedom, the rule of law and democracy, and offered to extend 'the hand of friendship and cooperation' to the Soviet Union and all other European countries. Such policy line was repeated by the London Declaration of 6 July 1990, at the NATO summit, making it the alliance's new practical orientation.[5]

Together with the successful conclusion of CFE talks and negotiations on Confidence and Security Building Measures in Europe, along with the signing of the resulting documents in November 1990, the unification of Germany represented a milestone in the whole *perestroika* of Cold War diplomacy, a change which had seriously contributed to the prospects for international peace and security. It equally constituted a giant step in freeing all ECE from diplomatic isolation.

Almost simultaneously, two other fundamental events had staggered the world – the violent anti-Ceausescu popular revolt, on the eve of 1990, in Romania, and the Velvet Revolution in Czechoslovakia. Opposites in method, they were common in substance, both resolutely rejecting the old autocratic power and further dissolving the Soviet alliance-system and rendering it incurably fractured.

ECE had been often regarded by the United States and its allies during the Cold War as a 'forgotten region',[6] or a region 'of secondary importance in itself and of primary importance only in so far as it represented an adjunct of Soviet power'.[7] After the cascade of anti-Communist upheavals of 1989–90, inspired by Gorbachev's doctrine of *perestroika*, ECE increased, unfortunately not for long, in its importance for the Western powers. The Bush Administration had even sided with Congress by passing the Support for East European Democracy (SEED) Act of 1989, which still governs many American political actions toward the region.

Western interest developed as a result of the continuing liberalization of ECE but it also revealed all the shortcomings of previous 'Eastern policies' of the West, notably the United States. The latter did not expect revolutions in ECE. SEED came as a partial answer to events and initially was directed only toward Poland and Hungary, later embracing Czechoslovakia. It proposed activities which have since been undertaken by more than thirty US government agencies, frequently working in conjunction with the American private sector and advocating private-sector development. The brightest proposition, so far, involved the deployment of the Peace Corps to ECE. With foreign aid growing increasingly unpopular in the United States, even for fiscal year 1993 – thus, well after the break-up of the Soviet Union – the Bush Administration requested nearly ten times more for military aid throughout the world (well over $4 billion) than for bilateral assistance to ECE ($450 million).[8]

Many observers admitted in those times that, while carefully tracing the painful transition of ECE from political totalitarianism and central planning systems to a democratic and free-market society in 1991–93, political leaders and economic experts in the West were either rather restrained in their appraisals and expectations, or tried to impose on the newly democratizing nations models of development which, in practice, entailed mass pauperization of the population. John Kenneth Galbraith pointed out that, in calling for ECE to move quickly toward privatization and the free market, the West was 'urging on it a kind of capitalism that we would not care to risk'.[9]

Nevertheless, a process of international recognition of changes in the region, initiated by the Gorbachev's 'new thinking', as a new and developing *modus vivendi*, not as another passing pseudo-reform, had been gaining acceptance and the nations of ECE gradually began to feel confident enough to demand more of Western support in strengthening their security and their reviving identity as part of the European civilizational cradle.

THE SOVIET UNION'S DISSOLUTION AND EMERGENCE OF RUSSIA: THE IMPACT ON REGIONAL REVOLUTIONS

Gorbachev and his team had greatly underestimated the consequences of the changes they propagated for the whole system and society, including their own. The reforms, carried out at an increasingly rapid pace after 1985, demanded the acknowledgement of necessary truths about the country's condition, which had been worsening even as the reforms proceeded. By that time, Gorbachev had already been pronounced 'man of the decade' and awarded the Nobel Peace Prize. At the same time, within the country, the percentage of citizens who expressed loyalty to the Communist Party, when polled on the matter, had declined to 14 per cent; between 80 and 90 per cent (in November 1990) rejected socialism, leaving its supporters only among older citizens.[10]

Gorbachev deprived the party of its monopoly status as the country's only legitimate political organization, reduced the Politburo to impotence and stripped the party of the bulk of its revenues. Members had been resigning at an alarming rate: 700,000 turned in their cards in the first eight months of 1990 alone, among them, many of the country's prominent political figures. *Pravda*, the party's main newspaper, had lost so many readers that its very survival became an issue. The Communist Party had to give up many of its economic privileges, including exemptions from taxes, rent-free tenancy of government buildings and the monopoly on publishing, its principal source of income.

Opinion polls, held at the end of 1990 in the Soviet Union, showed that approximately two-thirds of the population of the country favoured a free market and democratization of public life. In May 1990, opinion surveys indicated that 43 per cent of the inhabitants of the Russian Federation wished to secede from the union.[11] Polls also confirmed that there existed a widespread feeling that the Russian Federation, which had half the union's population but accounted for 70 per cent of its industrial output and 80 per cent of its exports, would be better off on its own.

The proposals for a new union treaty, made public in November 1990, came too late. By that time, the mood of disintegration had already seemingly reached a point of no return. Russia acquired a dynamic leader in Boris Yeltsin, who increasingly looked like a champion of Russia's sovereignty. Gorbachev had been feeling uneasy, despite the revolution he started, and the common man blamed his worsening economic conditions, resulting from the immense social and political turbulence, exclusively on him. The rise of Russian nationalism reflected the growing lack of support for life in the union state.

In 1991, the Soviet Union ceased to exist. Gorbachev's policy of reform – apart from his efforts to keep the system modernized but workable – had turned out to be completely destructive of the formerly autocratic governmental laws implemented by the party apparatchiks for more than seventy years. Unfortunately, Gorbachev could not cut himself free of many 'imperial ideas'. That pushed him into the arms of conservatives and made his retreat final. The coup d'état in Moscow put an end to his career as the first and the last Soviet President.

For a few years after becoming sovereign, Russia seemed to be collapsing into economic chaos and social unrest, although not the civil war which had been repeatedly predicted by anyone who could possibly voice an opinion on the air. In Russia, there never existed any of the prerequisites for a civil war – the society was wholly different from that of 1918.

The events of August 1991 constituted a violent attempt by the right-wing *nomenklatura* to reverse the Gorbachev line and all the achievements already gained in domestic and foreign policy. It failed, and a half-year later, in November, the accords were signed which eliminated the state named the Soviet Union.

The international mood concerning the decline of the superpower created a dominant scepticism as to the prospects of a sovereign Russia's chances of overcoming such a perilous episode in social and political life. Forecasts had been mainly discouraging because

Sergei Bolshakov

post-Soviet society was fundamentally unprepared for any transition to democracy; so many generations had grown to maturity oblivious to the democratic achievements of the twentieth century.

The media and political observers in ECE were no exception, replete as they were with prophecies of an already vanishing and disintegrating Russia. That generalized perception swiftly developed into an almost hysterical campaign, especially in such countries as Poland, where Russia was predominantly depicted as a state in a condition of agony, of no importance, of no value, with no prospects for the future, and certainly having no claim whatsoever to belong to Europe. Later, after three years or so, there emerged an equally distorted view, that of Russia as a menace destined to invade and enslave the democratizing nations of ECE anew.

This propaganda effort was not in vain – it basically disrupted the initial stage of new diplomatic and political relations between the countries of ECE and Russia, to say nothing of economic contacts. Instead of becoming a valuable source of information about Russia and the post-Soviet states for their own benefit, and increasingly for the West, instead of employing their accumulated stock of knowledge about all features of life on the territories of the former Soviet Union, thus creating an indispensable basis for a new kind of relationship with a strategic neighbour, the political media in the region created an image of an impoverished, dangerous, unpredictable, and hostile Russia, unable to revive as a civilized political partner. A chance for a mutually beneficial diplomacy was lost.

Such opinion had been carefully and consistently cultivated, although the most pragmatically oriented students of Russia in the West, for instance Graham Allison and Robert Blackwill of Harvard University, emphasized that 'even Russia alone would remain a great European power. It possesses about twice the population of Germany or France and many multiples their land mass and military capability; not mentioning nuclear arsenals and geopolitical location'.[12]

The damage to the new diplomacies of the regional countries in the course of 1991–94 has been immense. They have been reasonably demanding from the West admission to the Western political, economic and military institutions and rightfully define these activities as an essential move toward resuming their lawful place among the Western democracies. But a lack of geopolitical vision, the predominance of an emotional anti-Soviet (Russian) element in foreign policy, coupled frequently with a mere reluctance to act according to the changing mentalities of international peace and security processes – which include far more components than was the case even twenty years ago – kept harming an otherwise viable vision of a peace-zone in Eastern and East-Central Europe. Dogged with instability on the domestic political scene, and an evident failure to introduce a model of a well-functioning regional alliance-system (Visegrad), of all the countries of the region, only the Czech Republic and Hungary possess political agendas which look credible to the West.

Shock therapies in economic life, combined with the repeated inability of democratic forces in some countries of the region to work out a smooth politically and socially focused platform of action, with foreign policies increasingly becoming victims or hostages of geopolitical games, have transformed the recent stage of democratic revolutions in ECE into a turbulent, sometimes dramatic process. Russia is not an exception, and the size of the country automatically makes this process markedly harder.

Russian political development through the 1990s has been very complicated, not always consistent, often an erratic and slow process, fully reflecting all the problems of a society in transition. President Yeltsin and his team, led by the remaining democratic reformers (Mr Chubais & Co.), have done the job with comparative success, taking into consideration the immense, sometimes abnormal complexities of the transfer to political democracy and market economy in a country with no historical experience of political pluralism. The very fact of a peaceful (that is, short of any kind of civil war) transfer to a liberal capitalist model by a country which has for almost eighty years been ruled by one of the most authoritarian regimes in the world's political history, should be recognized as a dazzling success, even if practical achievements are still far from perfection.

The results of the elections to the Russian Duma, held on 17 December 1995, show how uneasy is the process of freeing the mass political consciousness from the social demagogy practised, for instance, by the Communist Party of Gennady Ziuganov or the so-called Liberal Democrats of Vladimir Zhirinovsky. The former, nevertheless, received far fewer votes (predominantly in provincial or rural areas where the high cost of reform or an almost complete lack of such caused social frustration) than a few years ago. The number of their seats in the Duma, however, gives the Communists only a measure of blocking capacity against governmental reform activities, and not of curtailing them, bearing in mind that the new Communists are already not the same kind of party that ruled the country in the past.

The Liberal Democrats are actually not winners, either. What they depend upon is simply the residue of a naive faith, operative at a certain grass-roots level, in a Messiah who would come and solve all problems. This limited, but rather natural belief, still persists, explicable in a society which has for centuries been dominated by all sorts of Messianic leaders. On the other hand, the main reformist party, Our Home Russia, was victorious in many big cities, Moscow and St Petersburg included, where signs of reform are the most visible.

In any event, the results of the parliamentary elections in Russia should not be deemed as a retreat to the past. They simply reflect the conspicuous and logically understandable peculiarities of a hard transitional period in a country which had never experienced any easy political solutions. The Presidential elections of June 1996 were certain to be a crucial test for the emerging Russian democracy. But even the 'worst' winner could not reverse a process of reform which has already passed the point of no return.

The future of security in Europe is closely intermixed with further developments in all European states, both East and West. A process of re-defining security collaboration is going on, and none of today's decisions are likely to upset the perspective. The concept of NATO enlargement concerns not only today's contenders, it leads to reassessment of the whole post-Cold War political environment, and thus should not be treated only as an awkward triangular diplomatic game named 'ECE – NATO – Russia'. There is a whole wide world encompassing the process and a bloc diplomacy is surely not its future.

Recently some students of Russian affairs have been focusing on 'Yeltsinism' as a certain political category capable of negatively influencing events in ECE or limiting the pace of its reform in different directions. The very idea, in my opinion, is inaccurate and basically wrong, because President Yeltsin himself is not the bearer of any concept, either harmful or favourable to the developments in the region and to those in Russia itself. Under the present conditions of advancing reform, he is – or rather has been – the right man in the right place at the right time.

The government of Russia, with its Prime Minister Victor Chernomyrdin, seems very devoted to reform and has already risked too much and has much at stake, to turn it down, suspend it or let some political forces do that.

Surely, the time is not ripe to hold final conclusions, predicting all the details of Russia's political future as well as the steps of the steady reform movement in ECE. Forecasts in politics have never been a sure thing, especially when it comes to ECE which was once named by the founders of geopolitics as the most vitally important (and often equally unpredictable) region in the world.

At least one thing looks more or less certain – with the conclusion of the Balkan War – peace and democracy in ECE and, though more painful, in Russia, are destined to succeed, no matter how tempestuous the roads to them might appear.

NOTES

1. H. Luers, 'The U.S. and Eastern Europe', *Foreign Affairs*, vol. 65, no. 5 (Summer 1987) p. 976.
2. Ch. Gati, 'Gorbachev and Eastern Europe', ibid., p. 961.

3. K. Kaiser, 'German Unification', *Foreign Affairs*, vol. 70, no. 1 (Winter 1991) p. 183.

4. Kaiser, op. cit.

5. J. Simon, 'Does Eastern Europe Belong to NATO?', *Orbis*, vol. 37, no. 1 (Winter 1993) p. 29.

6. An expression of Charles Gati used by him in one of the issues of *Foreign Policy* in the 1980s.

7. S. McElwain, 'The US Response to Events in Eastern Europe', *Peace Review*, vol. 4, no. 4 (Winter 1992) p. 16.

8. McElwain, op. cit.

9. McElwain, op. cit., p. 17.

10. *Izvestia*, no. 332 (Nov. 1990).

11. *Argumenty i Fakty*, no. 21 (26 May – 1 June 1990).

12. G. Allison and R. Blackwill, 'America's Stake in the Soviet Future', *Foreign Affairs*, vol. 70, no. 3 (Summer 1991) p. 85.

4

The new East-Central Europe and European security: snakes which divide

Janusz Stefanowicz

For 45 years East-Central Europe (ECE) was in a political and military sphere completely subordinated to the Soviet Union. Its subordination was an integral element of the bipolar structure of world security and so it was deprived of any identity or national specificity in the field of international relations. Only on the ruins of the Soviet empire and the Cold War system has ECE emerged as a distinct and peculiar geostrategic area. It is characterized by a state of suspension between the West, with its collective defence structures of NATO and a still inoperative WEU, and Russia, with its ambiguous leadership over some of the former Soviet republics in the field of military security. From this perspective the region's situation is neither advantageous nor desirable.

In spite of all the uncertainties – which we shall discuss later in more detail – the majority of experts and policy-makers, as well as public opinion of the area countries, see the threats to their security similarly, in the following rank ordering of importance and probability:

- internal threats caused by a lack of political and economic stability;

- external non-military threats of a political and economic nature;
- internal military threats of civil war or strife in nature and character;
- paramilitary threats connected with minority issues;
- oganized crime transcending national borders or rackets undertaken by undisciplined and badly provisioned neighbouring forces (for example from Kaliningrad military district);
- lastly, classic external military threats that are conventional rather than nuclear.

This perception, which seems to be wholly justified, reflects the systematic development of a new typology of threats to European security which Jeffrey Simon offered us at the beginning of the latest period: after 1989, 'Europe has moved from a high military threat/high stability environment to low military threat/low stability environment'.[1]

A similar opinion was expressed in a colloquial way by the retired Director of the CIA, James Woolsey: 'we have dealt successfully with the dragon who threatened us for forty years but there are still an awful lot of poisonous snakes about in the jungle'. As was aptly observed, 'in contrast to the dangers emanating from the dragon, which united us in the West, the dangers emanating from the snakes divide us!'[2] This is true not only in relation to the Western coalition in its present shape but much more so to Europe as a whole, and especially the relations between its Western and Central and Eastern parts.

Let me now make a digression of an historical kind. Throughout the centuries, the great European dividing line – in all dimensions: political, security and economic, and, to a lesser extent, cultural – ran between the western border of Poland in the north, to the topmost littoral of the Adriatic Sea in the south. 'Europe A', to the west of this approximate line, was the Europe that was modernizing and was in the van of advancing civilization; although it did not avoid conflicts and bloodshed, some international order functioned, at least on the level of rules of conduct (balance of power, the Holy Alliance, Concert of Powers). 'Europe B', on the eastern side of this line, was always backward, equally as far as security arrangements and guarantees are concerned. This division, in spite of radical changes in the European political and security landscape, was not overcome in the aftermath of World War I. And it was one of the ironical coincidences of history that when the Soviet Union, with the Western powers' tacit approval, created its zone of satellites after World War II, the great dividing line between Western and Eastern Europe turned out to roughly match the traditional divide: in Winston Churchill's words, the 'iron curtain' fell from Stettin to Trieste. In fact, one-third of Germany found itself on the eastern side, Greece on the western; otherwise the line was almost the same.

The 'iron curtain' disappeared suddenly and unexpectedly in the autumn of 1989. The collapse of communism and the Soviet empire seemed to provide a chance to create 'one Europe', based on the same common values and on a similarity of political and economic structures. These hopes were more or less fulfilled; with all the turbulence and uncertainties which abounded, the countries of ECE have reached the 'point of no return' on the path to democracy and the free-market economy.

In spite of this, however, the vision of 'one Europe' did not become much more real. To put it bluntly, the heavy and repulsive 'iron curtain' was replaced, this time by Western hands, by two different dividing drapes. They are certainly softer, more transparent and undoubtedly more civilized. Let me call them 'velvet curtains'. The 'iron' version deprived the nations of 'Europe B' of freedom, both internal and external. This has now been regained. But to enjoy freedom, nations must feel secure and must have a chance to develop. The first perspective became bleak due to Western evasiveness as to the enlargement of NATO eastward or its *de facto* postponement; the other – which is indirectly linked with our subject and therefore only indicated here – by a similar aversion to enlargement of the European Union by inclusion of the countries 'converted' to capitalism. Certainly we should not overlook some positive movements in both directions – especially in the first one – but it is probably still a long way off.

SECURITY DIVISION

On the 'security map' of Europe we can clearly see two separate zones: the NATO countries (plus formal neutrals, practically covered by the collective defence system) and territories eastward of it, most commonly called a 'grey zone', a 'no man's land' or a 'security vacuum'. These phrases may be too dramatic when, as presently, there are no direct external threats to the security of the countries of ECE. But even if we use a softer term like 'region of unsettled security', the realities remain as they are; the dividing line once again is drawn from Stettin to Trieste.

Certainly, there is a second layer of the 'security map', lying underneath and somewhat less visible. On examination, it discloses that 'Europe B' consists of three zones which can be usefully distinguished from the viewpoint of security risks and threats. It may be also interesting to note that, here again, some historical patterns are reemerging. In the regrouping of the nations of ECE, the old fault lines separating the three great empires which came to an end in 1918 – the Russian, Habsburg and Ottoman – are once again apparent, although with meaningful shifts: the most important being the case of Poland, which has since then preserved its independence and unity regained after 123 years of partition.

Central Europe embraces, first of all, the four countries of the so-called Visegrad Group (Poland, the Czech Republic, Slovakia, Hungary), and Slovenia (recently admitted to membership of CEFTA); the three Baltic states – former Soviet republics – may be added to them. All eight of these countries currently enjoy a fairly high degree of *de facto* security due to combination of internal and external factors. Their internal conditions include a more or less solidly developing democracy, a remarkable economic growth with good prospects for further advance, and (except for two of the Baltics and Slovakia) no serious ethnic problems. Their external situation includes an end to being pawns in the Cold War, a low probability of any military threat from outside (with the possible exception of Hungary because of its ethnic tensions with neighbours). Nevertheless, there remains a Russian 'residual risk'. It is plain to Poles, Czechs, Slovaks or Hungarians and even more so to the Baltic states, that a military threat from the east could arise in the future, should Russia take the dangerous course of expanding the notion of 'near abroad' to the confines of the Warsaw Pact (with the obvious exclusion of the German Democratic Republic which has simply ceased to exist) and by insisting on its *droit de regard* in this area.

There is a specific regional advantage, through the Visegrad Group mentioned above, which developed from Vaclav Havel's initiative in 1989, in a situation where the relevant political elites were excited by the euphoria of the fall of Communism, and believed in the power of factors that united them. The effect of such political cooperation – especially in the area of common security – has brought disappointment. However, in the economic sphere, they have established the Central European Free Trade Agreement, which, after Slovenia's admission, covers an area from the Baltic to the Mediterranean, inhabited by 70 million people. We can also achieve some modest but practical success in the security sphere: I mean the establishment of a common air traffic control system.

Eastern Europe refers to the countries of the former Soviet Union (except for the Baltics), west of the Urals. These countries are in a quite different security and general situation. Their condition is stigmatized by political chaos, dim prospects for democracy, and economic misery, all of which engender great social disorder, including extensive organized crime. Against this troubling internal background, we can observe a nearly infinite manoeuvring of these countries, motivated by two great forces. One is Russia's seduction of the others into rebuilding the Soviet Union, in which Russia will have the upper hand, above all in security matters. The second is the urge of the others to find real independence and their own identity. With respect to security, varying concepts have been considered in the Ukraine and Belarus since 1991. The options for the Ukraine – to side with the group of Black Sea states (under the aegis of Turkey since 1992) or with the entente of the Central

European countries (Visegrad) – are no longer relevant. This also applies to the occasionally discussed Baltic Sea–Black Sea security area. For Belarus, the discussions about the extension of the EU and NATO to its western frontier have led to growing pressure from Moscow and to the revival of the 'corridor model', which threatens to turn the country into a transit territory for Russian supplies and a minion of Russian politics. Eastern Europe – in distinct contrast to Central Europe – has a future that is unpredictable in the extreme: virtually, a black hole of invisibility.

South-Eastern Europe consists of the Balkans as traditionally defined, except for Slovenia. This region is rent by intense ethnic problems which have already caused Yugoslavia to disintegrate and plunged Bosnia into genocidal horror, and which may spill over yet further borders. Rivalries and tensions in South-Eastern Europe involve Albania and Bulgaria, as well as the former Yugoslav republics, and on the 'western' side Greece and Turkey. Hungary may also become a party because of its proximity to the Bosnian epicentre and the thorny issue of the Hungarian minority in Romania (although softened somewhat by the 1996 treaty on good neighbourship) and other neighbouring states. There is a possibility of intervention by outside powers (as distinct from their participation in international peace-keeping or peace-making operations), with potentially explosive results. Russia might intervene; Ukraine could; Western European powers might also, less possibly the United States. A suitable security image of South-Eastern Europe is a kettle, boiling and perhaps about to boil over.

NATO: AN IDEAL HUSBAND?

It may seem paradoxical that the countries of Central Europe, whose security situation – both in internal and external dimensions – is relatively (that is, in comparison with other parts of the post-communist area) most favourable, are at the same time the most ardent advocates of their joining NATO. But the paradox is apparent for two reasons. First is the Russian factor. Let me state it clearly. The Russian factor limits Belarus and Ukraine to a strategic political choice between full independence and some dependence within the framework of a 'democratized Soviet Union' (the Commonwealth of Independent States), Ukraine being closer to the first, Belarus to the second choice. For the Orthodox Balkan countries both tradition and geopolitical reasoning may make active Russian participation in the affairs of this area quite desirable. But for the countries of Central Europe, a Russia again reclaiming the region as its sphere of influence is the grimmest and most awesome of all scenarios. They know that currently, and in the near future, Russia will be unable to regain its hold on them by military or other means. However, they also know full well that this is a felicitous circumstance that may not endure. Security is forever a goal to be achieved, not a fate that is guaranteed. So the first motif is to obtain a reliable military guarantee against external – that is, practically speaking – Russian threat.

But there is also another important consideration: NATO seen as a vehicle for promoting internal political and economic stability and democratization. In our eyes, NATO has always been more than just a military alliance. It has served as a vibrant community of democratic states and played an important role in bolstering democratic systems in Spain, Greece, and Portugal after those countries emerged from many years of dictatorship. We hope that the alliance can serve as an equally effective stabilizer for the democratic changes and sweeping economic reforms underway in our own societies.

Poland and, I am convinced, other countries of the Visegrad Group, base their options on the following premises.

First, they are not begging for membership. Rather, they offer NATO important assets in return for support for their national security on a give-and-take basis.

'Poland in NATO would be an asset and not a liability [for several reasons – J. S.]. One: in the last four years we have made remarkable progress in our drive toward democracy and stability [...] Two: we are a stability exporter in the region, which is still far from being stable. Three: Poland in NATO would be an example and an incentive to other countries in the region, including Russia, that the world of the rich and secure is not an exclusive club.'[3]

Let me add that this condition expressed by centre-right politicians is fully shared by their leftist successors – from the President of the Republic through the Prime Minister to the Minister of Foreign Affairs.

Next, in Polish eyes, regular membership in NATO would be achieved not overnight, but as a result of a gradual process of a functional rather than structural character. For some time to come, this can be a middle-of-the-road approach between the extremes of doing nothing and a costly and complicated full-scale expansion of the Pact. One can also anticipate that, in the coming years, NATO will be increasingly ready to react to situations to its east, but on a case-by-case basis. No automatic formula is to be expected. NATO is likely to act pragmatically, and chiefly by reference to the extent to which the vital interests of the United States are at stake. And these interests may differ from those of other Western powers, not to speak of the interests of the Central European countries themselves.

Finally, one can imagine a gradual, technological, logistic and organizational adaptation of the military structures of those countries long before full membership.

A large question nonetheless remains, namely, how to combine two seemingly incompatible, vital interests of the Central European countries, both being particularly clear-cut in the case of Poland. These are: the enlargement of NATO and maintenance of good neighbourliness with Russia. Certainly it is the most difficult problem of Poland's – and, to a lesser extent, the other countries of the Visegrad Group – strategy in foreign and security policy. But is it really impossible to square this circle?

Let me put aside the opinion (albeit not ungrounded) that Moscow's current objections are, at least in part, something of a bargaining chip and assume that Russian opposition to NATO enlargement is of a deeper – historical, psychological and geostrategic – nature.[4] How might it be possible to appease, if not finally eliminate, its fears? From the Polish perspective – and I repeat, it is not substantially different from those of the other countries of the area – we can envisage three principal ways:

1. Strict observation of the Polish–Russian treaty of 22 May 1992, which enriches the traditional formulation of non-resort to force in bilateral relations by the obligation that 'neither side will allow that from her territory a third Power or Powers will make an act of aggression against the other Contracting Power' (article 3, point 2). To make this credible, in my opinion, it would be necessary to introduce into the treaty of Poland's accession to NATO a clause concerning the non-stationing of nuclear arms (the Norwegian precedent) and of an absence of foreign troops, bases and permanent infrastructures on her territory (the Danish and Spanish precedent). This certainly would not exclude periodical exercises concordant with the rules of confidence-building measures agreed upon by the OSCE partners, nor facilities aiming at improving NATO forces capability for peace-keeping or peace-making operations in ECE.

2. Shaping NATO's political and military doctrines in a way which would signal to Moscow that they are not directed against her. Here, the Partnership for Peace initiative is an important move: a genuine attempt to build a Europe without competing country groupings driven by ideological, nationalistic or historical considerations, without military blocs or lines of division. However, the PfP cannot be a substitute for the enlargement of NATO.

3. It is, therefore, essential that an offer of partnership is extended by NATO to all relevant countries, that all partners are encouraged to engage in close cooperation with NATO, and that none of them is deprived of the right to seek full membership in NATO [provided that those would be partners – J.S.] have completed their democratic transformation and, sharing the values and standards of NATO, are able and willing to share the responsibility for their protection.[5]

One should not hide the fact that the original PfP programme aroused more suspicion than approval among the countries aspiring to full membership, especially Poland. It has turned out, however, to be a flexible instrument-cum-framework, in which the enlargement programme, while not addressing specific countries or time frames, has given a chance to those who wish to do so, to pursue, on an individual basis, intensive bilateral and multilateral consultations.

Poland's perception of NATO as the best guarantee of its security does not eliminate the perspective of collective security in Europe. Building up a 'new security architecture for Europe' is a difficult and long-term task.[6] Indeed, in historical experience, collective self-defence – as currently embodied in NATO – for the areas in which Poland wants to find herself, has a long tradition and sometimes proved to be effective; collective security, however, has remained an unproductive ideal. Nevertheless, Poland favours an expansion of OSCE mechanisms and institutions in the field of early warning, conflict prevention and crisis management, including missions and peace-keeping operations. And also – perhaps even more important – in full implementation of arms control, disarmament, confidence and security building provisions and their further development.

One should note, with satisfaction, that this Polish scheme of 'squaring the circle' is in consonance, if not identical, with the way of thinking of the 'Study on NATO Enlargement' officially presented to the interested governments at the end of September 1995. It reads *inter alia* that:

'a broad concept of security should be the basis for the new security architecture which must be built through a gradual process of integration and cooperation brought about by an interplay of existing multilateral institutions in Europe, such as the EU, WEU and OSCE'; new members must commit themselves 'to contribute to the development of peaceful and friendly international relations'; 'enlargement will occur through a gradual, deliberate, and transparent process, encompassing dialogue with all interested parties'; 'implementation of Russia's Individual Partnership Programme under the PfP and of our dialogue and cooperation with Russia beyond PfP will together renew and extend cooperation between the Alliance and Russia'; 'enlargement will have implications for all European nations, including states which do not join NATO early or at all'; 'there is no *a priori* requirement for the stationing of nuclear weapons on the territory of new members'.[7]

ALTERNATIVE: THE CHAOS REPRISE

All in all, however, it cannot be excluded that the West will, both on account of a wish to draw in Russia and, more important, in order to avoid tensions within its own ranks created by the diversification of great-power interests, postpone decisions to expand the sphere of integration and the sphere of security to include ECE. Sixteen parliaments which must, without exceptions, ratify the enlargement (or enlargements) would be an ideal tool of a 'stop-go' policy. The NATO leadership and particular national leaders are decisively for, but... By the same token, the age-old division of the continent will be prolonged beyond the end of the twentieth century.

What answers to such discrimination might, theoretically and practically, be found by that 'second-class Europe'? Three variants are conceivable. The first is that some of the countries bordering on Russia and the non-NATO Balkan states succumb to its suggestions that their security can be guaranteed only by Russia. The second is that they will respond to the 'security vacuum' by creating a subregional grouping without the participation of Russia, but based on the nuclear capability of Ukraine. Both the lessons of the past and contemporary experience afford grounds for scepticism in the respect. The fate of the Visegrad Group has already begun to resemble the fate of the pre-war Little Entente and the Central European Initiative is as hollow a creation as the Balkan Entente of the same period. If the Baltic republics do indeed assemble the declared alliance, it will be an exception confirming the rule and caused by a solidarity thrust upon them by direct Russian pressures. But is even this a viable proposition?

The most probable variant seems to be the third, namely 'little nationalization' in the form of a return to traditional sympathies and antipathies with respect to adjoining nations, though modified by the broader European context. Thus, proceeding from north to south: Estonia and Latvia will seek support in Finland as a bridge to Scandinavia and thence to the West. Lithuania will put its trust in Germany as a protecting power in the light of an unloved Poland, an unpredictable Belarus and a dangerous Russia. Poland will once again have to embark on the arduous exercise of seeking a balance between Germany (as the outpost of the West and its integration and security structures) and Russia. If Ukraine survives in its present shape, it will o

scillate between Russia and its Western neighbours; if it loses the left bank of the Dnieper and the Crimea to Russia, it will of course move firmly towards the West, Poland not excluded. Slovakia will see in Poland and Ukraine a safeguard against Hungarian expansionism. For the Czech Republic and Hungary, certain fears of an economic nature notwithstanding, the natural pole of attraction will be, as for Croatia and Slovenia, the Germanly-dominated economic bloc. Moldova will, of course, gravitate towards Romania, even if formal unification proves impossible. Romania, new Yugoslavia (Greater Serbia) and Bulgaria will eagerly enter the Russian sphere of influence. In fact, the policy of all the countries of ECE will, to a greater or lesser degree, be determined by these two powers which form a frame of reference which their *raison d'état* can ignore only at their peril.

Over the watercolour landscape of contemporary European security there will of course also hover dreams of a state of international happiness in the form of collective security: the UN, the OSCE, a WEU roused from lethargy and a reconstructed North Atlantic Treaty as mutually reinforcing elements of the 'new architecture' of the European order. They are needed by people and nations since they delineate a certain ideal goal for which we yearn. But there is also much sense in the warning that: 'such a system is hard to imagine because the crux of the matter lies in mutual security, including perhaps mutual defence against the danger of invasion or against actual attack. This can become a realistic prospect only in conditions of far-reaching stabilization and broader cooperation on our continent.'[8]

Therefore, in the foreseeable future, the extension of NATO as a collective defence structure – interlocking with collective security arrangements of the OSCE variety, and supported by special relations with Russia – seems to be the only reasonable way to secure ECE against real or potential threats but also to put an end to the centuries-long division of our continent.

NOTES

1. J. Simon, 'An Overview of Security Issues', in J. Simon (ed.), *European Security Policy after the Revolutions of 1989* (Washington: National Defense UP, 1991) p. 2.

2. Both quotation and comment from Ch. Bertram, 'NATO on Track for the 21st Century?', *Security Dialogue*, vol. 26, no. 1 (March 1995) pp. 65–72.

3. *Seven Statements on Poland's Security*, by Minister of Foreign Affairs Dr Andrzej Olechowski, in Washington DC, 14 December 1993, Polish Embassy in Washington, duplicated document.

4. See Y. Davidov, 'New Parameters of European Security', *Perspectives* (Prague), no. 5 (Summer 1995) pp. 19-24.

5. Quotations from the *Letter of Polish Foreign Minister Andrzej Olechowski to the General Secretary of NATO*, Warsaw, 22 December 1993, duplicated document.

6. See D. Smith, 'Between Urgencies and Impossibilities: New Security Architecture for Europe', *Security Dialogue*, vol. 24, no. 3 (September 1993) pp. 305-16.

7. *Study on NATO Enlargement*, Brussels, September 1995, duplicated document.

8. Foreign Minister Krzysztof Skubiszewski addressing the Sejm Foreign Affairs Committee on 17 April 1992, reported in *Gazeta Wyborcza*, 19 April 1992.

PART II

Progress reports

5

Albania: beyond the Hoxha legacy

Terence Duffy

As early as March 1995, the influential London-based journal, *WarReport*, carried a feature on Albania entitled 'Hoxha is dead, long live Berisha'.[1] This significant article crystallized the extent to which Dr Sali Berisha had consolidated control in the style of his ultra-communist predecessors. To those who knew Albania, this process came as no surprise. Albania is, without question, the most problematic of the post-communist states which experienced political transformation in the period 1989–96. All the countries of East-Central Europe (ECE) started from varying levels of potential for democratization and mass politics, and Albania was actually the last one to hold multi-party elections. But while the others are struggling with the legacy of state socialism, Albania has embarked on nothing less than a metamorphosis from a rigid Stalinism. As an ultra-communist maverick entity, poised between Greece and the Balkans, Albania is truly the exception to all our generalizations about post-communist transitional states. Economically, the new regime has started virtually from scratch.[2] The political climate has been no less bleak. Between 1994 and 1990, the ruling Albania Workers' Party (AWP) banned all independent political organizations. Therefore, Albania's December 1990 Decree of the Presidium of the People's Assembly (providing for a multi-party system) constituted a political revolution.[3] Subsequently, five parties participated in the first democratic elections of March and April 1991. These brought the revamped Communist Party back into power, but their stewardship of the new Albania was remarkably short-lived, as the Democratic Party (DP) under Sali Berisha won a resounding victory in March 1992. Berisha's success occurred amidst a wave of popular democracy which seemed to sweep a way the memories of communist repression and central party economic planning. However, like so many of its former Communist neighbours, Albania has experienced severe difficulties in forging a new state grounded in democracy and civil liberties. The 'euphoria' of the immediate 'transitional' period has given way to political chaos and economic quagmire as Berisha struggles to maintain decisive leadership. Significantly also, the May 1996 elections highlighted the resilience of the communist heritage in Europe's most Stalinist country. International support masked some of the most shameless vote-rigging and intimidation recently seen in any of the 'new democracies'. Thus, Gramos Pashko refers to Berisha's presidency as 'The New Albanian Dictatorship'.[4] In the past few months, Berisha's rule has virtually collapsed amidst mounting allegations of corruption. The failure of 'pyramid banking schemes' and the loss of personal investments throughout Albania have produced widespread popular unrest. These financial maladies have cut to the heart of the bankruptcy and repression which are inherent in Berisha's policies.

Albania is an 'extreme case' of a wider East-Central European phenomenon. The years that have followed the collapse of communist governments in ECE have been marked by 'transition'. Competitive elections were thrust on most countries of this region in 1990 and 1991 with the only fixed pole being opposition to the communist system. These early years were characterized by 'stand-offs' between the *new politics* and the *old regime*. In the Albanian case, the early rift in the Democratic Party between the right wing, led by former Agriculture Minister, Petrit Kalakula, and the DP majority behind Berisha, proved intractable. It was revealing, as a warning shot to Berisha about dictatorial politics, that his political fortunes were initially so mixed. He did not 'learn any lessons' and now seems unlikely to survive. As early as 6 November 1994, Albanian voters had refused to ratify a proposed constitution which, the opposition claimed, would have given President Berisha overwhelming political power. The proposal was rejected in a substantial vote of no-confidence of some 54 per cent against 42 per cent. Although Berisha tried to allay public fears by saying that he had always been in favour of parliamentary democracy, not executive presidency, the opposition parties were unconvinced. Moreover, it appears that in many of the more remote districts, the SHIK security service had been active in suppressing opposition to the failed referendum.[5] After decades of authoritarian politics, Albanian voters challenged the further heavy concentration of presidential influence. In recent elections, Berisha has simply 'over-ruled' the vote and ignored popular by ever-increasing reliance on the security services. It is hardly surprising that opposition violence flared up so intensely in February 1997. By March, large areas of Southern Albania were beyond government control, including the port cities of Vlora and Sarande.[6] As 'international confidence' rapidly drained from the regime, Berisha proved determined to use every means at his disposal to retain power. In this process, the Albanian government showed contempt for the rule of law and for fundamental democratic principles of free media and free activity for the opposition.[7]

DEMOCRACY AND HUMAN RIGHTS IN A POST-TOTALITARIAN SOCIETY

The international community had seen in the recent history of Albania some hope for a future embryonic democracy. The Albanian elections of March 1992 certainly marked the fall of Europe's last hard-line socialist state. Ramiz Alia had preserved and venerated much of the Hoxha inheritance against an increasingly cold climate for socialism. Under Hoxha and his successor, Albania isolated itself not just from the western, but equally from the communist, world. This produced a unique authoritarian insularity characterized by totalitarian interference in every aspect of life.[8] Consequently, Berisha's Albania confronted a legacy of anti-state bitterness. Predictably, his state officials, whilst espousing democracy, changed little in method. From the start, there were reports of police attacks on journalists and newspaper vendors. Moreover, the attempts by Democratic Party activists to disrupt the opposition Democratic Alliance meetings in January 1995 were symbolic of the set-backs in the development of a multi-party system. Berisha struggled with both opposition leaders and hostile press attention throughout 1996. Then, in early 1997, came an absolute crackdown on political opposition and press freedoms. Opposition leaders were jailed or arrested on 'suspicion of activities subversive of the state'. The 'independent' Albanian newspaper, *Koha Jone*, was burnt down. Surprisingly, Berisha had repeatedly stressed his reforms of the of the security system. Indeed, former secret police officers probably participated in the pro-communist demonstrations held in July 1993 in favour of former Prime Minister Fatos Nano, who had been jailed on corruption charges. Politically, the Nano affair was damaging for Berisha, and scandals of this kind harmed Albania's relations with its European partners. Moreover, foreign aid and investment will now have to be renewed in the light of the increasingly oppressive style of government. In the course of 1996 it became clear that Berisha had to resuscitate the secret police network in order to survive.

KOSOVO AND MACEDONIA: REGIONAL TINDER-BOXES

In the mid 1990s, Albania – given the potentially explosive situation in Kosovo and Macedonia – became a key player on the Balkan stage.[9] Albanian political forces helped preserve the peace in Macedonia, but still face increasing frustration because of the absence of will on the Slav Macedonian side to create a positive climate for resolving the Albanian issue.[10] These maladies have empowered Berisha as a statesman with regional interests, and also presented him with a collection of problems. On the highly sensitive issue of ethnic identity, Berisha has endeavoured to stand by his pledge of citizenship to all Albanians. Whereas Albanians in Macedonia have managed to a achieve a modicum of gain from the emerging political pluralism, the situation of Albanian Kosovars, a 'persecuted majority' in Kosovo, remains dire.[11] Islamic and Catholic leaders in Kosovo have strongly criticized Belgrade's violent repression of Albanians in the statelet. Representatives of both faiths have maintained supportive political relations with the Albanian political leadership.[12] Since Berisha took power in 1992 he has noted, on numerous occasions, that Albania would not stand by if war broke out in Kosovo, but he has stopped short of the Kosovar call for independence.[13] Nevertheless, Berisha's stance has threatened to destabilize the region with its overwhelmingly Albanian population. Ethnic Albanians make up 90 per cent of the population of this autonomous satellite of Serbia. Kosovo is former Yugoslavia's poorest province, and suffers acute regional problems.[14] Direct rule from Belgrade since July 1990 has not repaired its economic dislocation. Nor has it diminished the Serbian regime's wasteful political expenditure.[15] The political and iconographical significance of constructing a new Serb Orthodox church in the centre of the Kosovo capital, Pristina, are obvious.[16] In Kosovo, Serbia has tried to demonstrate that Albanians shall not have autonomy 'without a war'. In this situation, Kosovo Serbs – such as those in the Serb-populated town of Gracanica – have also been placed at risk.[17] However, by mid-1996, Berisha had too much to occupy him at home to devote time to the Kosovo issue.

In any case, Kosovo Albanians have gradually taken measures to establish their own state organization in a clandestine manner. Albanian leaders have repeatedly declared that 'ethnic cleansing' in Kosovo would not be tolerated by Tirana.[18] In the 1980s, Belgrade endeavoured to relieve tension there by pouring subsidies into economic schemes and industrial projects.[19] However, since the beginning of the Croatian crisis, Serbia has ruled Kosovo by severe political and cultural repression. At first victims of socio-economic deprivation, the Kosovars are also denied political autonomy from the Republic of Serbia, following the constitutional changes obtained by Slobodan Milosevic in September 1990. It is widely recognized that Kosovo and Albania will probably be united in some model of confederation.[20] However, full unification is a possibility only in the very long term unless Serbia's historical claims on Kosovo can be assuaged by some form of 'special status region' encompassing Serbian cultural monuments in Kosovo.

However, the conclusion of the 'Pristina Show Trials', which started in November 1994, and in which more than 150 Kosovar Albanians were charged with various 'political offences', suggest the continued flouting of human rights standards by Belgrade. Kosovo, say political activists, 'is itself a trial against a whole nation'.[21] Since the 1970s, Kosovar Albanians have been losing their young men at an alarming rate – as they join the lists of refugees in Western Europe. This haemorrhage of the Kosovo population has fitted the plans of the Serbian administration as it has contributed to a significant transfer of the Albanian population. It has achieved a 'bloodless' ethnic cleansing.[22] Nevertheless, the political problems facing the Albanian community has worsened in response to the crisis in ex-Yugoslavia. Not least, the arrival of Serbian refugees has produced increasing ethnic tensions.[23] This worsening tragedy places Berisha in an increasingly difficult position as he strives to support the Kosovars but cannot hope to gain at home with an Albanian electorate notoriously preoccupied with local issues. With the country gripped by the worst civil unrest in its history, Kosovo seems 'far away' to Berisha and his colleagues.

The exodus of Krajina Serbs to Kosovo has impacted significantly on Serbian–Albanian relations. Belgrade's insistence on the sovereign right to decide refugee issues 'on their own territory' has alarmed the governments of Macedonia, Albania, Greece and Turkey. However, Serbian refugees have not reacted positively to re-settlement there. Psychologically and politically, this is the end of the Serbian myth of Kosovo. Even for those most unfortunate, displaced, homeless Serbs, Kosovo is clearly 'Albanian land'.[24] Without a resolution of the problem in Kosovo, no real peace will last in the Balkans. As for the situation in Macedonia, Macedonians and Albanians desperately need to create mutual confidence based around the exercise of minority and human rights. In this respect, the Macedonian government must make further concessions. Slav Macedonian intransigence threatens the patience of Albanians in Macedonia. But raising the pressure in favour of the Albanians may well exacerbate Macedonian fears that the Albanians ultimately aspire to autonomy.[25] In this region equally, Berisha must tread a delicate tightrope between concern for the fate of Albanians in Macedonia, and the dangers of adding to potential regional dangers. The tasks facing Berisha are unenviable and may further threaten his presidency. By mid-1995, it had become clear that the 'greater Albania' issue was no longer relevant to the daily live of Albanians proper.[26] It is interesting that in response to the political violence across southern Albania in March 1997, Macedonia immediately deployed its military in anticipation of a wave of illegal immigrants pouring in from Albania.[27] As for Kosovo, in early 1997, the activities of the Kosovo Liberation Army (particularly its alleged bombing of Serbian public monuments in Pristina) continued to symbolize Albanian Kosovar hostility towards the Serbian administration.[28]

ALBANIA'S GREEKS: A CASE STUDY IN HUMAN RIGHTS POLICY

Disrupting Albanian national aspirations (especially regarding Kosovo) is one of the main objectives of Greece's Balkan policy.[29] Greeks in Albania raise for Berisha a key question that may prove a 'litmus test' for all post-communist societies. The break-up of former Yugoslavia has revealed the worst nightmares of ethnic consciousness.[30] For such a small country as Albania to have minority problems, in addition to a nascent economy, places a tremendous additional burden on state structures. Albania has three minority ethnic groups and two minority religions. Ethnically, it has southern Tosks, northern Ghegs, and an estimated 350 000 ethnic Greeks. The population is 70 per cent Muslim, 20 per cent Greek orthodox, and 10 per cent Roman Catholic. However, the principal pressing 'minority issue' in Albania concerns the treatment of the ethnic Greeks who were subjected to systematic human rights abuses under the communist regime. From the outset of the Berisha regime, it was apparent that the Albanian president would take a 'hard-line' position regarding the Greek minority. Hoping to raise his standing at home, Berisha actually tarnished his image abroad while offering Greece an 'own goal' – a perfect opportunity for them to exploit Tirana's tough policies *vis-à-vis* the Greek minority. Moreover, and predictably, the widespread human rights violations inflicted by the Albanian authorities have only contributed to the consistent radicalization of the Greek minority.[31]

The internal economic difficulties facing Albania have caused Greece to experience an influx of Greek Albanian refugees returning to their homeland.[32] The motive for this emigration seems primarily economic but may suggest human rights concerns. Instances of ill-treatment by Albanian officials certainly elicited strong warnings from Athens.[33] The issue has become an especially sensitive one for Berisha's presidency. Tirana wants Greece to take back the Muslim Albanian Cams (expelled from northern Greece after 1945 for collaborating with Italian occupation forces) and to return their lands in northern Greece. Athens has conceded nothing and shows no intention of doing so. The deterioration in relations with Greece since the August 1994 trials of ethnic Greek Omonia activists has had a major domestic impact because of Albania's dependency on remittance earnings. By September 1994 more than 60 000 Albanians had been deported and this number probably went up to 70 000 by the close of 1994. The problem continued into 1995. The Greek government's intention to destabilize the Berisha regime and thus force fresh elections was only narrowly staved off by Berisha's increasing political aggressiveness – a drift which has dampened his popularity at home and in the West.

The other side of the Greek issue is Albania's increasingly warm relations with Turkey. Ankara attaches particular importance to Albania – partly because of its closeness to Sandzak and Kosovo, where there are more than 10 000 ethnic Turks, and because Turkey invariably competes with Greece in fostering relations throughout the region. It may well be that the issue of the Greek minority in Albania will prove to be crucial for human rights policy and practice under Berisha. As evidence of Berisha's positive intent, a number of European non-governmental organizations, such as the Norwegian Human Rights Foundation, have conducted human rights courses in cooperation with the Albanian Foreign Ministry and Ministry of Education.[34] The Red Cross have also been active.

One hopes that on this evidence, Berisha will address the human rights situation in Albania as a key aspect of government policy. As armed revolt against Berisha's government shook Albania in March 1977, government war-planes bombed several houses in a predominantly Greek district. This prompted officials in Greece to urge the Albanian authorities to refrain from using force against the Greek minority, while the Albanian defence ministry denied that any orders were given to bomb the protesters.[35] Whatever the formal denial from the Albanian authorities, this incident does not reflect well on how Berisha is to be perceived either by the Athens-administration or by the international community.

REALIZING DEMOCRACY: POST-ELECTION BLUES

It was inevitable that post-election Albania would be characterized by a sense of negativism after the apparent excitement of democratic transition. This has been further reinforced by the failure of the new regime to deliver on its economic promises. Any assessment of Albania's political and economic performance since the 1992 elections must be a pessimistic one. The new government had a most insecure economic base upon which to build. Oil production, a potentially lucrative export, fell dramatically during the 1980s and early 1990s, and mineral exploitation was equally unimpressive. In the past five years, Albania has endeavoured to promote economic cooperation with the West and has been visited regularly by IMF and other international aid officials. Berisha praises the Albanian people for overcoming communist occupation and 'walking the path to freedom and democracy'.[36] In recent years the fragility of that democracy has been exposed – and, in any case, it has not brought social improvements. Unless the challenge of political and social is tackled, the new society is unlikely to be more pluralistic or more egalitarian than that which it has replaced. This process of reconciliation must also define Albania's foreign policy. Balkan cooperation has a long and inglorious reputation but intra-Balkan activities have recently developed in many domains, including common regional security policies. It is to be hoped that these regional relationships will assist Albania's process of transition economically and politically.

From the early days, the limited nature of Albanian democracy was symbolized by the degree to which Prime Minister Aleksander Meksi's cabinet proved secondary to Berisha in all major political decisions. By 1995 there was a growing challenge to Berisha which a wholesale purging of non-DP loyalists only briefly forestalled. In an effort to stave off tensions Berisha attempted to re-establish political direction to his ruling Democratic Party by a campaign of centre politics while also eliminating factionalism. As a broad post-communist movement, political fragmentation was inevitable. The challenge to Berisha was increasingly rural and from the North. Traditionally, the Balli Kombetar (BK) Party stomping ground has been in central and southern Albania, not in the north, so from 1995 it was surprising to see their influence grow so close to Berisha's own 'safe constituencies'. With Berisha courting centralism, the BK emerged as an effective opposition party.[37] All of this was made increasingly irrelevant by the groundswell of popular opposition to Berisha in late 1996.

ALBANIAN POLITICAL LIFE: A NEW TOTALITARIANISM?

In response to growing opposition, the Albanian security service rapidly became an adjunct of the president. On the economic front, although the G-24 nations had pledged an adequate financial cushion for the Albanian government in the summer of 1992, economic progress has taken a 'nose-dive'. The reality of 50 per cent urban unemployment was accentuated by the collapse of the industrial and technical infrastructure. Roads, railways, the electricity network, water purification and communications all need urgent attention. The largest source of remittance earnings continues to be Albanian economic migrants in Greece, which currently hosts about 200 000 Albanians. More recently, Albania benefited somewhat from UN sanction-busting in former Yugoslavia. However, that economic avenue has ended with the emerging peace process there.

In all the 'new democracies' of ECE there has been an anxiety that the judiciary be genuinely independent of the state. In the Albanian case, since the second year of Berisha's presidency, there has been widespread concern about its operation. As early as September 1993, the SHIK chief was called to Parliament as opposition MPs expressed concern at the scale of telephone tapping, mail censorship, and surveillance. SHIK's declaration 'to treat all citizens equally' echoes the empty utterances of Ramiz Alia, back in 1986, that the Interior Ministry would be 'vigilant and fair'.[38] Yet as early as 1995 the Albanian public doubted the very status of 'democracy' in their country. The perceived revival of a *sigurimi*-style security police constituted an enormous body-blow to earlier hopes that (at least) quasi-democracy could be secured in the immediate post-election years. By early 1997 Berisha was employing every organ of state in a desperate effort to survive.

There were ample 'fore-warnings' of the disintegration of Albanian democracy. The 'press law', passed by Parliament as early as October 1993, was blatantly neo-Stalinist in complexion. In response, all newspapers apart from the DP mouthpiece *Rilindja Demokratika* went on strike. Intellectuals and academics assumed the 'low profile' which had allowed them to outlive the Hoxha regime. The judicial system – emasculated by Berisha as early as 1993 – was increasingly controlled by DP loyalists. From mid-1995, the death penalty was frequently employed and summary executions were conducted with the apparent connivance of the security apparatus.

The local elections held in Albania in May 1994 were accompanied by violent intimidation and electoral malpractice of every variety. The biggest offender, without question, was the Democratic Party. Thugs interfered with voting procedures and even kidnapped several Socialist Party MPs. In some areas, humanitarian aid was released on the day before the elections to ensure that people voted DP. In many districts the ballot boxes were tampered with and the locked front door of the Greshice polling station was dynamited so that access could be gained to the ballot boxes. In defiance, the Socialist Party MPs, led by Namik Dokle, staged a protest in Parliament. Thus in December 1994 Albanian voters had refused to ratify the proposed new constitution amidst opposition claims that it would give Berisha too much power. After decades of authoritarianism, the voters felt threatened by Hoxha's reincarnation.[39] By May 1996 the Albanian government was engaged solely in a desperate effort to secure the re-election of the Democratic Party. The DP called for co-operation with all 'who want Albania to become part of the west, a truly democratic Albania'.[40] This appeal came as the DP's policies metamorphosed into 'one party rule', manipulation of the legal system and human rights violations. The Genocide Law effectively crippled opposition parties by excluding them from participation because of ties to the communist regime. By the end of 1996 it was clear that the polarization between Berisha's DP and the Socialists could not be bridged.[41]

CONCLUSION: A RETURN TO AUTHORITARIAN POLITICS

By March 1997, plagued by an eruption of civil unrest caused by a failed 'pyramid investment' fiasco, Berisha's Albania was effectively isolated.[42] The government concealed its reaction by banning all independent media and imposing a widespread curfew. Even as this crack-down proceeded, Berisha was elected, by means of his party's majority, to a second term office. With armed opposition growing throughout the South, and the Albanian population pitted against a crumbling, corrupt government, Berisha and his confidants resorted to repression in a desperate bid to restore order.[43] Albania is politically polarized. The DP label all opposition as 'dangerous communists' while the opposition parties, in their turn, refuse to see the DP as anything other than the source of criminality, corruption and repression. The chief beneficiaries of this political and civic crisis have been Albania's mafia – a further body-blow to any prospects for democracy.[44] The safeguarding of Albania's slender progress towards democracy had been dependent on continued cooperation with the rest of Europe. This demanded equal effort from the west European countries and from NATO – initiatives which lacked commitment. From the Western perspective, a promised concern to formulate 'new security concepts' was not met with positive action. This threatens to condemn ECE, and thereby the whole of the continent, to recurrent trauma. On the Eastern side, such concepts required the genuine implementation of democratic principles. Albania, like other East-Central European governments, faced the formidable challenge of 'rapid democratization'. Most post-communist governments have been substantially worse-off as 'transitional actors' than their 'right-wing' counterparts – such as Spain in the 1970s. The financial market was never the target of systematic elimination under such authoritarian regimes, as it was under communism. Moreover, previous regime transitions have not manifested the ethnic complexity of many former communist countries. Still more seriously, post-communist societies, like Albania, lack any genuine commitment to a democratic 'civil society' which would sustain autonomous social and political organizations interacting within an established framework of institutions.[45] They are thus vulnerable to the sort of political extremes which have allowed Berisha to 'outlaw democracy' in the name of 'state security'. It is easy 'to be wise after the event' but the international community should not have anticipated a 'transformation' in post-communist states of Albania's ideological nomenclature. Moreover, on the financial front, the international economic environment is even more unfavourable than it was for earlier examples of 'authoritarian transition'.[46] There are no easy solutions from Western Europe that could ease the 'transition process' for countries like Albania. Perhaps our expectations for either the Albanian economy or polity were simply too high.

It has become abundantly clear that President Berisha rapidly abandoned the ubiquitous political pluralism which he lauded upon his election. The virtual demise of the centrist opposition parties encouraged the Democratic Party of the Right (DPR), led by Petrit Kalakula and Abdi Baleta. Berisha responded by trying to steal the nationalist right-wing vote. As the DP encountered a torrent of domestic problems, their political campaigns suggested little recognition of past failures or of the necessity for new methods.

Their principal tactics were to rubbish the opposition parties thorough the state-run television and radio services. Claiming to be the only true defender of the centre-right, the DP has vociferously attacked its splinter party, the Democratic Alliance, and has accused it (and other right-wing coalition parties) of 'collaborating with the socialists' and being 'enemies of democracy'. Predictably, these internal wranglings between the DP and other centre-right parties only benefited the left, particularly the Socialists and Social Democrats whose popularity increased.[47]

It is obvious that Berisha and the DP have fallen foul of a catalogue of political miscalculations. The DP sought to 'mend fences' with the Athens administration to its own political cost – as time after time Athens has ignored such promises as to provide Albanian refugees with legal status. Berisha has also tried to exploit Kosovo and the Albanian minority in Macedonia but these 'national consciousness' issues have failed to find strong support amongst Albanian voters. Albanians have lost interest in political parties, whom they perceive as having failed to provide concrete policies for the pressing matters of housing, employment and shortages. Whereas the DP began as a collection of the best-known figures of the democratic opposition, it now revolves around Berisha. Berisha's fall in popularity caused the DP's ratings to plummet. For the Albanians in Albania, water and power shortages remained the real challenge for the Democratic Party campaign in March 1996.[48] They failed to deliver and the electorate reacted. The DP's response was to 'change the goal-posts' so as to manipulate the electoral process. Albania is not a post-communist state which has 'transformed' but a state still 'in transformation'. It is far from clear what this activity may ultimately produce.

In 1996, Berisha's Democratic party won the national elections for a second time in a contest which was boycotted by the opposition and criticized by the OSCE and the international community. In order to dampen domestic criticism, Beret's government permitted a number of unregulated business ventures to operate, including the alleged 'pyramid schemes' which have appeared (and mostly collapsed) in other post-communist countries.

Berisha's government is now accused not only of negligence but of profiting from these flotations. Certainly, one of the biggest of these companies, Vefa, helped fund the DP's campaign in the 1996 general elections.[49] There have also been persistent allegations that Albania's government has been involved in organized crime, including sanctions-busting and drugs trading. These accusations have been strenuously denied, but express a wider lack of public confidence in the Albanian state.[50]

Worsening political violence in March 1997 forced the then European Union President, Hans van Mierlo, to travel to Tirana for meetings with government and opposition officials.[51] The Italian Ambassador to Albania, and Italian president, Lamberto Dini, also endeavoured to mediate to lessen mounting tensions in the south of the country. Rome has been concerned about a threatened exodus of Albanians arriving at Italian sea-ports.[52] The OSCE Mission led by former Austrian Chancellor, Franz Vranitzky, persuaded Berisha to extend an amnesty to rebel factions in the countryside, and to work with opposition figures towards fresh elections.[53] In response to international pressures and internal violence, Berisha and opposition leaders also agreed to form a multi-party commission to investigate 'pyramid scheme investments' – the collapse of which had cost thousands their life savings and had ultimately triggered the armed conflict. Berisha also agreed to hold early elections.[54] The US State Department welcomed Berisha's resolution to work with opposition leaders.[55] However, rebel forces were insistent that Berisha should go, that Albania should have a new coalition government, and that compensation should be made to those who lost their life savings in the investment schemes.[56]

Aleksander Meksi's government 'resigned' (sacrificed by the President) while Berisha himself held on – invoking a state of emergency decree.[57] The European Broadcasting Union Satellite used by foreign networks was closed down and journalists were ordered to leave southern Albania. Only the DP's organ, *Rilindja Demokratika,* has been published and the offices of the liberal paper *Koha Jone* were destroyed.[58] Berisha has agreed to the formation of a government of national reconciliation that will include the opposition and also acceded to calls for early elections.[59] Now opposition politicians, who have for long argued that Berisha's departure is necessary to safeguard Albanian democracy, insist on radical change. They argue that Berisha has violated the very ideals Albanians fought for in December 1990.[60] The fate of Berisha and Albania are equally uncertain. Against this depressing scenario, it is to be hoped that Albania may find the conditions to move beyond authoritarian politics and to embrace a new climate of political pluralism.

NOTES

1. E. Gjoni, 'Albania: Hoxha is Dead, Long Live Berisha', *WarReport* (March 1995) p. 11.

2. M. Fromont, 'Reconstructing Albania from the Ruins', *The Magazine of the ILO*, no. 7 (March 1994) pp. 22-3.

3. T. M. Duffy, 'The Reconciliation of Memories in Albania: Dealing with the Communist Legacy', *Reconciliation Quarterly* (Summer 1992) pp. 32-5.

4. G. Pashko, 'The New Albanian Dictatorship', *WarReport* (June 1996) p. 3.

5. Z. Noli, 'Albania: Referendum Results Shake the Government', *WarReport* (January 1995) p. 12.

6. S. Markotich, 'Albania on the Brink of Civil War?', *OMRI Publications* (5 March 1997).

7. S. Markotich, 'Albanian President under Fire', *OMRI Publications* (5 March 1997).

8. R. Alia, *Enver Hoxha – The Banner of Struggle for Freedom and Socialism* (Tirana: Institute of Marxist-Leninist Studies, 1985) esp. p. 5.

9. R. Hibbert, 'The War in Bosnia: Can the Balkans be Saved from Balkanisation?', *The World Today* (August–September 1995) pp. 155-6.

10. B. Geroski, 'Macedonia: The Letter to Clinton', *WarReport* (September 1995) pp. 17-18.

11. T. Arifi, 'Political Pluralism for Albanians', *WarReport* (July/August 1995) p. 42.

12. A. Berishaj, 'The First Battlefield', *WarReport* (April 1996) p. 38.

13. F. Nazi, 'The (Democratic) Party's Over', *WarReport* (June 1995) p. 18.

14. A. Karaosmanoglu, *Crisis in the Balkans* (New York: UNIDIR Research Paper, United Nations, 1993) pp. 6-7.

15. Interview by author with Mr H. Alidema, Partia e Unitetit Kombetar, Malta, January 1993.

16. M. Palaiet, 'Ramiz Sadiku: A Case Study in the Industrialization of Kosovo', *Soviet Studies*, vol. 44, no. 5 (1992) pp. 900-1.

17. V. Orosi *et al.*, 'Kosovo: Mutual Fear', *The Intruder*, no. 5 (May 1992) p. 30.

18. P. Moore, 'The Widening Warfare in the Former Yugoslavia', *RFE/RFL Research Report*, vol. 2, no. 1 (January 1993) p. 9.

19. Palaiet, *op. cit.*, p. 900.

20. H. Kekezi (ed.), *What the Kosovars Say and Demand* (Tirana: Nentori Press, 1990) esp. pp. 3-11.

21. V. Orosi, ' Kosovo: The Pristina Show Trials', *WarReport* (June 1995) p. 10.

22. V. Surroi, 'Kosovo: Blues for '78', *WarReport* (March 1995) p. 10.

23. I. Rexhepi, 'Kosovo: Where Yugoslav Refugees are Welcome', *WarReport* (October/November 1994) p. 10.

24. S. Maliqi, 'Kosovo: The Least Desirable Place of Settlement', *WarReport* (September 1995) pp. 16-17.

25. Geroski, *op. cit.*, p. 18.

26. F. Nazi, 'Tirana Votes West', *WarReport* (May 1996) p. 41.

27. M. Wyzan, 'Macedonian Army Placed on War Footing', *OMRI Publications* (5 March 1997).

28. S. Markotich, 'Bomb Blasts in Kosovo', *OMRI Publications* (6 March 1997).

29. S. Maliqi, 'Kosovo', *Balkan WarReport*, no. 28 (September 1994) p. 9.

30. T. M. Duffy, 'Conflict Resolution and Political Violence in the Former Yugoslavia', *Review of International Affairs*, vol. XLII, no. 1 (1992) pp. 6-10.

31. F. Nazi, 'The Greek–Albanian Conflict', *WarReport* (October/November 1994) pp. 3-5.

32. Y. Valinakis, 'Greece's Balkan Policy and the Macedonian Issue', *Stiftung Wissenschaft und Politik* (April 1992) p. 15.

33. D. Nelson, 'Europe's Unstable East', *Foreign Policy*, no. 82 (1991) p. 144.

34. *Report of the Norwegian Foundation for Human Rights on Human Rights Seminars Conducted in Albania* (Oslo: Norwegian Foundation for Human Rights, 1993), esp. pp. 2-4.

35. S. Markotich, 'Is the Albanian Crisis Spinning Out of Control?', *OMRI Publications* (6 March 1997).

36. *The European* (26 March – 1 April 1992).

37. *Eastern Europe Newsletter*, vol. 7, no. 20 (October 1993) pp. 6-7.

38. R. F. Staar, *Communist Regimes in Eastern Europe,* 5th ed. (Hoover Institute Press, 1988) p. 14-16.

39. Noli, *op. cit.*, p. 12.

40. Nazi, 'Tirana Votes West', *op. cit.*, p. 40.

41. H. Miall, 'Healing Social Divisions', *WarReport* (May 1996) p. 49.

42. J. Robertson, 'Albania Cuts Links with the World', *The Guardian* (4 March 1997).

43. A. Gumbel, 'Albania Enters the Twilight Zone', *The Independent* (4 March 1997).

44. A. Gumbel, 'Albania's Democrat Turned Dictator', *The Independent on Sunday* (9 March 1997).

45. S. M. Terry, 'Thinking about Post-Communist Transitions', *The Slavic Review*, vol. 52, no. 2 (1993) pp. 333-6.

46. *Ibid.*, p. 336.

47. Nazi, 'The (Democratic) Party's Over', *op. cit.*, p. 18.

48. *Ibid.*, p. 19.

49. I. Beshiri, 'Albania on the Brink of Civil War', *OMRI Analytical Brief,* no. 560 (7 March 1997).

50. F. Schmidt, 'Is There a Link Between the Albanian Government and Organized Crime ?', *OMRI Analytical Brief,* no. 553 (17 February 1997).

51. S. Markotich, 'Death Toll Rises', *OMRI Publications* (6 March 1997).

52. I. Beshiri, 'A Busy Weekend in Tirana', *OMRI Analytical Brief* (11 March 1997).

53. *Ibid.*

54. S. Markotich, 'Amnesty in Albania', *OMRI Publications* (8 March 1997).

55. S. Markotich, 'International Support for Berisha', *OMRI Publications* (11 March 1997).

56. S. Markotich, 'But Rebels Set to Continue Fighting', *OMRI Publications* (8 March 1997).

57. Beshiri, 'A Busy Weekend in Tirana', *op. cit.*

58. Beshiri, 'Albania', *op. cit.*

59. S. Markotich, 'Albanian President Offers Deal', *OMRI Publications* (10 March 1997).

60. Pashko, *op. cit.*, p. 5.

6

Bulgaria: a stop-go modernization

Evgenii Dainov

The collapse of the communist system in Bulgaria was as spectacular as elsewhere and took place at virtually the same time. Symbolically, the resignation of Todor Zhivkov, Europe's longest-serving dictator (*in situ* since 1953), exactly coincided with the demolition of the Berlin Wall. Vigorous reforming governments in 1991 and 1992 ignited a reform package no less dramatic than the Polish 'shock therapy'. But by 1993–95, as differences between the different former 'socialist countries' appeared, Bulgaria slid back into the ranks of slow developers. Reform sagged and at the end of 1994 the ex-communist Bulgarian Socialist Party – the least reformed of its kind between the Oder and the Dniester – returned to power on a platform of a further slowing down of the transition process and a recovery of some aspects of the totalitarian system. In the meantime, however, strong indicators had appeared that the agenda of the transition had become part of society's life at the everyday level in spite of weaknesses at the level of the decision makers. By mid-1996, as the economy slumped dramatically, the banking system suffered a series of collapses, the currency slumped and shortages appeared, it had become clear that the Socialists' attempt to turn the clock back had failed. A national protest movement led to the resignation of the Socialist Cabinet at the end of 1996, and to the dissolution of parliament by March 1997, with new elections – expected to mark the demise of the ex-communists as a major force – called for April.

POLITICAL SYSTEM AND DIVISION OF POWERS

In retrospect, the construction of a political system based on a plurality of political forces, free and fair elections, and a balanced system of division of powers was easiest of all. By 1993 the system was obviously in place and functioning. It had passed through a peaceful dismantling of the one-party system, through four governments and through three elections. The Socialists had won and lost power peacefully, as had the Democrats. The political landscape had settled into a surprisingly stable – given the traditions of the region – two-party system, with the BSP on the one side, the UDF (and its split-off groups) on the other, the MRF acting not only as a pivot in parliament, but also stabilizing the system by ensuring the parliamentary presence of the Muslim minority.

Constitutionally, Bulgaria became, under the 1991 Constitution, a 'parliamentary republic' with strict division of powers and a directly elected President with largely symbolic – but nevertheless real in some fields (security, foreign policy) – powers. The various components of this system rapidly came to enjoy and guard their constitutional independence, evolving beyond loyalties to political party and ideology. In the early 1990s, the President refused to toe the (increasingly sectarian) UDF line, as did the Constitutional Court which overturned a number of 'de-communizing' pieces of legislation passed by the UDF-dominated National Assembly of 1991–92. Ultimately, the only 'de-communizing measure' which survived in the country (until it was voted out by a Socialist majority in 1995) was an Act banning leading former communists, for a period of five years, from holding senior administrative posts in the academic world. Attempts to conduct political trials against former Communist leaders fizzled out as the judiciary as a whole refused to move beyond current legality for political reasons. The army and police, 'de-politicized' (that is, banned from party memberships) since 1990, took a non-political stand, refusing overtures from all sides of the political divide to become less neutral.

The system was placed under severe pressure in 1995–96 with the return of the Socialists. An early bid to concentrate power in what the BSP called 'the triangle of power' – the BSP itself, its government and its parliamentary group – collided with the unwillingness of other powers to abandon their independence. Pledging their allegiance to 'the values of the transition agenda', first the President, and then the Constitutional Court resisted Socialist pressure and torpedoed significant amounts of legislation which was directed at the recovery of the dominant role of the state in the economy and society. A particularly high-profile and visible battle took place over the Socialists' repeated attempts to overturn previous legislation on land return, hedging it with provisions designed to encourage land owners to return to socialistic co-operatives. After a year of this, the Socialists suffered a definitive defeat at the hands of the Constitutional Court but, refusing to let the situation revert to the *status quo ante* (land return Acts of 1990–92), froze the process and created an effective ownership vacuum which led to the collapse of the 1996 harvest and to grain shortages.

CIVIL SOCIETY

Another evident progress in the transition effort in Bulgaria was the rapid stabilization of an independent media and of key components of civil society.

Possibly due to the intellectual beginnings of the democratic process, one of the first and most visible trends in Bulgarian society was the explosion of independent media, mainly newspapers, in the opening years. In 1990, the sum total readership of newspapers reached 4 million – half the entire population of the country. While, by 1995, this had dropped to under two million, nevertheless Bulgaria had, in the mid-1990s, 54 daily newspapers and 323 weeklies. In late 1992, the first regional independent radio station started up in the capital Sofia. By the end of 1994, there were some 20 of these around the country, together with local TV channels in most of the major cities and a number of cable networks. Only the National Assembly's incapacity to produce legislation to allow national independent TV operators has held back their emergence.

Through 1995 the Socialist government placed the state-owned media (National Radio and National Television), as well as some independents, under severe pressure. Although leading journalists were ultimately sacked from both radio and TV, and the leading independent newspaper, 24 Hours, was brought to heel, the independent media largely held out. More, investigative reporting set off a series of Cabinet changes and prosecutions against 'persons close to the government' for embezzlement of funds and fraudulent accounting.

Trade unions, as major components of civil society, also rapidly abandoned their ideological connotations and took an independent stance as early as 1991–92. One of the major Labour Confederations, Podkrepa, left the UDF in 1992 and even engaged in a series of strikes against the then UDF government. The other, the formerly official Communist Confederation of Independent Syndicates, also rapidly left the umbrella of the Socialists and, by 1996, was in the forefront of protests against the Socialist government. At the same time, the Unions faced the usual problem in a former communist country: their membership shrank together with state employment, while they have signally failed to take a foothold in the private sector. Attempts in 1995 by the Socialist government to delegitimize the two Confederations failed, demonstrating the capacity of established civil society bodies to survive government pressure. The Cabinet tried to appoint as its partner in tripartite negotiations a Socialist-created dummy, and to send this body to international meetings as the 'official Bulgarian trade union'. Under domestic and international pressure, the dummy union faded by mid-1996 and the government had to accept again the two Confederations as the legitimate representatives of hired labour.

As the 1990s wore on, and society continued to re-define its way of life away from reliance on the state, ethnic relations also settled into a new balance. Relations between the ethnic Bulgarian majority and the various minorities (primarily the Turks, making up some 8 per cent of the population, and up to 15 per cent together with other Muslims) had been severely disturbed throughout the

1980s. The then Communist Party, in a bid to find a new 'national' legitimacy after the loss of previous legitimacies ('overtake the West'), engaged in a series of efforts to re-name with Bulgarian (that is, Christian) names various Muslim groups, to ban the speaking of minority languages and the wearing of minority dress, outlaw Muslim holidays and festivals and so forth. Once the pressure was off after 1989, the various ethnic groups on the ground made consistent efforts to mend fences and recover their routine communal daily life in concert with other groups. The most visible of these, by the mid-1990s, were 'cross-religious activities': in mixed areas Christian communities engaged in financing the building of mosques, while Muslims financed the building of Orthodox churches.

At the same time, the economically depressed areas – black spots with failed state industry and high unemployment – tended to coincide with ethnically mixed regions. This placed economic pressure over the mixed communities, hitting particularly the Roma (Gypsy) groups particularly hard and reviving, in the other ethnic communities (Bulgarians and Turks alike) the traditional prejudice against the 'thieving Gypsy'. Only in the mid-1990s did the government start targeted employment programmes for such areas, while the massive effort targeted by the NGO sector at the Gypsy community also started bearing fruit in terms of producing regional development schemes, self-help initiatives and organizing the Gypsy community for a more effective presentation of their problems and demands to government.

It is worth noting that, during political crises, major parties tried to introduce – 'from the top' – ethnic tensions anew, in order to split up mixed communities along ethnic lines and turn one or other of the groups into a captive electorate. Such efforts have been particularly evident as regards the areas with a strong Turkish presence, where the Socialist Party repeatedly launched campaigns – unsuccessful to date – to rally 'all Bulgarians irrespective of ideology' against the MRF. Such initiatives have been underpinned by a massive campaign, by noted nationalistic writers and novelists, against the 'Turkification' of non-Turkish Muslim populations in the Rhodope mountains, as well as by efforts of a number of freewheeling latter-day Christian missionaries – father Saraev being the most famous case – to christen ethnic Bulgarian Muslims (Pomaks).

By 1995, as the Socialists increased pressure on such areas, local communities organized along mixed lines and launched a number of initiatives to preserve their way of life together against political meddling from the top. In early 1996 the Socialists lost a spectacular trial of strength when the Supreme Court ruled against the government on a dispute over the election, the previous autumn, of an ethnic Turk as mayor of the mixed region of Kardjali in the south of the country.

As civil society settled into a new mode of existence, observers were struck by the notable absence from this process of the Orthodox church. Formerly subservient to the communist regime, and since 1992 internally split along political lines, with just 1,550 priests nationwide in the early 1990s, the church, unlike the situation in other post-communist countries, has failed to become any kind of significant agent of civil society development and of progress in the transition agenda.

Civil society revealed its decisive political capacities during the national protest of 3 January–5 February 1997. *Ad hoc* citizen committees, student organizations, trade union–NGO alliances managed and kept within bounds a nationwide explosion demanding the resignation of the Socialists and early elections. The democratic sections of the Church also joined in the first time, bringing out into the streets its gonfalons – holy banners which are taken out of churches only during great festive days and wars. Ranged behind these banners, civil society declared war on its Socialist rulers and, by the evening of 4 February 1997, the country was in the throes of a national rebellion: a national political strike coincided with most cities declaring themselves 'communist-free zones' and sprouting barricades. Barricades blocked towns, some villages, all major roads and the exit points of the country (in Sofia alone there were upwards of 30 manned barricades). In the evening, the Socialists climbed down, agreed not to attempt to form a new government (their right under the Constitution) and to early elections. Civil society's self-organization capacity was revealed by the fact that, within hours, the rebellion was ended, all barricades cleared and life returned to normal.

PUBLIC OPINION AND THE CHALLENGES OF THE TRANSITION

The attitude of the public to the leading themes of the transition process – freedom, private property and initiative, emergence of the individual, retreat of the state and so forth – illustrates the well-known thesis that the 'transition', in order to succeed, involves a major change in culture, values and attitudes.

As early as the end of 1990, analysts and pollsters noted that Bulgaria was a cultural schizophrenic. Older age groups, the less educated, the inhabitants of smaller towns and villages – the Socialist-voting heartland – continued to hold on to dependent, pre-modern, collectivistic, state-dependent values and outlooks. This culture rejected the major values of the transition effort and, in particular, the move to a minimal state and to a market economy based on private property. The better-educated, the younger age groups, and the inhabitants of larger urban centres as early as 1990 embraced independent, modern, individualistic and state-independent outlooks. This group – at the last count (1995) a large minority in the population, and a majority in the working population – went through several peaks (winning the 1991 elections for the reforming UDF) and troughs (losing disastrously the 1994 elections to the Socialists), producing something of a new dominant culture by the end of 1994. In the mid-1990s, it formed an electoral body slightly larger than that of the Socialists, but continued to find minority representation in parliament due to the incapacity of democratic parties to effectively use the available non-socialist vote.

It proved to be a lucky break that the peak of belief in the reforms coincided with the drastic reform actions by the reforming governments of Dimitar Popov (1991) and Philip Dimitrov's majority UDF government of 1992–93. Through the hardest first

stage of the 'shock treatment' in the economy – 1991 – for
example, approval for the economic measures rose from 10 per cent
in March to almost 30 per cent in the autumn; disapproval fell 50
per cent to 38 per cent over the same period. The trend continued
through 1992 and, by the end, approval of the new economic
realities became a majority opinion. During the weak government
of Lyuben Berov (1993–94), which lost the capacity to provide
society with a vision of the future, belief in the reform eroded,
returning the Socialists at the end of 1994. Through 1995, as the
Socialist government placed pressure on all achievements of the
reform – particularly in squeezing the private sector and blocking
investment opportunities – faith in the transition agenda recovered,
forming a majority again by late 1995. For example, compared to
only 20 per cent in 1990, by the middle of the decade a full 53 per
cent of Bulgarians agreed with the watershed position, 'Free private
enterprise is best for this country'.[1]

But in the mass mind in particular the trends which have ensured
the chequered development of Bulgaria since 1989 are also very
evident. Although basically satisfactory for any reformer, the mass
backing of the transformations in society has been undermined
from the start by several factors, which have repeatedly ensured
shifting majorities for governments that deviate from the original
agenda. On the one hand, large minorities in public opinion have
never come to reject the pre-1989 *status quo* out of hand, and
continue to hanker after the 'security' of those days. On the other,
having never attained an industrial and urban modernity before the
advent of the communists in 1944, Bulgarians demonstrate
deficiencies of imagination which again hamper the reform effort.
For example, there has never been a majority convinced that 'large
industry' should be taken out of the hands of the state. As in any
small-scale, largely traditional society, it is difficult for the average
person to imagine that something as big as a steel works can in fact
be run by one owner. Sizeable minorities – or even thin majorities –
repeatedly opt for 'left-leaning' poll options which favour a state-
guaranteed social security: such as a modestly paid, but secure
(state), job; low prices even though garnished with queues and

shortages; price controls by the state; suspicion of foreign investors and so forth.

It is on the back of such sentiment that the Socialists, pulling a fresh contingent of some 400,000 votes, won the parliamentary elections of 1994. By mid-1996, having tried out policies to return to the 'secure' past, the government demonstrated that such a return was an illusion: industry collapsed for a second time since 1990 (with a 10 per cent drop in GDP over 1996 alone), the banking system registered failings and blockages, the currency halved its value in just the three summer months of 1996 (and lost a further nine-tenths in January 1997 alone, opening the floodgates to hyper-inflation), there was a return to shortages, bread queues and other paraphernalia of classic socialism.

From then on, analysts expected that this demonstration will ultimately result in a new realignment of public opinion away from the communist tradition and towards the agenda of reform. This, indeed, is what happened in the opening weeks of 1997. Following the success of the national protest, polls confirmed that the public had formed an outright rejection of the BSP for its anti-reform ideology and had rallied in unprecedented numbers around the Democrat alliance, newly re-legitimized as the carrier of the reform agenda. An early February poll, by the MBMD agency, indicated a 70 per cent readiness to vote for the Democrat alliance (compared with under 30 at the last vote in 1994), with a backing of only 8 per cent for the BSP (compared to 44 per cent in 1994) and further 8 per cent reserved for a hypothetical 'European left' party expected to be established by reformers streaming out of the ex-Communist Party.[2] Another (unpublished) poll, by NOEMA, indicated a strong movement towards crucial reform themes, such as the desirability of private as against state economy (an almost 60:40 majority).

The continuing refusal of popular opinion – as revealed by opinion polls and debates – to entertain 'strong arm' options in politics, in spite of almost universal dissatisfaction with party politicians, has been additionally heartening to the reformers.

INTERNATIONAL CHALLENGES

Following 1989, Bulgaria faced a particularly tough set of challenges on the international arena. Together with the other post-communist countries of Europe, the country attempted a radical realignment to the West. But this was an extraordinarily complicated procedure given the specific characteristics of pre-1989 Bulgaria in relation to the Soviet Union. *One*, never having been occupied by Soviet armed forces, the country found it difficult to form a clear majority view of abhorrence for the Kremlin and, as a consequence, a clear mandate for a radical break with its rulers. *Two*, Bulgaria was the country most enmeshed with the Soviet economy – to the point of virtually losing its economic independence in the early 1970s and becoming an economic province for the USSR's specific market needs. This situation resulted in an economy entirely orientated to service the Soviet Union's disturbed markets, and a break out of this was more difficult than for any other post-communist country. Moreover, the Socialist government of 1990 declared a 'moratorium' on foreign debt repayment, which threw Bulgaria into a severe international isolation precisely within the community of nations – the West – it was trying to join. *Three*, the major component of the political system – the former Communist Party – at no stage managed to free itself from psychological and political dependence on Moscow. This additionally complicated the process of foreign policy realignment – which, given the arguments above, was particularly in need of full political consensus in order to succeed unequivocally.

Nevertheless, helped along by the collapse of the Soviet markets themselves (and the collapse of the Soviet Union), the UDF government of 1991–92 managed to realign foreign policy priorities away from Moscow. By mid-1992, turnover with EC countries overtook turnover with the former Soviet Union for the first time. In 1993 the National Assembly voted to steer Bulgaria towards full NATO membership; in 1994 Bulgaria became an Associate member of the EC, and in 1995 it joined NATO's Partnership for Peace initiative. Bulgarian armed forces took part in several international peace-keeping operations, notably in Cambodia and, following the Bosnian peace accord, in former Yugoslavia. As the 1990s wore on, Bulgaria became increasingly credit-dependent on 'the West's' key, last-resort credit institutions, such as the IMF, the World Bank and, closer to home, the EBRD. This process of rapid absorption into the tissue of relations spawned by the community of democratic nations has ensured that internal wavering and shifts of political alignment have not been able to place a question-mark over Bulgaria's foreign policy direction.

Through the 1990s, the country had to solve several foreign policy challenges. First was the intractable question of Moscow; second was repayment of the foreign debt, which stood at some 12 billion US dollars by the time of the 1990 'moratorium'; third was the embargo against former Yugoslavia and the very severe complications arising out of Bulgaria's adherence to it.

For some time following the initial break with Moscow, Bulgaria did not figure on the Kremlin's mental map. In 1992, Russia's new rulers even signed a new Friendship Treaty with Bulgaria which, for the first time since Bulgaria's liberation by Russian forces (1878), did not place this country in a clearly subservient position. By 1994, however, with the appearance of the new toughness demonstrated in Chechenya, Russia's decision-makers woke up to the fact that NATO was poised to start a procedure of expanding membership which, to the Kremlin, looked like a definitive loss of its Central European *cordon sanitaire*. Foreign policy makers concentrated on pressuring at least one Central European country into deviating from the path to NATO and – ideally – returning to the Moscow fold. Initially, the Russians put pressure over the two countries of the region with, at least on the surface, the least democratic political establishments, Slovakia and Bulgaria. As the Slovak rulers, in spite of their non-democratic temptation internally, took a clear stand against Moscow, pressure concentrated on Bulgaria alone. The Socialist government, formed in early 1995, clearly signalled that it would 'revive traditional links' with Moscow and, indeed, a stream of senior Socialists passed through Moscow in a few short months. Misreading the signals, during the preparation of the new confederation accords inside the CIS, President Yeltsin specifically invited Bulgaria to join the envisaged confederation around Russia, immediately dubbed USSR Mark 2. This came on top of repeated overtures by Russia's Defence Minister, Pavel Grachov, for a reconstruction of a defence alliance around Russia as a counterweight to NATO. Public opinion in Bulgaria exploded unexpectedly against the Yeltsin invitation, mass rallies were held for the first time in a number of years, President Zhelev replied scathingly while the BSP hovered on the verge of a split between pro- and anti-Westernizers. The pro-Moscow faction lost the day and, given also Russia's express lack of willingness to provide credit to the Socialists, Bulgaria's foreign policy re-settled into its pro-Western mould.

Nevertheless, as industry remained in state hands due to vacillating privatization policies, and as the Western markets proved tough to penetrate on a durable basis, through 1994–96 the Russian markets again formed a major component of Bulgaria's turnover, making certain that Moscow would remain a major factor in Bulgaria's development. Turnover rose from 1.6 billion US dollars in 1994 to almost 2 billion in 1995. Plans to construct pipelines through Bulgaria for Russian gas and oil reinforced Moscow's significant position in the mental landscape of Bulgaria's decision-makers.

The foreign debt repayment negotiations, repeatedly undermined by frequent changes of governments, were finally signed in 1993–94. By the end of 1995, the debt had shrunk from more than 12 billion US dollars to slightly over 9 billion. In 1996, however, severe socialist mismanagement of the economy resulted in a serious drop in production, a halving of foreign trade turnover, of the national currency reserve and of the value of the lev. Bulgaria's capacity to meet debt payments for 1996 and 1997 were thrown openly into doubt, particularly given the Socialist government's vacillating attitude to the international credit institutions which support the repayment effort, the IMF and the World Bank. The government spent 1995 blocking negotiations due to mistaken assumptions that these institutions were not needed. When the scale of the 1996 economic dislocation became clear, the government went into panic negotiations with the IMF, which, however, failed to produce fresh IMF money to back the debt repayment effort when the Cabinet attempted, within weeks of signing the agreement, to hoodwink the Fund by evading agreed enterprise liquidations.

In the closing weeks of the Socialist government (which resigned days before Christmas of 1996), the IMF judged the situation severe enough to demand the instruction of a 'currency board', that extreme monetary measure designed to ensure the end to financial profligacy and combat inflation by imposing outside discipline on weak national banks.

The embargo on former Yugoslavia in the early 1990s turned into a major foreign and domestic policy challenge. Due to the previous, ill-judged credit policy, on the eve of the Yugo-wars Bulgaria had lost, in sanctions against former allies, some 2 billion US dollars in Iraq, and a similar sum in Libya, Iran and other countries placed under restriction by the international community. When the Yugo-sanctions were announced, Bulgaria immediately declared its strict adherence to this initiative, together with a clear stand of non-involvement in any way in the Yugo-conflicts. It had been the first country to recognize Macedonia internationally and had a particular stake in keeping a high and pro-Western profile in the region. Ultimately, the losses to the Bulgarian economy are now estimated at between 2 and 4 billion US dollars.

The internal dimensions of the embargo are considered, however, as more serious. Coming at a time of institutional vacuum and loss of direction which accompanies major shifts in any society, the embargo created almost ideal opportunities for the appearance of organized crime. It was an open secret that whole regions of the country subsisted on embargo-busting activities, which inevitably sparked off routine corruption of state officials at all levels. In this sense, the internal effect of the embargo is seen as akin to the Prohibition regime in the US: creating a corrupt environment for officials, a whole 'black economy' and crime syndicates which threaten the security of the state. By mid-1995 analysts estimated that up to 90 per cent of profit in the country was realized in the 'black economy'.[3]

MACROECONOMIES AND MOVING TO MARKET ECONOMY

The most visible failure of the transformation process under way in Bulgaria has been in the economic field. To date, it is the only country which, following stabilization and growth, has found itself abruptly thrown back to the original 1989 situation. Until the collapse of 1996–97, the basic indicators seemed to point to a course of economic reform congruent with the hesitant nature of the country's support for – and understanding of – the challenges of the economic transformation. Further – given the previous extraordinary dependence on Soviet markets, and the consequently deformed economic structure – indicators for a number of years were optimistic rather than pessimistic.

GDP dropped by 9 per cent in 1990, hit bottom with a drop of 17 per cent in 1991 and thereafter started climbing out, reaching a 1.4 per cent increase in 1994 and a 2.5 growth in 1995. This was accompanied by a positive foreign trade balance, attained by 1995, and a trend of inflation diminution (apart from a 'blip' of 122 per cent in 1994), which reached 33 per cent in 1995. In spite of the very slow rate of privatization, and the increasing taxation squeeze on private entrepreneurs, a transition to private initiative was also evident. Starting with 9.5 per cent of GDP in 1990, the private sector's contribution by 1996 was estimated at around 40 per cent.[4] Against overall GDP growth of 2.5 per cent in 1995, the private sector demonstrated a growth of 25 per cent. Private initiative clearly dominated in trade, agriculture and services, and – until the 1996 taxation package which not only increased all taxes, but also placed a profit tax on investment – was making serious headway in manufacturing, increasing its share by more than half in 1994–95 alone. Some analysts estimate that at least half of the private sector is still invisible to statistics, and that in reality GDP is already dominated by the proportion produced by private initiative. As elsewhere, employment dropped severely after 1989 – from more than 4 million to slightly more than 3 million in 1995. At the same time, a virtual parity in employment between the state and the private sector was attained by 1996; if analysts are to be believed, here again the private sector is the bigger employer, given that a lot of it is invisible to statisticians. The unemployment rate, hitting a ceiling of 15.7 per cent in 1993, dropped to 12.5 per cent in 1995. Through the period of reform average wages also held, in spite of backslides and turbulence, at around 112–120 US dollars per month, dropping sharply to around 65 by mid-1996 as a result of currency collapse and the renewed economic turmoil, and reaching – for the first time – under 10 US dollars in early February 1997. Foreign investment turned out to be the Achilles' heel of Bulgaria's economic effort. By mid-1996, direct foreign investment made since 1990 totalled only 610 million US dollars.[5] Investment fell by half during 1995 (compared to 1994) – the first full year of Socialist government.

The barely satisfactory macroeconomic parameters and the failure at the heart of the reform – the transition to an economy based on private property – can be laid at the door of all governments after 1989. The reforming Cabinets of 1991–92 ran out of vision and evaded the problem of enterprise liquidations inevitable in a privatization procedure of such scale. The BSP government after 1994 specifically banked on a revival of the state's dominant role in the economy and produced the mid-1996 crisis which was without analogue through the region.

Throughout the period, as governments and the public vacillated, it has been the international credit institutions, such as the IMF, which have turned into the key guarantors of the economic agenda of the transition. Following the collapse of the Socialist government and the Socialist majority in the winter of 1996–97, it was evident that the future Democrat government, set to win the forthcoming early elections in the spring of 1997, would be tackling these issues in an adverse economic environment and under severe pressure from both the impoverished domestic public and the international financiers.

THE PROBLEM OF ELITES

By the mid-1990s it had become clear that, against a not very heartening horizon, Bulgaria had at least escaped one major trap on the road to Europe: the reconstruction of an effective power elite around the security 'organs' of the communist regime. As early as the 1990 Round Table, clear decisions were enforced regarding the de-politicization of police, army and other security structures. A purge of these structures was conducted by a series of Socialist and non-Socialist governments, and the intelligence and security apparatus was re-structured along modern lines under the new Constitutional provisions. Great numbers of former security officers took their intelligence-gathering skills and their networks into banking and business. While forming, in the early 1990s, a number of unholy alliances with former communist dignitaries and the new crop of mafiosi, the former security officers could not manage – or did not wish – to form the backbone of a new power oligarchy. Their presence did, however, contribute to the lack of transparency and trust in business, and limited opportunities for the formation of a truly fresh business class along European lines of openness and cooperation.

The problem with the political elite of post-1989 Bulgaria turned out to be rather more serious. The problem, visible with great clarity from the vantage-point of the mid-1990s, is different for the two basic groups of political decision-makers: those affiliated to the Socialists and those affiliated to the 'democratic parties'.

The Socialists, although re-naming their party from Communist very early on (April 1990), and passing several years of heavy internal debate, did not manage to complete the process of transforming themselves into Social Democrats – something achieved elsewhere in the region. By late 1993, skirting around the question of the future shape of the country and the priorities arising for themselves, the BSP re-defined itself around its traditional 'productionist' mentality centred on the state's dominance of the economy. Accordingly, the government's policy package constructed a rather simple pseudo-Keynesian chain: inflationary stimulation of state industry, increase of demand, increase of taxation income and a 'just' social security policy as a result. This led directly to the economic collapse of 1996–97. Failing from power under pressure from a national protest movement which hovered on the verge of rebellion, the BSP entered into 1997 increasingly split between out-and-out communists and a dwindling reformist fringe.

The anti-Socialists have also had problems with their vision of society. They impressively tackled the early stages of the reform – liberalization of prices and macroeconomic stabilization, new taxation and business legislation, the drive to return nationalized property and land to their former owners. By the end of 1992, this had a visibly stimulating effect on private business and initiative as society began to realign itself around the new business and profit opportunities. But through lack of previous managerial experience – and hands-on knowledge of modern democratic societies – the UDF government of 1992 failed in its attempt to set up a system of rapid privatization. Since then a new generation of better-informed and more pragmatic leaders has come to the fore in the UDF and its allies, offering society something akin to a coherent reform horizon in a package called 'The New Beginning'. The public, by the end of 1996 turning definitively against the BSP and realigning around the reform agenda in unprecedented numbers, endorsed this package by voting for a Democrat President, Mr Petar Stoyanov, by a 60:40 margin against the Socialist pretender, on 3 November 1996.

CONCLUSION: ACHIEVEMENTS, FAILURES AND CHALLENGES

Judged by the standards of countries such as the Czech Republic or Poland – with whom it had much in common in the opening years of reform – Bulgaria's effort at transformation must be judged as a failure. While these countries are entering the OECD and have moved beyond reliance on last-instance creditors such as the IMF, by 1997 Bulgaria was again in the throes of economic dislocation directly resulting from an inability to stick to the original reform agenda and due to political confusion and pusillanimity.

Judged, however, by standards closer to home – Balkans, the former Soviet Union – Bulgaria has, at least, been a partial success. It remains unique in avoiding the trap of ethnic conflict and nationalist politics. It has evolved a stable two-party system and a settled division of powers, holding up against repeated attempts at constructing a Balkan-type oligarchical and/or repressive regime. The structures of civil society are in place and have proved resistant to political and government pressure. The country has, in spite of internal squabbles and temptations, remained on course for EU and NATO membership, and has managed to remain out of all Balkan conflicts.

Past history and existing mentalities have ensured that Bulgaria is a slow society, shrinking from enthusiasms, basically conservative, requiring a long time to weigh pros and cons and make up its mind about going in a new direction. The fact that Bulgarian progress has been not only slow, but repeatedly interrupted with back-sliding, can be traced primarily to the inadequacies and lack of decisiveness on the part of the decision-making elite. Unable to translate the diffuse popular backing for the reform process into real government policy and vision, the decision-making elite has effectively blocked those processes – such as decent business legislation and energetic privatization – without which society's potential remains unutilized.

As the country, in its unprecedented anti-Socialist mood, and given its also unprecedented backing for the reform process, moved to elections in the spring of 1997, the Democrat political establishment faced its greatest challenge to date. The public mood was unequivocal, but the country had run out of time and money and margins for political manoeuvring and vacillation at the top had shrunk to nothing. Resolute and imaginative leadership alone could save the day – both for the country and for the transition.

The basic lesson – if any – at the time of writing is, however, more poignant. There is no way back available to any post-communist country, no matter how big the electoral backing – nor how strong government will – for such a return may be.

NOTES

1. *The Insider*, no. 1 (1993) p. 11.
2. *Demokratsia*, 9 February 1997.
3. *168 Chassa*, 15-21 May 1995.
4. *SEGA Magazine*, 23-29 January 1997.
5. *Trud*, 30 July 1996.

7

Czechoslovakia: the break-up and its consequences

Ivan Gabal

The post-1989 development towards democracy and the market in Czechoslovakia was divided into two main periods. The first phase ran until June 1992, when the second parliamentary elections resulted in the massive victory of two somewhat incompatible political forces in the Czech and Slovak parts of the Czechoslovak Federation. The second began on 1 January 1993, when Czechoslovakia split into the Czech Republic and the Slovak Republic.

The following report chronicles important features of the political and economic development of the two new states. I will begin with a brief summary of post-1989 developments prior to the divorce in order to understand the background of the separation of the two countries.

THE 1990–92 PERIOD – UNIFIED CZECHOSLOVAKIA

The Czechoslovak, that is unitary, phase immediately following the fall of communism was driven by certain common as well certain diversifying processes contained within the general framework of the dynamics of post-1989 change. The common aspect of development was characterized by the implementation of the main political goals articulated in the early days of political change. These were:

- Re-establishment of basic political rights and the institutions of parliamentary democracy including early democratic election of the three parliaments (Federal Assembly and the two National Councils). The elections provided full legitimacy and legality to the 1989 changes as well as to the new governments and political programmes.
- Reconstruction and development of national sovereignty based on (1) dismantling of the Warsaw Treaty; (2) negotiation of the complete withdrawal of Soviet troops; (3) change of the geopolitical orientation of Czechoslovakia (Visegrad Group and the EC Association Agreement); (4) developing an active policy and role for Czechoslovakia in the security area (CSCE, participation in the international operation in Kuwait as well as participation in peace-keeping operations in several regions); (5) development of normal relations with Western neighbours (mainly Germany).
- Implementation of the main steps of macrostabilization and liberalization of the economy as well as full – scale privatization.
- Protection of the full legality and legitimacy of all changes by the mechanism of parliamentary procedures and votes on all key government decisions.

All these changes were subject to debate and vote by the Federal Assembly. The structure of the Czechoslovak Federal Assembly was carefully designed to balance the interests of the two nations through a powerful anti-majority voting system in the Chamber of Nations. The main systemic changes were accepted by the deputies of both the Czech and Slovak parts of the Federation. The general direction of the country's development was not subject to greater disagreement due to the close political and personal affiliation of the winning political forces in the 1990 election in both parts of the Czechoslovak Federation (Public Against Violence in Slovakia and Civic Forum in the Czech Republic).

This first period also exhibited increasing tendencies to diversification. The existence of significant differences between the

Ivan Gabal

Czech lands and Slovakia was well known before 1989 from sociological and economic research. Following the early period of euphoria, the dynamic economic and political development increased the significance of inherited differences.

The Slovak population, which was used to stabilized growth under the socialist system to a greater degree than the Czech population, was less ready to absorb the consequences of radical change. However, though the change represented a new historical opportunity for the Czechs, for the Slovaks it was rather a threat to their stability. Industrialization and modernization of the Slovak economy in the post-war period was concentrated in heavy industry and in branches closely tied to the markets of the COMECON. The collapse of Eastern markets, combined with poor industrial performance and lack of competitiveness resulted in the rapid growth of unemployment, which had been previously unknown. The military hardware industry in Central Slovakia became a major force in the political bargaining surrounding the impact of Czechoslovakia's new foreign and security policy on armaments production and exports. Havel's declaration to decrease military production and exports had more of a political than an economic significance. Accompanied by international diplomatic and media pressure against all military exports, the presidential declaration provided strong political ammunition for Slovak nationalists.

From the Fall of 1990, public opinion in the two republics started to differ in the level of acceptability shown towards liberal policies and the costs of transition.

The future structure of relations within the Czechoslovak Federation was a subject of transformation as well. There were two main reasons fuelling the desire to restructure the pre-1989 communist constitutional system. The first one was the explicit duty of the Parliaments, elected in 1990, to establish a new democratic Constitution. The second was the increasing pressure of the majority of Slovak political leaders to gain more autonomy and control over the economic and political development of the country. Difficult negotiations were conducted during the whole period of 1991–92. The possibility of a referendum pushing political representatives into an agreement emerged as a real alternative during 1991. President Havel failed to persuade the Federal Assembly to accept it. The poor results of the negotiations among the national representatives and Havel's withdrawal of the referendum brought the country to a constitutional crisis and deadlock.

All of the-above mentioned factors were political nourishment for the rise of populism and nationalism in the Slovak political environment. Populist politicians in Bratislava took advantage of the worsening economic conditions and the leading role of Federal bodies in the introduction of painful policies to blame the Federation and Prague for the exploitation of the Slovak nation by the Czechs. In the 1992 elections, the majority of Slovaks voted for political parties and leaders promising a more autonomous and sovereign Slovakia inside Czechoslovakia. A confederation was presented as an ideal solution. However, what Slovakia finally received was not more autonomy inside a united state, but full sovereignty outside the previous coexistence with the Czechs.

THE INTERIM PERIOD – THE NEGOTIATION OF THE DIVORCE

Continuous monitoring of public preferences related to the Czechoslovak constitutional arrangement was carried during the period of 1991–92. On both sides, a stable majority supported the continued existence of Czechoslovakia. The Slovak support for secession never reached the level of 15 per cent. Less than 10 per cent of Czechs were of a similar opinion before the elections in June 1992.

The preferences for ideal constitutional arrangements slightly differed. The Czechs were more in favour (on average approx. 35 per cent) of a unitary state model of one government and one Parliament. The existing model of the federation of two republics with strong centralized powers for the federal institutions was the second preference among Czechs (approx. 26 per cent). The confederative model (ruling position of the two republics with minimized and weak federal institutions) was considered the worst alternative among Czechs (support on the level of 4 per cent).

At the beginning, the federation of two states was the most favoured preference structure of the Slovaks (27 per cent). With the passing of time, support for the confederative model started to grow. By the end of 1991, support for confederation was equal to the support for federation. The unitary state model was considered an inappropriate solution, as it enjoyed the support of less than one-fifth of the Slovak population.

The prevailing feeling among Slovaks of the need for a more autonomous position was a fact. However, the mood of Czechs and the approach of the Czech political parties strongly focused on economic reform was different. At least one party (the Civic Democratic Alliance) started to encourage the idea of a tough policy towards Slovakia: 'either federation or nothing'. Although the Czech public did not overreact on the issue, it was becoming more and more uncomfortable with the dispute. The level of satisfaction with the overall situation in the Czech Republic declined in this period to the Slovak level of 20 per cent.

Neither the Czechoslovak constitutional arrangement nor the future existence of the country were election issues for the Czechs or Slovaks in the parliamentary elections in June 1992. The most general subject of the vote was the vision of the economic future. Czechs were more eager to see further and faster changes while the Slovaks desired more economic autonomy and less radical economic transformation. The political space for a uniform common economic reform became narrow. The future of Czechoslovakia was once again vitally dependent on the political skills and ability of the election winners in both parts of the federation. However, the two leading politicians, Vaclav Klaus and Vladimir Meciar, were not ready to negotiate a compromise. The split-up of Czechoslovakia was the only outcome.

The end of Czechoslovakia was characterized by several political facts that are important for understanding subsequent developments in the two independent states:

1. The post-election atmosphere increased public support for the split on both sides. Strong support for dissolution was displayed by 22 per cent of Czechs and 19 per cent of Slovaks in November 1992. Another 25 per cent (31 per cent) identified their support for the split as being accompanied by serious doubts. However, even one year after the elections the split had not succeeded in winning the support of the majority of Czechs or Slovaks.

2. The split was ideologically supported on both sides by the notion of economic profit gained from avoiding 'costly' coexistence. The Czech side defined the Slovak economic programme as neo-socialist, by this meaning a threat to democracy, the economic transition, and future prosperity.

3. The split was carried out clearly and reached by political agreement between the two leaders and their political parties (the Civic Democratic Party on the Czech side and the Movement for Democratic Slovakia on the Slovak side). All other parties were excluded from the negotiating table. Their agreement was mostly conditioned by their access to the governing coalitions on the national level. President Havel did not oppose the agreement and resigned immediately after a second unsuccessful attempt at re-election as Czechoslovak President in the newly composed Federal Assembly. His preliminary agreement to become candidate for President of the new Czech Republic provided legitimacy to the split on both sides.

4. The split was legally decided by a vote of the Federal Assembly. The Federal Assembly declared the end of Czechoslovakia and abolished all federal institutions including the Assembly itself. Czechoslovakia was succeeded by the two sovereign republics.

5. A political agreement on the immediate administrative consequences in the practical division of all federal properties by a ratio of 2:1 in favour of the Czech interest.

AFTER THE SPLIT: DEVELOPMENT IN INDEPENDENCE

Public climate

In October 1992 only 10 per cent of Czechs and Slovaks expected that the split would be conducted smoothly. One-third expected more or less serious conflicts. From this point of view, the fast and peaceful nature of the process brought relief to both nations. The public observed the end of Czechoslovakia with visible passivity and resignation. Only 25 per cent of Czechs and 23 per cent of Slovaks considered the division very important, while 35 per cent of Czechs and 28 per cent of Slovaks attributed to the division little or no importance at all. This was mainly the result of negligible public access to the decision-making process.

The fact that the divorce was accomplished apart from the democratic and public interest is an important feature of the political foundations of the new national states. The lack of identification with the new states among the majority of citizens on both sides is an important feature of the new citizenship.

The suppression of direct public involvement in the decision to dissolve Czechoslovakia can be explained by politicians' worries about further developments in the event of a contradiction between their political decision and the likely referendum vote favouring the continued existence of Czechoslovakia. To these ends, the case of Yugoslavia was manipulated by politicians as an example of what could happen in Czechoslovakia. Contrary to the Serbs and Croats, in the case of the former Yugoslavia, a majority of Czechs and Slovaks were interested in the continuous existence of the existing nation.

On the eve of sovereignty the feeling of Slovak society was dark and pessimistic. Viewing the impending split, Slovaks reconsidered their opinions on different features of post-1989 policies. The strongest shifts occurred in areas of economic reform and foreign and geopolitical orientation. In September 1992, 49 per cent of Slovaks already agreed with the need for systemic changes in the economy. Between April 1992 and March 1993, trust in NATO increased from 21 per cent to 28 per cent and continued to rise to

44 per cent in October 1993. In October 1992, immediately prior to the split, 86 per cent favoured orientation towards the EU and 53 per cent supported membership in NATO.

For the Slovaks the paradox of the split is that Czechoslovakia became a kind of historical standard against which future developments in Slovakia would be measured.

Retrospective evaluation of the split one year after it happened confirmed the existence of a large degree of nostalgia. The number of Slovaks who would have voted for the split if there had been a referendum decreased between March and October 1993 from 29 per cent to 23 per cent. The number of potential NO voters increased from 50 per cent to 60 per cent. The majority of Slovaks look back on Czechoslovakia as a valuable country. In October 1993, 63 per cent saw some (federative or confederative) form of coexistence with Czechs as valuable. The model of two independent states was approved by only 32 per cent. However, the Slovak public is aware of the low probability of some form of reunion and 68 per cent expect the future to be built on two fully independent states.

Low support for the separation of the nations in the Slovak perspective seems to be rather incompatible with the high level of approval of the Slovak Government (47 per cent) in March 1993. Moreover, the Parliament and the President, which are also the political forces and personalities responsible for the split, enjoyed significant support (58 per cent and 78 per cent respectively).

General disillusionment with the costs and results of sovereignty were evident already in October 1993. The condition of the economy worsened according to 80 per cent of Slovaks, unemployment increased in the view of 93 per cent, whilst the standard of living fell according to 85 per cent, and opportunities for honest people were fewer in the opinion of 69 per cent. The realities of the new Slovak state already accorded with the pessimistic expectations and new policies did not provide the desired social security and economic stability. In this worsening situation, the economic orientation of Slovak society towards a mixed market model with strong state intervention remained dominant or even strengthened (51 per cent), while support for the free market model with less state intervention was found in less than one-third (28 per cent) of the Slovak population. Therefore, it seems that the Slovak vision of Czechoslovakia is that of a type of socialist state – one that provides full safeguards for social welfare and economic assistance.

The climate of Czech public opinion has been somewhat different since the breakup of Czechoslovakia. In January 1994, 54 per cent of Czechs regretted the split. However, only 35 per cent would vote for some form of reunion and two-thirds would clearly vote against any coexistence with the Slovaks. Approximately one year after the split, 51 per cent of Czechs were satisfied with economic reform, 43 per cent expected economic improvement in two years and 44 per cent were satisfied with the political situation. The major political institutions (government, presidency) attracted majority approval. Czechs were and still are somewhat sorry for the loss of Czechoslovakia, but they feel a certain relief and satisfaction with the development.

The Czecho-Slovak issue rapidly disappeared from Czech public attention immediately after the split.

BUILDING AND STABILIZING THE NEW STATES

The starting positions and conditions of the two new states were rather unequal.

The Czech Republic

The institutional stabilization of the new state was accomplished in the Czech Republic simply by the relabelling of an already existing infrastructure and filling in a few gaps where necessary. There were three significant tasks to be accomplished: the creation of a new Constitution, which was accepted just two weeks before 1 January 1992; the transfer of responsibilities from federal institutions and laws to Czech institutions and legal infrastructure; and the construction of a full regime border system with Slovakia. However, the international and bilateral succession to the position of Czechoslovakia has not yet been completed.

Following the split, the Czech Republic is developing towards a model of a strong centralized government and executive power. There are several reasons for this. The first is the relatively weak position and composition of Parliament caused by political design rather than by constitutional definition. The second factor strengthening the dominant position of the government is a significant decline in the influence of the President. The third factor is an increase in the role of political parties.

A relatively new issue is the quality of democracy in the Czech Republic. Further improvement of the institutionally established democratic system is principally desirable in three areas. A legally regulated system for channelling economic and political interests must replace a political culture based upon diminishing moral appeals. The second area of needed improvement in the quality of democracy is a strengthening of civil society as a counterbalance to the overexposed role of political parties. The third area is de-centralization introducing a subsidiary system functioning in favour of regions.

The new Czech Republic, relatively early, reached both political as well as institutional stability based on transparent political processes. However, even before the election in 1996, the Czech government failed to complete some of the fundamental constitutional tasks imposed by the new constitution in 1992. The absence of the second chamber of parliament (the Senate) exposed the constitutional system to the risk of a possible deadlock in parliament. The second was the failure to establish a new regional structure for elected self-administrative regional government. In both cases the government of Vaclav Klaus did not respect the Czech Constitution but favoured the protection of centralized powers in Prague.

The Slovak Republic

The development of Slovak statehood has been different in nature. The state was and still is being built and perceived as a fresh, new state. Slovaks experienced discontinuity through the creation of a sovereign state. Slovakia had to expand or build from scratch a large part of its state structure. Under the Czech and Slovak Federation, both republics had their own administration, government and national Parliament. However, their position, responsibilities and executive powers were defined by federal laws and limited by federal executive powers controlling all vital external and internal functions of the unified state. The offices controlling the national currency, foreign policy, national defence, transportation and communication, state intelligence and security, constitutional legislation, strategic energy infrastructure, foreign trade, transportation, and jurisdiction, were all in Prague. The transfer of administrative know-how was further complicated by distrust, in Bratislava, of those Slovaks working in the federal administration in Prague.

It is definitely too early to evaluate how successful Slovakia has been in establishing a fully functional and efficient democratic state. The first years after partition are insufficient to give any final answer about the main political, economic and geopolitical features of the Slovak Republic. However, the simple fact that the Slovak state was institutionally established in all main areas was a significant achievement of the period 1993–94.

In the constitutional sense, Slovakia has developed a system that fulfils formal democratic standards and the requirements of parliamentary democracy. Starting with Meciar's strong and rather authoritative government controlling almost all parts of executive and legislative procedures, Slovakia moved towards increasing political and public influence under the new President Kovac. Moreover, the Parliament, fully controlled by Meciar's Movement for Democratic Slovakia since the split, has been gaining more influence and a more active position. Once independence was achieved, a set of questions about Slovakia's direction of development arose in all main areas, thus introducing new political diversification in the Parliament. The main pro-independence forces divided when addressing issues of economic transformation, privatization, foreign and defence policy (NATO and the EU) issues and so on.

The result of this new differentiation was the no-confidence vote in the government of Prime Minister Meciar in March 1994. Strong governance has been replaced by the more developed practices of parliamentary democracy inaugurated by the interim government composed of former opposition and pro-reform politicians of Meciar's movement. The role of the presidency, as well as of the Parliament, has created a stronger political equilibrium. Slovakia seemed to be on a rough road toward rapid political and economic stabilization including relations with all its neighbours.

The third come-back of Vladimir Meciar to power started another round of large-scale upheavals in the constitutional and democratic stability of Slovakia. A new coalition, composed of Meciar's populist Movement for Democratic Slovakia, the nationalist Slovak National Party and the neo-communist Association of Slovak Workers, gained power by exercising full control over the public media, by a focused campaign to remove President Kovac and by using the intelligence services and police force to intimidate the electoral support of some opposition parties. The relatively successful stabilization of the new parliamentary and constitutional democracy became a battleground for power games rather than respect for constitutional duties or international reputation.

1995 and 1996 brought further strengthening in the main political principles of Meciar's policies, in particular the conduct of a continuous confrontation with opponents using all possible methods. The country experienced an ongoing, open conflict between the main constitutional institutions and the Presidency. The conflict was pursued by increasingly unconstitutional methods such as the blackmailing of Kovac, via his family, by the secret services.

The second main dimension of confrontation was an increasing and threatening pressure against the Hungarian minority in Slovakia. Beginning with the attempt to abolish or weaken Hungarian language-based schooling and concluding with a draconian 'language law' establishing the full dominance of the Slovak language in all areas, including the private media, the Slovak government was guided by the extremist nationalist demands of the Slovak National Party. The nationalist confrontation is likely to increase with the new regional administrative division of the country aimed at administrative weakening of the Hungarian population's ratio in southern districts and, consequently, the Hungarians' access to local, regional and central governance. The political polarization of Slovak society is becoming counterbalanced by unifying anti-Hungarian sentiments.

Against the background of the main domestic political conflicts, the government continued its purge of the administration and state bureaucracy, the army and police by positioning party members in managing positions in all levels and areas, including the state-owned economy. The Slovak opposition is probably right when speaking about new nomenclatura principles being introduced to the state bureaucracy.

The government was successful in re-gaining control over large parts of the economy via politically driven privatization of profitable enterprises by officials of the governing parties or politically affiliated business community members. In several instances, 1995–96 witnessed a weakening of private ownership when the government administratively took control of large businesses and investment banks considered as politically unfriendly.

All attempts at weakening democracy were closely investigated and reported on by the private media. Generally, the press represents a stronghold of free information flow to the public. With public media (radio and TV) fully controlled by the government, the private print media became subject to severe political and economic pressure by the government. Two anti-free-press strategies were followed. First was the disruption of the free advertising market by allocating all advertisement resources of state owned or shared (or influenced) companies to pro-government media. Practically all the opposition media ran into financial or cash flow difficulties, some of them were sold or collapsed into government hands. Direct violations of a free media environment occurred through blocking or blackmailing of printing companies, by threatening journalists, and so on. However, in spite of all the attempts of the Slovak government the free press still exists and protects democracy; they solve problems with the enthusiasm of the media staff and some foreign assistance.

Supported by official EU and USA complaints, there is serious concern about the declining standard of and perspectives for democracy in Slovakia. Slovakia still keeps the institutional features of a functioning democracy (Parliament with an opposition, independent Constitutional court, free press). On the other hand, there are new features of the government's behaviour which impel Slovakia closer to political standards of a distinctly lesser kind.

Public opinion, in the majority, prefers the continuation of the democratic process and rejects the undemocratic excesses of the current government. The government's control over public media was rejected by 71 per cent in December of 1995. The harsh criticism from European institutions is largely shared by the population, and the language law is predominantly perceived as a significant step toward an increase in ethnic tensions in Slovak society (46 per cent).

The Slovak paradox of the 1990s continues to be constituted by the coexistence of pro-democratic attitudes on one side and pro-government feelings on the other. A hypothesis might be that if there is no pro-democratic government then the majority of society would follow, in the absence of democratic forces, the paternalistic, populist and authoritarian Meciar as leader of the country and gaining in popularity.

INTERNATIONAL AFFILIATION OF THE NEW STATES

The peaceful nature of the Czechoslovak divorce did not justify certain international nervousness about the split as a direct source of regional instability. However, the expectations of consequent geopolitical changes in the region proved to be justified. The split of Czechoslovakia introduced several probably irreversible changes:

(1) The end of Czechoslovakia has further diminished the co-operation of the Central European region among the four Visegrad countries. (2) The split in the region provided a space for strong

opposition by Russia to any NATO enlargement. Russia renewed attempts to diversify and influence political developments in Central Europe. (3) Czechoslovakia was replaced by two states with rather different foreign policies as well as different relations with their neighbours. This results in a different attitude on the part of the international community and international institutions. (4) The divorce re-introduced historically rooted problems with neighbouring states (Germany in the Czech case and Hungary in the Slovak case) that had been successfully controlled under the Czechoslovak umbrella. Most of these problems concern national minorities.

The two states have been developing different policies from the very beginning. The Czech Republic, in comparison to Czechoslovakia, became more oriented westward; to the contrary, the Slovak Republic became oriented more eastward, and this has defined their future foreign policy.

The Czech Republic

The foreign policy of the Czech Republic has three main aims: (1) international justification and legitimization of the division of Czechoslovakia as a step towards security rather than insecurity in the Central European region; (2) maximum individual capitalization of the more westward location of the Czech Republic; and (3) the successful appropriation of the positive international position and recognition of Czechoslovakia and presentation of the new Czech state as the political and historical successor of democratic Czechoslovakia. The more specific goals of Czech foreign policy are the following:

1. Stratification of the connection between the CR and other Central European countries as well as with the rest of the post-communist world;

2. Putting an accent on the promotion of economic achievement and a single national economic performance and interest resulting in the 1995 accession to full membership of OECD;

3. A high priority was put on winning a seat as a non-permanent member of the UN Security Council;

4. The Czech Republic also strengthened its participation in the peacekeeping efforts in the former Yugoslavia (UNPROFOR, IFOR, SFOR) and increased general activity within the frame of the Partnership for Peace (PfP). However, participation in other security structures (for example CSCE) decreased significantly;

5. The 'as-soon-as possible' strategy towards EU membership became rather complicated due to the necessity of re-negotiation of the Association Agreement which was not transferred automatically from Czechoslovakia to the two successor states. The approval of the Association Agreement by all EU members' parliaments had been completed only by the end of 1994. By early 1996, CR submitted the EU membership application. However, the position of the current Czech government can be defined as Euro-sceptic, or Euro-critical, mainly in the area of the Maastricht standard of unification, in relation to the common EU currency prospects and, last but not least, its harsh criticism of EU agricultural policy;

6. Separation from Central Europe effected by low-profile relations with the four Visegrad countries while simultaneously increasing efforts to build bilateral relations with Western countries. In 1995, CR revitalized bilateral relations with Poland mainly due to the strategic position of Poland in NATO expansion plans;

7. 1995 brought a new initiative by CR toward improvement of bilateral relations with Germany which, historically speaking, have been heavily influenced by the demands of the Sudeten Germans transferred from Czechoslovakia in the post-war period. However, the proposed declaration of parliaments closing this chapter of the past was not agreed upon due to the fears on the Czech side about possible negative consequences of weakening the legal basis of the transfer effected by the post-war presidential decrees. Long-term deadlock in Czech–German relations became a source of bitter domestic political disputes on both sides (the final agreement was signed only in January 1997).

The Slovak Republic

The foreign policy of the Slovak Republic has been developing in different circumstances. In the beginning, its foreign policy faced the accomplishment of several important tasks:

1. Institutional establishment and stabilization of the foreign service of the independent Slovak state. Development of a full infrastructure, including diplomatic relations, signified by the presence of embassies in Bratislava;

2. Introduction of the Slovak Republic to the international community as well as to the main international organizations as a new, yet mature and reliable state;

3. Changing the international image of Slovakia as being the party more responsible for the collapse of Czechoslovakia;

4. Changing the dangerous historical parallels to the Slovak fascist state existing in the period 1939–44;

5. Redefinition of relations with neighbours within the new geopolitical situation in Central Europe;

6. Improvement of Slovak–Hungarian relations.

Most of these goals were achieved by 1994. Other new developments were evident in 1995 and later on.

The change of government in Budapest in 1994 decreased the significance of the Hungarian minority's interest in shaping Hungarian foreign policy and international pressure (for example, the Balladur plan) led to a new Slovak–Hungarian treaty being negotiated and signed in Paris. The treaty allowed for more protection of the minority from the Hungarian perspective and brought border stability guarantees from the Slovak perspective. However, in bilateral development and in relation to the climate surrounding the 'Hungarian issue' in Slovakia, the Treaty did not yield the expected fruits and the situation even worsened.

Anti-democratic measures and policies executed by Meciar's cabinet attracted more and more adverse attention and increasing official criticism. The USA, the EU, the European Parliament and other international institutions (including the Catholic Church and the Vatican) publicly warned the Slovak government about the possible negative consequences of anti-democratic policies.

Consequently, Slovakia became less frequently mentioned among countries to be included in the EU and NATO in the first round.

The Slovak government introduced policies counterbalancing the western pressure by closer co-operation with Ukraine and also with Russia, including military and security co-operation. Thus, 1995 brought real problems for the geopolitical orientation of Slovakia and, simultaneously, the danger of a new east–west geopolitical division fixed on the Czech-Slovak borders.

Part of this development was a significant decline in Czech–Slovak bilateral relations in all aspects, including economic co-operation and international political support of Slovakia by Czech foreign policy and diplomacy.

During the first two years of sovereignty, Slovakia succeeded in achieving its main international goals as a new independent state: being recognized as a member of the group of most advanced post-communist countries struggling – via the PfP and the Association Agreement – for European identity and full integration into the international democratic environment.

However, during 1995, and under radical nationalist pressure in the coalition, Slovak foreign policy did not succeed in building the necessary level of independence and stability in the main features of its foreign policy which was subject to currents operative on the domestic political scene. Its foreign policy proved to be another victim of domestic political instability.

Another important feature of 1995 developments is an increasing gap between foreign policy shifts by the government on one side and public preferences on the other. Public opinion manifests a clear stability in its geopolitical preferences. EU/NATO membership was supported in December 1995 by 50 per cent and opposed by 27 per cent. In the event of a referendum, the pro-EU vote would be 59 per cent and the pro-NATO vote 43 per cent (an increase, compared to July 1995, of 7 per cent). The idea of affiliation with Russia (instead of other geopolitical alternatives) is extremely unpopular (3 per cent). A non-affiliated status (neutrality) was supported by 27 per cent.

The geopolitical orientation of Slovakia is also subject to national dispute. Contrary to the government's policies, the majority of the public supports a Euro-Atlantic identity as the future of Slovakia and reflects the unease of the West about the direction of Slovak development. Even among supporters of Meciar's movement, pro-NATO attitudes climbed to 44 per cent, slightly outnumbering NATO opponents (38 per cent).

The tension between prevailing support for current government on one side and the equally prevailing interest in NATO/EU membership on the other is a feature of the current climate of public life in Slovakia. However, there is probably no political party strong enough to represent and defend the pro-European development of Slovak society. Last but not least, we have to speak about the continuous positive impact of certain Central European interests, well perceived and understood by educated Slovak society.

ECONOMIC DEVELOPMENT

The economic integrity of Czechoslovakia was based on extensive economic co-operation between Czech and Slovak enterprises, as well as on the reallocation and investment of resources from the Czech regions in favour of Slovakia. The size of the common market of 15 million consumers and the relatively successful economic transition were put at risk at the time of the split.

The divorce contained several agreements dealing with the smooth shift from one economy to two separately operating markets. The agreements allowed for the continued use of a common currency, the establishment of a free-trade zone and a clearing system for payments connected with Czech–Slovak trade.

This monetary union did not survive longer than a few weeks. Increasing differences in monetary and financial development resulted in the introduction of separate national currencies in the Spring of 1993. A clearing system for payments with a strictly defined acceptable variation in exchange rates in relation to the ECU was ended by 1995 and replaced by a standard hard currency regime of payment. The free-trade agreement had a rather difficult period due to Slovakia's protectionist measures implemented in an effort to improve the balance of trade between the two states. Collaboration in manufacturing has decreased most dramatically. This development is mostly characterized by the declining position of the Slovak market in Czech exports while the position of the Czech market in Slovak exports remains one of the strongest.

The economic development of the two republics experienced a similar post-split shock strengthened by the introduction of VAT taxation at the same time. Budget imbalances and a rapid decrease of hard currency reserves occurred on both sides during the first months after the split.

The Czech Republic

The Czech Republic achieved stability earlier in all aspects including control over inflation. Three per cent growth, 10 per cent inflation, unemployment below 5 per cent and a balanced budget in 1993 were much better results than expected. 1994 brought further recovery and stabilization by modest growth (2.4 per cent), one-digit inflation, and still the lowest unemployment in Europe. 1995 brought an already significant growth up to the 6 per cent level, approximately the same level of inflation and unemployment continuing below 5 per cent. Czech currency became fully convertible in 1995. Such convertibility was one of the preconditions for full membership of the OECD achieved by CR in the Fall of 1995. The private and privatized sector now represents 80 per cent of production after the completion of the second round of voucher privatization.

The main problem confronting current Czech economic development is the substantial deficit in exports (4 billion US dollars in 1995) which is likely to continue. The deficit threatens the macrostability of Czech economy and currency. Disputes about the deficit's causes point to the declining export capacity resulting from the lack of restructuration of the economy as well as to the import requirements necessary for economic growth. The Czech economy also needs further deregulation and liberalization in the areas of housing, energy, and telecommunications. Cuts in the rather large volumes of government expenditure and the budget, and a significant decrease in high taxation are all needed. Major restructuring of the economy and the labour force are also priorities for the Czech Republic. To encourage growth and better export performance of the economy is more of a political than an economic problem. The recent election results in Hungary and Poland have probably pushed the Czech government towards a more social democratic rather than, as previously, the conservative and monetarist approach mandated by the election results of 1992. A slow-down in the dynamics of economic transformation for political reasons continued even through 1995 and brought major crisis in the health care system and its financing, in the school system and public transportation.

The Slovak Republic

The post-split economic shock was deeper in Slovakia and stabilization took longer. The further worsening of the economic situation – in comparison to the 'Czechoslovak' period of 1990–92 – was strongly reflected in public opinion and influenced macroeconomic stability. Early after the split, Slovakia ran up a large budget deficit due to its lower budget income. Stabilization of the new state was also impeded by the lack of tax discipline. Hard currency reserves dropped dramatically to a critically low level. The active pro-stabilization policy included devaluation of the new Slovakian currency and further regulations targeted towards balancing the budget. The stability achieved has been renewed and recovery occurred in 1994 when Slovakia experienced modest growth and inflation fell to 12 per cent.

The economic reform slowed down mainly in the privatization process. Stabilization policy during 1994 incorporated administrative measures and trade regulations were imposed on imports from the Czech Republic. With this manoeuvre, Slovakia achieved a trade balance at the probable expense of the agreements pertaining to the clearing payment system. After Meciar's second removal from the office of Prime Minister, the new broad coalition government re-introduced preparations for a voucher privatization and further stabilization policies. However, it was stopped and postponed for political reasons after Meciar's re-election in the Fall of 1994. In 1995, the voucher method was replaced by government bonds at a fixed price. The major privatization method became direct sales mostly into politically affiliated hands. The number of public bids, as well as bids open to foreign investors, dropped significantly. Consequently, the inflow of foreign investment declined in 1995. The strongest trade partner was still the Czech Republic.

The main feature of 1995 has been the largest economic growth in Central Europe (over 6 per cent), accompanied by an inflation below the 8 per cent level, a dramatic drop in budget deficit (close to a balance) and a modest export surplus. The main problem was unemployment, decreasing slightly from 15.2 per cent in 1994 to 12 per cent during 1995. In the Standard & Poor agency rating, Slovakia climbed to the rating Baa3 (investment level) and the country is expected to join the OECD this year.

In conclusion, we can see that whatever problems Slovakia experienced in its political and democratic developments following 1994 and Meciar's come-back, the economy has already produced the fruits of transition. The only question is what result may emerge from the combination of democratic decline and economic growth. Slovakia will probably experience more complex political and economic adjustment with results difficult to predict. The country and the society contain both possibilities for political stabilization as well as an instability unsettling the security situation throughout the Central European region. Part of the risk is the general possibility that the split of Czechoslovakia may result in division of Central Europe into two different geopolitical regions with distinct systemic features in all areas, beginning with political systems and ending with ethnic and economic instability.

REFERENCES – SOURCES OF DATA

Attitudes toward the Split of CSFR in the Czech Republic (Prague: STEM Research Agency, January 1994).

Current Problems of Slovakia after the Split of CSFR, March 1993 (Bratislava: FOCUS Research Agency, 1993).

Current Problems of Slovakia, Spring 1995 (Bratislava: FOCUS Research Agency, 1995).

Current Problems of Slovakia, December 1995 (Bratislava: FOCUS Research Agency, 1996).

Czech Attitudes toward Germany and Germans. Survey report (Prague: Friedrich Naumann Stiftung, Gabal Analysis & Consulting, July 1995).

Czechoslovakia on the Eve of Split (Prague: AISA Research, November 1992).

Development of Attitudes toward Czechoslovak Constitutional System during 1991 (personal archive of I. Gabal).

Ethnic Climate in the Czech Society. Survey report (Prague: MENT, Gabal Analysis & Consulting, 1994).

Gabal, I. (ed.), *National Minorities in CR and Europe* (Prague: Institute of International Relations, 1996).

Political Scene in Slovakia, December 1995 (Bratislava: FOCUS Research Agency, January 1996).

Selected Attitudes toward the Security Situation of the Czech Republic (Prague: STEM Research Agency, May 1994).

Smoke, R. (ed.), *Perception of Security: Public Opinion and Experts Assessments in Europe's New Democracies* (Manchester and New York: Manchester University Press, 1996).

8

Estonia, Latvia, Lithuania: the way to Europe

Eugenijus Maldeikis and Gediminas Rainys

THE BALTIC STATES: GEOGRAPHICAL DEFINITION OR A ZONE OF COMMON INTERESTS?

What do we mean by saying the Baltic states? What is that separates them and what unites them? The features by which these three small neighbouring countries differ, one from the other, are quite obvious.

Different languages. A third language, usually English or Russian is used for interstate communication. The Lithuanian and Latvian languages are of the same origin, though they differ significantly at present. *Different religions.* The main religion in Lithuania is Roman Catholicism, while it is mainly Lutheran Evangelical in the other countries. *Different histories.* Historically, Lithuania's closest relationships were with Poland, while Latvia and Estonia were more closely tied to the Scandinavian countries and Germany.

What is it that unites them? It is quite peculiar that the strongest argument for the development of an image of the Baltic States as a common region is that East and West consider them a single region with the same problems. To Russia, they are *blizneje zarubezje* (close foreign countries), a zone of national security and economic interests, and a zone of protection for the Russian speaking population. Western countries and the European Union – as can be seen from its actions, programmes, and agreements – do not separate these states, either. For that reason, the Baltic states' foreign policy with respect to their Eastern neighbours is integrated and well coordinated. The steps towards European integration are coordinated too, though to a lesser extent. The process of social-economic reforms, and the development of an adequate legal foundation remains uncoordinated. The latter fact determines the fact that the transformation process in the Baltic States is not identical, but differs in its political evolution and the general speed of reforms.

The present state of interstate relationships among the Baltic States can be illustrated using the words of the President of Latvia, Guntis Ulmanis. Answering the question 'how do you evaluate the relationships between Latvia, Lithuania and Estonia?' he said:

> Our unity is not really strong. I see neither possibilities nor arguments for it to come into real effect and to become a solid foundation, because there are a lot of disagreements standing behind our backs. The occupation – when all three states were under one hammer – is gone and only that episode of history unites us. However, before the occupation [the interwar period – E. G. and G. R.] we were quite separate. To most of the people the real and objective need for unity remains unclear.[1]

The necessity for the Baltic States' internal and external policy coordination, common market development and, finally, their closer relationship, has been publicly expressed at the highest level. There are even common institutional structures – the Baltic Assembly, the Baltic Council of Ministers. However, such declarations have not been backed by any real work, actions or steps leading towards coordination of any kind. Today, the Baltic states are three different countries. Why is that so?

Many reasons and opinions can be advanced. The answer, first of all, should probably be sought in the popular mentality formed by the tortuous historical development of the Baltic states. During the last few centuries, the Baltic states sought their independence and the achievement of their individual national identities. This desire was fulfilled only in the two interwar decades of this century. After the collapse of the Soviet Union, independent states were re-established, and the perceptions of state sovereignty predominating at the beginning of the twenties were revived. Such perceptions of independence could not be separated from the understanding of sovereignty, from the necessity to resolve the internal and external policy issues of *sovereignty*, to establish an *independent* legal foundation and institutional structure. Thus, for many people, any integration resulting in a partial loss of sovereignty is still undesirable and unacceptable.

Yet another factor is the significance of historical interstate relations and links. The connections between Estonia and Finland, as well as Lithuania and Poland, are developing much more dynamically than any relationship among the Baltic states themselves, due to the long-standing historical relationships between those countries.

However, history not only separates, but also unites. The incorporation of the Baltic states into the Soviet Union at the beginning of the Second World War, as the result of Molotov–Ribbentrop pact, absolutely equalized the conditions of social-economic development in all three countries. The common history of the Baltic states started somewhat earlier – in the times of the Russian Empire's disintegration and the establishment of three independent states. These states functioned independently during the two interwar decades. A network of governmental institutions was established, as well as a market economy system and an independent foreign policy. Two decades is a very short historical period for the establishment and strengthening of any independent state. However, the same two decades of the 'lost' Soviet episode have a huge influence on the starting-point of the transformation process. This is the main feature that separates the Baltic States from the other Soviet republics. 'The Baltic states have destroyed the Soviet Union' – this is a widespread expression which also depicts the Baltic states' eagerness for independence. On 11 March 1990, Lithuania – which had fewer nationality problems – proclaimed the restitution of its independence and actually finished the era of Gorbachev's *perestroika*.

The Baltic states can readily be distinguished from the Central European countries. At the beginning of the transformation process, those countries which used to belong to the Soviet bloc had an absolutely different starting position as compared to countries that were part of the Soviet Union. The unitary system of the country produced a situation in the Soviet republics, the Baltic states among them, where the majority of commonly found institutions functioned only formally or not at all. Thus:

1. The states' Supreme Councils were only formally functioning institutions, working for only a few days a year;

2. The activities of the ministries of foreign affairs, too, were merely formal;

3. There was no commercial banking and no national currencies: these market elements have had to be developed from scratch;

4. And total economic integration into the Soviet economy (the so-called unified complex) existed. Economic relations with the rest of the world were not direct but centralized through Moscow institutions.

These are the main features which differentiated the Baltic states from the former Soviet bloc countries.

The same internal and external conditions for socio-economic development, the same starting-point in the process of transformation, and the above-mentioned features both uniting the Baltic states and separating them from CIS countries as well as from former Soviet block countries, enable us to reach conclusions on the similarity of transformation process in the Baltic states.

All the Baltic states have declared a clear and definite willingness to join in the European integration process. Unity of the Baltic states will not be a result, but the *precondition* for integration processes. Integration is a goal that could be achieved by mutual coordination of the processes of socio-economic transformation. Despite all the difficulties, a process of integration among the Baltic states is going to be the first step, showing the competence, ability and capability of the countries to integrate into Europe.[2]

THE NEW INTERNATIONAL ENVIRONMENT

The new international environment that forms the background of changes for the newly independent states is a crucial matter. This environment in the Baltic region and in neighbouring countries is very dynamic. The Baltic states are clearly attempting to integrate into European political and economic structures in order to ensure minimal political and military guarantees for their sovereignty. This also produces effects on the political position and influence of Russia. However, during the last few years a clearly evident 'one-way traffic' tendency has not engendered any new disequilibrium in the space East–Baltic States–West. This is due to a starting position which was itself a departure from total integration with the East.

Evaluation of the geopolitical position of the Baltic states clearly discloses a collision of political-military and economic security aspects. Western countries are interested in the creation of a buffer zone for the European Union from any realm of potential conflicts. This interest has gained further momentum with Sweden and Finland joining the EU. Bearing in mind Russia's highly negative response to the Baltic states' attempts to join NATO, this region can be characterized as a zone of high military-political risk. From the economic point of view, the geopolitical position of the Baltic states is very favourable for European countries (as well as the Baltic states themselves) considering trade and economic relations with Russia and other CIS countries. This collision creates a dilemma for the Baltic states when trying to find optimal forms, and political as well as economic instruments for protection of their perceived national interests.

The question of ensuring independence and national security for the Baltic states has three aspects.

Political aspects. One of the most acute issues is the stabilization and provision of a legal foundation for a political relationship with Russia, all of which will require goodwill, great diplomatic skills and efforts from both sides. The scale of the problems can be illustrated by the following examples. The Estonia–Russia border question remains unresolved and legally unregulated. Under the terms of the bilateral peace treaty signed by countries after the First

World War, Estonia's territory should be larger than it is now. After the annexation of Estonia, a part of its territory was attached to Russia's Pskov region. Estonia is constantly stressing the necessity to resolve this issue legally. The specifics of Lithuania's geopolitical situation are that it lies between the CIS countries and Russia's Kaliningrad region. Russia's military forces are situated in this region and the territory of Lithuania is virtually the only acceptable transit, including military, route. The issue of military transit has already been used by Russia as a pretext for economic pressure. The imposition of double tariffs on Lithuanian goods resulted in companies losing $125 million, according to some estimates. These tariffs were kept in effect until a bilateral agreement on military transit was agreed. The third instrument of political pressure is the protection of the human rights of the Russian-speaking population. The problem is emphasized to the international community and is used in order to put pressure on Latvia and Estonia.

In another, western, direction there is a clear 'Europeanization' tendency, which is unanimously accepted by all Baltic states' political parties. The Baltics have already signed Association treaties with the EU. Nevertheless, these agreements, signed by all three Baltic states, show the different readiness of the countries for integration. Lithuania has chosen a six-year transitional period for implementation of a free-trade regime, while Latvia has chosen a four-year period. Estonia has rejected the possibility of using protective tariffs. In our opinion, these chosen options depict very clearly the economic transformation credos of the Baltic states. In the case of Estonia, one can generalize as follows: 'Maximum openness, maximum foreign investment'. The different degree of openness determines the different speed of integration with Europe and provides an insight into the inadequacy of inter-Baltic integration.

Military aspects. After half a century of occupation, there is no foreign army in the Baltic states. The countries are strengthening their state borders and air-space control systems, creating their own armies. The might of the CIS block in military terms and the facts of historical experience (the annexation of Baltic states) has produced a unanimous desire to join NATO. According to the NATO authorities, there is no queue for entering the organization. However, taking into account the current level of the Baltic states' readiness to join NATO, and notwithstanding their accumulating experience of practical cooperation, there are, ultimately, Russia's objections. In such a context, it is clear that membership of NATO is a matter for the distant future. Actually, the queue in front of the Baltics is formed not in Brussels but by differences in the East-Central European countries. At present, the 'Partnership for Peace' is a proper initiative to enhance stability and security in the Baltic region.

Economic aspects. Russia is interested in preservation and expansion of its interests in the region; therefore it is not difficult to forecast that it will further enhance its economic influence. This tendency has been becoming clearer during recent years, with Russia trying to develop economic integration among CIS countries. The important changes in the Russian–Belarussian relationship reflect the features of this integration. A typical opinion of the Russian experts influencing Russia's strategy towards the Baltics is as follows:

> Russia's strategy towards the Baltic states should be particularly careful. On the one hand, it should not give the Baltics the opportunity to accuse Russia of having imperial ambitions, and, on the other hand, it should protect Russia's interests in the region to the utmost extent. It would be useful to propose significant initiatives [...] Besides, it is absolutely necessary to utilize the possibilities for economic influence on the Baltic states, which still overwhelmingly depend on Russian resources and energy.[3]

It may be paradoxical, but an 'escape' from the Eastern neighbour's influence is not only impossible, but also undesirable. Russia is still the main trade partner for all three Baltic states. Almost 100 per cent of the Latvian and Lithuanian, and a great part of the Estonian, demand for energy resources is satisfied by Russia. Today, Russia is an immense, though frequently insolvent market.

The seaports of the Baltic states handle 90 per cent of the transit cargo of the CIS countries. The economic stability of the Baltics is especially dependent on re-export possibilities. The share of re-export in Lithuanian export volume constitutes from 30 to 80 per cent, depending on the type of goods. These figures sustain the image of the Baltic states as the bridge between East and West and vice versa. And this is not only a matter of words. In our opinion, trade still remains one of the most effective buffers lessening the impact of the transformation's burdens and ensuring internal political stability.

DEMOCRATIZATION

The progress of the Baltic states' democratization, which began in the late 1980s, is primarily tied to changes in the political system, particularly the shift to a multiparty system. This process is characterized by: (1) the growth of national democratic movements and their subsequent transformation; (2) the reform of the ruling communist parties.

The national democratic movements, which functioned actively for only two or three years, were political products of the transitional period, and they have lately evolved in different directions. The Estonian movement 'melted down'; in Latvia it split into several parties; in Lithuania, it was transformed into a coalition of parties.

The transformation of communist parties and their members during the period of democratization was also differentiated. In Estonia, the members of the communist parties joined other political forces; in Latvia, the orthodox Communist Party was preserved and at the same time reorganized into a new reformed party. In Lithuania, the Communist Party was reformed, like the Bulgarian or Slovakian cases, by changing its title and programme, although in opposition it did not split and, fairly rapidly, re-acquired its ruling position. The results of a survey conducted in Lithuania show that, according to their views on economic reform, the elite of the ruling Lithuanian Democratic Labour Party can be evenly divided into three groups – left, centrist (moderate) and liberal.

The classic political parties (Christian Democrats, liberals and social democrats) are still relatively weak in the whole region and during elections are able to attract, jointly, only some 20–25 per cent of the electorate, while in the countries of the EU they attract more than 70 per cent of all votes. A relatively large number of votes are given to those parties which assert pragmatic or national policy slogans but do not have a clear system of values. The influence of radical populist parties is getting stronger. The groups of this type are given up to 15 per cent of the vote.

The election results in the Baltics produce a tendency to formation of a multiparty structure without any leading party. The obstacles and *difficulties* for the democratization process are related to: economic and social difficulties of the transitional period, and the aggravation of ethnic conflicts that could weaken the legitimacy of democracy; radical political and economic changes that cause social, political and property-related polarization in society; a still predominantly low level of political culture among the political elite and masses; dangers springing from nationalist funda-mentalism, which could be a basis for new forms of autocracy and populist dictatorships.

Free elections and adoption of new constitutions also signify the beginning of the democratization process in the Baltic states. Having identified four stages of the democratization process, that is (1) the weakening of the autocratic regime, (2) a transitional period, (3) a consolidation period, and (4) a stable democratic period, it is possible to conclude that the *Baltic states have already gone through the transition to democracy period and are currently starting the democratic consolidation period.*

The ongoing process of democratic consolidation is leading towards a wide and deeply legitimate democracy. It involves changes to institutional and spiritual values in society which reduce the uncertainties of democracy. It is worth mentioning the following features of consolidation which have gradually become stronger in the Baltic states: there is a firm commitment by the population and political elites to democratic principles; there is a consensus by the political elites that free elections are the only way to acquire political power; *political institutionalization*, that is (1) the effective functioning of governmental institutions, which absorbs social shocks and discrepancies; (2) well structured executive governance implementing necessary reforms; (3) an independent and professional legal system; (4) a system of political parties characterized by dominant centrist tendencies; (5) a society of active citizens with real channels for participation in the political process.

All this proves the formation of *representative democracies* in the Baltic states. The dangers and difficulties that accompany this institutionalization process could gain momentum if representative democracy is narrowed and transformed to a *delegative democracy*. This can be caused by the narrowing of the representation of societal interests, clientelism, patronage and corruption.

ECONOMIC TRANSFORMATION

The approach to economic reform in the Baltics generally was based upon a macroeconomic vision of the transformation process. The reform programmes were dominated by the classical steps of structural adjustment: microeconomic liberalization–macroeconomic stabilization–privatization. While the first two elements were supposed to bring socialist economies back to macroeconomic equilibrium, privatization was supposed to increase the efficiency of industry by introducing a new governance structure.

The initial structure of the independent, post-Soviet Baltic states' economies was a product of forcible incorporation into the Soviet economic system. As a result, the Baltics were compelled to develop in a distorted, unbalanced way, becoming heavily industrialized to the detriment of other economic sectors, especially consumer goods and the entire service sector. In 1990, the share of industry and agriculture was 60 per cent of Lithuanian GDP, while in 1994 it accounted only for 28 per cent. At the same time, the trade sector share of GDP has grown from 5 to 23 per cent, services and related activities from 25 to 40 per cent. These figures illustrate the deep structural deficiencies of the economy, as well as the scope and speed of the transformation.[4]

Having reviewed the macroeconomic indicators of the Baltic states, one can conclude that relative macroeconomic stabilization has already been achieved. After four years of decline, GDP and industrial output have bottomed out and improvement is expected. The annual inflation rate in Lithuania was 35 per cent in 1995 and 13 per cent in 1996. Similar tendencies were experienced in the economies of other Baltic states. In order to control inflation Estonia and Lithuania have adopted the Currency Board model. The Estonian kroon was pegged to the deutschmark, the Lithuanian litas to the US dollar. The Latvian lat remains a floating currency; however, its Central Bank is conducting a tough monetary policy that ensures a relatively low inflation rate. Although there can be contradictory opinions about the IMF's role in shaping the economic transformation policy, it is necessary to stress that the memoranda agreed by the governments of the region and the IMF lessen the probability of governments opting for voluntarist and populist decisions in the monetary and fiscal realms. The main difference between the Baltic states' transformation process and that of the Central European countries have been problems of state management – new state management institutions were introduced during this process: from Central Bank to customs offices. This was not the case in most Central European countries.

The marketization level of the states' economies is best depicted by indicators characterizing the economic relationships of the Baltic states with market-oriented countries. Starting from 1994, trade turnover volumes with non-CIS countries were greater than 50 per cent. This leads us to conclude that there has been a successful diversification of the Baltic states' economic relations. The best position in relation to the EU market has been obtained by Estonia. This was largely influenced by the fact that Finland and Sweden – Estonia's traditional trading partners – became EU members. Estonia has had, by far, the greatest success in attracting foreign direct investment. Lithuanian economic policy is oriented towards credits and loans from international financial institutions and foreign governments. The 1 billion dollars invested in the Baltic states over a five-year period indicates the attractiveness of this region to foreign investors.

Privatization and associated demonopolization have been, by far the most important element, forming the backbone of transition from plan to market. Analysis of the privatization process in the Baltic states shows the difference in privatization goals and methods adopted. The formal similarity of the processes is derived from the restitution of expropriated real estate and land, as well as the use of investment vouchers. However, though vouchers were the main instrument in Lithuania, in the other countries their use was limited. The mainly commercial Estonian privatization could be characterized by the following credo: 'a principal investor, openness for insiders and outsiders'. In 1997 the following opinion was expressed:

> No other country in the old East Bloc has gone so far, so fast. Private owners bought virtually all Estonian industries. With a final round of big infrastructure sell-offs in the works, Estonia stands to emerge with one of Europe's greatest concentrations of private ownership, with a planned 90 per cent of the economy springing from the private sector.[5]

The arguments for the distributional privatization model show that Lithuanian privatization policy was shaped partly under the influence of such populist slogans as:

1. *Social equity.* Free distribution of vouchers to the population was preferable for reasons of both political efficacy and equity.

2. *Social justice.* The State must compensate its citizens for the low wages which they were paid by the former regime.

3. *Creation of a capitalist class.* Acquisition of even a small amount of 'capital' (investment vouchers), the necessity to invest it and a desire to do it in the most effective way, will force ordinary people to use their 'creative capability' and thus the process will engender a capitalist class.

4. *High speed of privatization.* The comparison with British-style privatization was very popular. It was argued that adoption of such

a method of privatization would extend the process for 400 years and, of course, this was unacceptable.

5. *There is no capital in Lithuania to carry out commercial privatization.* The problem was considered as a question of national security with two types of possible negative consequences. First, the possible participation – and consequently political and economic influence – of Eastern neighbours; second, the necessary capital for commercial privatization would be acquired by representatives of hidden economy, the former *nomenklatura*.

In 1997, it was concluded that 'Lithuania tries to entice big-ticket investors, then it locks away most of its assets in a vault marked "strategic"; any wave of openness may be slow in coming'.[6]

The Latvian privatization process started later and its concept is closer to the Estonian privatization model.

The acute problem of political and economical stability in the Baltics in 1995 was related to the banking sector crisis, especially in Latvia and Lithuania. The crisis has led to the bankruptcy of some commercial banks. A sociological survey in Lithuania has shown that only 4.7 per cent of people have faith in banks.

The reasons for the crisis are related to the present state of the economy and to the quality of bank management. Another reason for the banking crisis in Latvia is the openness of its banking system: Russian-originated capital transfers back to Russia induced by a stronger rouble and the beginning of commercial privatization in Russia had serious repercussions. A specific feature of the Lithuanian crisis is the insider-oriented nature of the privatization. A major part of banks' loans was used for the privatization of entities hoping to resell them later to strategic investors. The banks' credit abilities and high investment risk were not taken into account. The bankruptcies of industrial – financial holdings caused instability in the economic situation.

NATION BUILDING, MORAL AND PSYCHOLOGICAL REVOLUTION

Human resource development is a crucial matter for the success of the overall transformation process. Five years of experience allows us to conclude that the success of transformation should be evaluated neither by macroeconomic indicators nor by the volumes of state assets privatized. Success should also be measured by changes in popular mentality, by erosion of the characteristics of *homo sovieticus*. The immense differences between the two systems and the speed of systemic changes were factors conducive to a mental and psychological vacuum, making for much discontent among many people. What are the main sources of such discontent?

1. The decline in living standards (however, this decline is most felt only in particular social groups – pensioners, workers of large (and mainly insolvent) state enterprises, farmers, and so on);

2. Such intangible welfare assets as country openness, possibility of travel, Western TV programmes and so on, are usually not ascribed any value;

3. The sudden increase in consumer demand dictated by visions of western prosperity;

4. Psychological difficulties in accepting marked income differentiation (this differentiation is fairly large: the middle class is still in the process of formation);

5. The feeling of social insecurity: former full employment versus unemployment or threat of unemployment.

Passivity in the former system ('Government, help me') is subjected to change through individualistic activity and acceptance of risk. The *new* institutions and functions of the economy (banks, financial markets, marketing, accounting and so on) require *new* knowledge. Newly emerging economies suffer from a lack of specialists in the field of public administration. This produces a situation where governmental management is brought to equality with corporate management. This fact is best characterized by the words of one Lithuanian state official, expressed during a private conversation: 'I do not need any programmes. If the right decisions are taken each day, then the transformation process is going in the right direction'.

The dissolution of the Soviet Union equally involves us in the birth of nations, emerging from the ruins of the great multinational empire. In the case of the Baltic states, having evaluated their relatively shorter period of sovietization, it is incorrect to claim that the ruination of the former empire also involves their national development *from the ruins*. It is more appropriate to speak about the problems created by this period of sovietization. The paramount issue here is about national minorities. Estonians comprise 64.1 per cent in their country, Latvians 53.5 per cent, Lithuanians 81.1 per cent. After the re-establishment of the Baltic states' independence, the question of granting citizenship was resolved in different ways.

In nationally more homogeneous Lithuania, citizenship was granted to all legal inhabitants of the country. Meanwhile, in Latvia and Estonia, a 'restitutional' approach was used, meaning that not all new inhabitants have instantly become citizens with attendant citizens' rights. What was the reason for such treatment? It was feared that the Baltic states' search for independence would be hampered by intractable internal problems – the fear of national minorities losing their rights and, consequently, creating resistance to the Europeanization process. Hopefully, the processes referred to will be closely related to assuring the rights of national minorities.

THE ESSENCE OF CONFLICT

One of the biggest problems for a transforming society is to ensure political stability. The main reason for instability is the ineffectiveness of political institutions, whose development is necessary for quick reforms and changes in all segments of society.

Society's expectations are still closely tied to the state, and when these expectations are not satisfied there appears a growing discontent with government activities. The political culture currently dominant in the Baltic states has partly absorbed some features of the former autocratic regime which held a superior position over its people and demanded their obedience. This mixture of a passive political culture and a developing democratic system produces a minimal level of control by political authority. On the one hand, the state institutions undergoing reforms cannot implement any effective control of political activity and, on the other hand, passivity in society is the cause of the non-existence of public control. The process of development of political culture and democracy in the Baltic states has not been absolutely even. During the autumn of 1995, in Estonia, the prime minister and the minister of internal affairs resigned after a highly publicized scandal connected with unauthorized telephone-tapping. Therefore, our previous conclusion about the passivity of political culture is, perhaps, more appropriate for Lithuania rather than for Estonia.

The results of Lithuanian surveys reveal popular attitudes towards the fairness of political decisions. Right decisions are made: (1) 'almost always' 2 per cent; (2) 'frequently' 14 per cent; (3) 'from time to time' 63 per cent; (4) 'almost never' 15 per cent; (5) 'do not have an opinion' 6 per cent.[7]

The five years of transformation have also been years of formation of a new elite which determines the direction of the transformation process, its scale and speed. This elite consists of representatives of the old political, administrative and economic *nomenklatura*, intellectuals and representatives of a 'new wave', who became well known during the period of national renaissance. This elite already has formed a general outline of future state and social development. The Lithuanian political elite, which is formed by representatives of different political movements, unanimously support the economic reforms. Of course, the division of the elite into a left and right wing – and its general political credo – is conditioned by its members' attitude towards the past but this finds little reflection in the programmes of the parties, most of which are very similar. The majority (two-thirds) advocate the market economy with a small, state-owned sector and limited state intervention. One half of the interviewed Lithuanian elite thought that economic reforms should be conducted more vigorously and only 29 per cent opted for a slower speed of economic transformation.

The political weakness of the Lithuanian elite is reflected in its lack of deeper analysis of transformation processes and strategic planning. The problem is clearly seen – only 5 per cent think that current government strategy was planned in advance. Social institutions are still unable to effectively control the behaviour of the authorities. The only accessible institution, capable of influencing matters is the free mass media.

Only about 1 per cent of Lithuanian citizens belong to political parties or social movements. Intellectuals like to stress their political independence. The negative attitude of intellectuals, who shape social opinion, towards the activities of political institutions and politics as a whole widens the gap between the elite and population. The state and its developing political system has not yet become a positive value for citizens and there thus remains the danger of conflicts between the authorities and society. Lithuanians are proud of the history of their state, architecture and moral values, but only 2 per cent of them mention government, 0.9 per cent parliament, 3 per cent the courts. In the structure of the political elite, the main role is played by the state bureaucracy. It is the strongest and so dominates. Other groups are simply too weak. The major means of influence embrace:

1. Financial resources (budget); (weak parliamentary control allows for manipulation of budget resources);

2. The procedure for drafting laws allows ministries to prepare them in favour of their interests (only stronger social groups and organizations representing their own interests could partially defend such interests);

3. Lobbying of industrial-financial groups.

According to the Lithuanian elite, the main actors in the process of formulation of economic policy are the Parliament majority and the Government (7.2 points out of a possible 10 point score). Almost the same weight is given to the influence of Eastern and Western countries, as well as criminal organizations, on the economy. Representatives of left-wing parties accord higher influence to Western countries and the representatives of right-wing parties to Eastern countries. The influence of public opinion is accorded the least place (2.1 points). The Parliamentary opposition is given very little influence on the country's economic policy (2.6 points), and the same is true for political parties (2.7 points).

Disregarding the mistakes associated with 'adolescent growth', the tendency to political stability, the growth of social and political culture, democratic consolidation and economic growth in the Baltic states enhance the formation of civil society, strengthen the ethical foundations of the new elite, and deepen the need for a better representation of popular needs.

NOTES

1. *Neatkariga Rita Avize* (Riga), 17 November 1995.

2. P. Ludlow, E. Fenech-Adami, G. Vassiliou and the CEPS International Advisory Council, *Preparing for Membership. The Eastward and Southern Enlargement of the EU*. 2nd International Advisory Council Report (Brussels, 1996). The study highlights the dynamics of the relationship between the EU and its partners in the East and conditions for membership – transparent criteria for assessing economic health, the quality of civil society and the security situation of prospective member states.

3. A. Vuskarnik, 'Baltijskaja Politika Zapada i Rossija', *Mezdunarodna Ekonomika i Mirovyje Otnoshenija*, no. 3 (1995) p. 122.

4. All calculations presented in this paper are based on data from the statistical offices of Lithuania, Latvia and Estonia, as well as from the Estonian and Latvian embassies in Lithuania.

5. M. Brzezinski, 'Country for Sale', *Central European Economic Review*, IV, no. 10 (December 1996 – January 1997) p. 13.

6. M. Brzezinski, 'Flip Flop', *Central European Economic Review*, IV, no. 10 (December 1996 – January 1997) p. 14.

7. In December 1994, the Institute of International Relations and Political Science at Vilnius University and the social opinion survey company Social Information Centre conducted sociological research. The social survey data used in this paper are taken from this research.

9

Hungary: in the midst of systemic change

Attila Agh

The socio-economic and political transformations in Hungary had already begun in the 1980s and the historical turning point of 1989–90 signified the culmination of this incremental process, as well as the start of a new democratization-cum-marketization process. Hungary was an early starter, along with Poland, and despite all turning-points, a strong continuity still connects the reform processes of the 1980s with the democratization processes in the 1990s; a strong political stability characterizes the whole period because of (1) the constitution passed in 1989–90; (2) the strong prime ministerial government; and (3) the presence of the same six parties elected to the parliament in both free elections.

Hungary has had great achievements as well as serious setbacks in the democratization process. Democratic institutionalization has taken place dynamically, but the first freely elected government produced some return to the past, to the Golden Age That Never Was in Hungarian history. Therefore we have to consider not only 1989–90, but also 1994, as a turning-point (although of a lesser extent), separating two markedly different political regimes within the new democratic system. We can analyse here the period of the national-conservative government between 1990 and 1994 fully, and in some detail, but that of the new social-liberal government only partially, that is until the end of 1996, and only in very general outline.[1]

THE PERIOD OF THE NATIONAL-CONSERVATIVE GOVERNMENT

Political transformations

There has been a fundamental political transformation in train since the early 1990s with the establishment of new democratic institutions in Hungary. This process has historical significance as a major turning-point; nevertheless, most Hungarians were dissatisfied with the first Antall government. Its public standing was rather low. In fact, the new government suffered a crushing defeat six months after the general elections in the local government elections. All international and Hungarian public opinion polls have shown, in turn, that the previous, Nemeth, government is still popular even now and its public standing has always been higher than that of the Antall–Boross government.

This can be considered a paradoxical situation only if we accept the sweeping generalizations of commonsense Western analyses. When the 'democracy barometer' shows that mainly Hungarians and former Soviet citizens have the greatest nostalgia for 1989, the year '1989' may mean the former system for Belarusians or Ukrainians, but it is certainly not so for Hungarians. For Hungarians, this period means the Nemeth government with an active transformation process towards democracy and market economy in the late 1980s. The socio-political transformation was full of contradictions, but it had a particular economic and social dynamism with high expectations and great optimism for modernization and westernization. This process in Hungary was broken, or slowed down, in the early 1990s by the Antall government. Therefore it would be for Hungary an oversimplification to associate the year 1989 and the Nemeth government with the former authoritarian regime. Nor can one associate the year 1990 and the Antall government with a fully democratic regime, either. In general, in the early 1990s, the citizens of Hungary, Czechoslovakia and Poland thought very precisely that *their countries were somewhere half-way between a new authoritarian rule and a future democracy*. In particular,

Hungarians perceived that both their political situation and their perspectives for democracy worsened between 1991 and 1992 as the divergence from mainstream democratization became consolidated.

This is not the legendary pessimism of Hungarians but a realistic assessment by them, in which disappointment has followed on high expectations and modest realities. Hungary had a very substantial modernization potential in the 1980s and its people felt, with justification, that the Antall government did not utilize it properly and optimally. There was a political swing to the other extreme, from the 'soft dictatorship' of kadarism, to a mild rightwing authoritarianism or traditional conservatism, which frustrated all those who were modernization- and westernization-oriented. The late nineteenth century and interwar Hungary merged to become a socio-political model for the Antall government, instead of aiming for the present political structure found in the West European states. This government also revived the role of religion – primarily Catholicism as a new-old quasi-state religion – in political life, although most Hungarians have secular habits and a very vague attachment to religion.[2]

This swing back to traditionalism-conservatism and the reappearance of the traditional Hungarian political class with its characteristic behaviour, symbols and mentality shook the optimism of the population. It led to the erosion of the popularity of the right-wing coalition government and to that of the former coalition parties themselves. The Hungarian Democratic Forum (HDF) went through a series of splits between moderate, traditional conservatives and extreme right-wing nationalists-populists (Antall versus Csurka). The rise of openly anti-European populist nationalism from inside the hegemonic party certainly damaged the international reputation and image of Hungary.

Between 1990 and 1994, the Hungarian party system of six major parliamentary parties changed beyond recognition. Concerning the parties, the party preferences, second preferences and dispreferences among the population indicated the loss of credibility of the three former governing parties and the increasing popularity of the three oppositional parties. The representatives of the former government always cast doubt on the results of public opinion polls because they were unfavourable for them. Numerous surveys, however, pointed in the same direction and the results of the surveys by the international and domestic institutes differed only slightly, almost imperceptibly. These results indicated very low preference and very high dispreference among the population for the former coalition parties, with one-third of the population completely alienated from politics. Yet Hungary had relative stability with the same government for four years, but it paid a very high price for this unique feature in the region. During these four years, a huge gap arose between the legal and political legitimacy of the government. Hungary for four years avoided a change of the transitional political elite. In the other countries of the region, around 70 per cent of MPs have been changed at each election, so the least talented politicians have already been weeded out, in some countries several times.

In Hungary there has been a classical combination of the 'Democracy Wave' and 'Reverse Wave', using Huntington's terms, with the dominance of the former but with too much loss of time and energy because of the so-called Authoritarian Renewal and distortion of democracy during the Antall–Boross government.

We can test the political transformation against the above-mentioned factors or dimensions as follows:

Structural problems: The Central European countries have developed a particular mixture of authoritarian and democratic traditions with long authoritarian periods and short, recurring reform-cycles for democratization. State socialism was not an alien element: it simply reinforced and easternized the long-extant authoritarian traditions. The recent democratization has had to break with these authoritarian traditions and tendencies towards de-Europeanization. The negative legacy is *the relative or partial lack of democratic institutions and political culture*, as an institutional and cultural deficit.

Transitional problems: The short period of democratic transition has been overburdened by too many transformations going on at the same time, partly strengthening, partly weakening each other. The deep socio-economic crisis certainly makes the political transformation more difficult and the necessary structural changes in the economy lead unavoidably to even more social problems (unemployment) which worsen political conditions and may threaten even the democratization process by producing mass dissatisfaction and extreme right-wing populism. The major problem was, however, a *missing political experience and skill in governance and also the lack of a clear European orientation.* The transitional political elite, and Antall himself to a great extent, returned to traditionalism-provincialism and this delayed the fundamental transformation of the economy and society. The early 1990s became a period of lost opportunities for Hungary.

Systemic problems: The new system has established democratic political institutions, but its first regime was also prone to deviate from the line of democratization as well. It created only a 'partyist' democracy, that is a democracy for the party elites. In this, there was a 'tyrannical majority' of the ruling parties which dominated, based on their simple parliamentary majority, which declined, incidentally, between 1990 and 1994, from 60 to 51 per cent. The basic democratic values of competition and participation were hurt and violated, and the re-institutionalization of democracy hardly reached the sphere of organized interests or civil society. I can describe these new systemic problems with the terms 'authoritarian renewal' for the structural dimensions, and 'politics running amok' for the transitional ones. On the level of macro-politics, with the former government as its leading institution, there were attempts to organize a political monopoly over the other political and socio-economic actors, and to establish a new order in which the ruling party had a socio-economic clientura in an 'Italian' way.

Situational problems: The West has to face its own problems and has forgotten about promises concerning Central Europe. The European Union has been unable so far to develop a Grand Strategy on Central and Eastern Europe with a differentiated approach according to the 'EU capacity' of the countries concerned. Thus, overgeneralization still dominates. Big words have been followed by small deeds in the EU treatment of the Central European countries; 'short-termism' prevails against long-term strategic thinking. Hopefully, this attitude will be significantly changed after the consolidation of the Maastricht process within the European Union.

Economic transformations

The economic transformations as 'marketization' were already present in Hungary with the 1968 reforms; this accelerated in the late 1980s. Before 1989 – that is, before the collapse of the former regime – Hungary had already begun the marketization of the economy and strategic reorientation from Eastern to Western trade: in 1982 57.1 per cent of exports went to the East and 30.0 to the West, by 1988 50.6 went to the East and 40.6 to the West. The majority of the laws for the market economy were also passed in 1988 and 1989, including a Company Law and Law on Free Profit Repatriation. Privatization made big strides in the late 1980s and big industrialists were already establishing their firms in the 1980s. It seemed at that time that, after the political changes, the socio-economic transformation would accelerate even more and Hungary would be integrated into the Western economy very soon. These opportunities were lost, again.

The economic transformations since 1989 can also be analysed from different perspectives:

Structural problems: The command economy created industrial giants, first of all in heavy industry, based on state subsidies. Their structural transformation was already unavoidable by the late 1980s, with a major shift from an industrial to a service economy. Yet in this 'creative destruction', destruction dominated and the creation was minimal. The GDP of Hungary has been decreasing since 1989, and this is most drastically apparent in agricultural production, but it is also quite stark in industrial output. Industry began a slight recovery in 1993, although the investment figures have remained negative. Over the last three decades, up until 1989, there has been a cumulative inflation of 300 per cent; yet since 1989 there has been yet another 300 per cent inflation – only this time it took only four years (despite these figures it is relatively still the lowest in the region).

Transitional problems: The transition period really needed a policy of efficient crisis management right from the start, and the government should have concentrated on socio-economic crisis management. Instead, crisis management was neglected, the Antall government pushed aside its own Kupa programme for systemic socio-economic crisis management in favour of its own legislative agenda. In contrast, it focused on historical justification and ideological issues. The major victim of the ideological approach was Hungarian agriculture – by far, the most developed and export-oriented among the former socialist countries – and having a relatively solid base for private business in the second economy. The agricultural economy was almost ruined, the legal regulations changed frequently and state assistance was denied. Landed property became over-fragmented because of the nostalgia of the Independent Smallholders Party for the traditional small peasant economy.

Systemic problems: Privatization was slowed down by the Antall government in 1990–91 to give way for a wave of renationalization, that is for regaining political control over the economy. The Antall government established a clientura with the appointments it made in state firms, and by the special favours it granted within the context of privatization. Only the Church was given the privilege of reprivatization; for all the others there was only a small and sluggish compensation scheme with high bureaucratic costs and delays. The compensation for property losses and personal damage left everybody dissatisfied. Nevertheless, it produced huge extra costs for the deficit-prone state budget. The private economy continued to develop significantly, despite the efforts of the government rather than because of them. However, Hungarian developments in this period failed to produce a large middle class which could be the bearer and promoter of marketization and democratization. In 1993, 55 per cent of the GDP was already coming from the private economy, but this was the result of a long process. The real economic opening, however, with genuine privatization, budget reform and conscious economic policy remained basically a task for the Horn government.

Situational problems: The Eastern markets have collapsed and EU commercial contacts have become predominant and vital for Hungary. Yet the associate membership in the EU has not yet opened a clear perspective for long-term economic modernization in Hungary, since the European agreement still contains many restrictions. Obviously, some interest groups within the member states can still over-represent their narrow interests in Brussels against the new East-Central European democracies, even though their market share at issue can be extremely small.

Social transformations

The social systemic change has, in my view, three major elements which, to a certain extent, can also be put into a chronological order, as they emerge and as they dominate during the social systemic change. A deep *social crisis* appears first and leads to both political changes and *social structure transformations*, and the radically changed social structure mobilizes *new social actors*. The latter might have been on the scene from the very beginning, but they can act with full vigour only when they acquire the support of the newly emergent strata, whom they will serve by articulating and aggregating social demands into political channels. The emergence of new social actors as an organized interest is, at the same time, the 'end' of the transformation of politics as well, since the incorporation of organized interests into institutionalized policy-making signifies a conclusion to transitional processes.

1. The social crisis. The social crisis was already manifesting itself in the late 1980s, with the lack of social mobility, declining real wages, housing shortages and tremendous overwork with its harmful health consequences. This increasing social crisis has been a prime mover behind social movements, re-organized trade unions and, in general, mass political pressures. The recent social crisis has three main aspects. First, there is a drastic worsening of material living conditions, from the relatively high level of Hungarian 'consumer society' of the 1970s and 1980s compared to the other state socialist societies. The whole population was shaken by the sudden drop in standards of living in the early 1990s. The second aspect is social polarization – the growing distance between winners and losers in the political and economic transformations. Although mass poverty (in the most extreme case, homeless people) has manifestly appeared, with two or three millions below the social minimum line (elderly people, unemployed, big families, Gypsies and so on), the real losers are not to be found among the poorest strata whose position has deteriorated only slightly, but among the lower strata of the middle classes. Thus instead of building a middle-class society with a large middle-income stratum predominant, social systemic change has so far produced the phenomenon of the 'missing middle' in the social structure. One-third of society is growing richer, reclining on islands of modernity, but two-thirds are growing poorer and the 'old' middle strata (clerical employees, teachers, skilled workers) have lost a large part of their incomes. Their social situation gave an entry point to nationalist-populist extremisms.[3] Finally, the social crisis was accompanied by a psychological crisis: people felt abandoned, cheated and frustrated; families and friendships fell apart, many people sold their political loyalties for better and secure jobs, and changed ideological colours shamelessly, becoming devoted Christians from devoted Communists overnight. The masses, however, were making their own subjective evaluations about the systemic change: they did not see it as a change for the better, as a success – they saw just the opposite, and they perceived it as a humiliation and defeat. People refused the nationalist challenge of the Antall government.[4]

2. Social structure transformations. The systemic changes have brought about a fundamental transformation of social structure, but the new social structure is only *in statu nascendi*; therefore it has to be analysed with special care. Obviously, the new social structure should serve as a base for the new political and party system as well, with the new entrepreneurial middle classes being the focus of these social developments. The former classes and strata of the lopsided and overextended industrial society have begun to erode and diminish, but their decline has been much quicker than the formation of new strata. During recent decades, a dual society has come into being in Hungary, the *state-society* and the *market-society*, and most people have participated in both. Although state redistribution and market incomes have had markedly different characteristics, they have been consolatory and complementary in Hungary. The two contradictory systems still coexist and compete with each other, while the decline of state-society and the rise of a market-society can be plainly seen. In late 1995, more than 60 per cent of the active population was employed in the private sector, whereas the separation between the two spheres is far from being finished. This is why most people still receive incomes from both.[5]

3. The social actors. The Antall government in 1990 began with an argument based on the absolute priority of national interests. In this paternalistic state model there was no place for organized interests, including the business interest associations which supposedly represented 'dirty, materialistic-particularistic interests' against the sacrosanct national interests represented by the Antall government. What is more, the interest organizations had been, so to say, only transmission belts in the state socialist regime, therefore they were supposed to be in the new regime completely unnecessary and delegitimized. This logic was false in many ways. Firstly, interest organizations can be delegitimized only by their members. If their members abandon them, they disappear; if they get support *en masse*, then they remain powerful social actors in any event. Secondly, the whole logic of the direct and exclusive representation of national interests by the government was false. Contrary to all the efforts of the Antall government, the interest organizations emerged and/or re-emerged as influential social and political actors. The government was forced to conclude a type of social pact in November 1992 with the national Interest Reconciliation Council, involving the principal organizations of the employers and employees. This led to an Act on Trade Unions in February 1993. In East-Central European countries there has always been an organizational or institutional deficit in the meso-politics of organized interests, also called, in this case, the 'missing middle'. The process of institutionalization in meso-politics, however, has accelerated in the last years with the growing support of newly emerging social strata. The trade unions arrived at the above-mentioned crisis earlier than business interest associations, but they also achieved consolidation and institutionalization earlier. The major trade union confederations are competitive, of course, but they are cooperative as well, for example in the national Interest Reconciliation Council. The trade union structure of Hungary at present shows both the 'Nordic' tendency of organizational unification and the 'Southern' tendency of political diversification. The confederations are very active domestically – representing both the 'old' industrial and the 'new' dynamic strata – and also internationally in pan-European organizations.[6]

We can now summarize the social systemic changes in the following way:

Structural problems: As an overreaction to belated industrialization, the state socialist regime extensively 'overindustrialized' the country; thus a mixture of two – urban and rural – archaic structures coexisted until the late 1980s as a division of labour between overindustrialized and backward agrarian regions. The traditional institutional deficit, the 'missing middle', the lack of interest organizations and that of political representation for the social actors was characteristic of both – right and left – soft authoritarian regimes, that is, throughout both the interwar and the postwar periods. Thus, the modernization of social structure as the mobilization-institutionalization of social actors has to overcome this common negative historical heritage.

Transitional problems: The deepening social crisis and the widespread appearance of crime (to a great extent 'imported' from neighbouring countries) have to be managed in paradoxical circumstances, that is in conditions of a shrinking GDP, yet with a growing demand for social security provisions. This results in an increasing inflationary pressure and a soaring state budget deficit; this threatens the economic recovery, which is the only way to solve the social crisis. The Antall–Boross government was unable to cope with this aggregation of problems (similar to a Catch-22 situation) and its negligence and poor performance even engendered some extra problems.

Systemic problems: The old social structure has almost collapsed but a new one has not yet emerged. The Antall–Boross government had two means to promote the social transformations and both resulted in new distortions. The first was privatization, which produced a quasi state-dependent bourgeoisie and fewer smaller independent owners, instead of a growing domestic bourgeoisie and broad middle classes. The second was agricultural transformation, where modernization was halted. However, the modernization drive, despite the renationalization and re-traditionalization efforts of the government, has proved to be the stronger, since both the new social strata and their representatives as new social actors have emerged.

Situational problems: There have been a lot of complicating external factors in the social transformation, but it is sufficient to mention the most important one: a mass migration to Hungary from the neighbouring countries. The Yugoslav war has caused a forced mass migration, with a lot of official and unofficial refugees, that is those in the camps and those commuting between their home territory and Hungary. In the last three years there have been more than 70,000 refugees in the Hungarian camps and about ten million visitors have come to Hungary every year from the neighbouring countries to conduct small business dealings. The situation has been complicated by the fact that many such visitors are ethnic Hungarians, who need, indeed, special care and support by fellow Hungarians and by the Hungarian state. The Western countries have regarded Hungary only as a 'filter' to stop these refugees. This has meant an extra economic and social burden for Hungary. Cost and crime have come together with the economic refugees, usually 'black' workers and traders. The international agencies have provided some assistance, but the regional, Central and East European, social transformation in general has caused an extra problem and burden for Hungary, worsening its own social crisis.

In general assessment of the 1990–94 period we have to point out that, in the short transition period of the Antall–Boross government,

Hungary went through a deep economic, social and political crisis. The economic decline in Hungary was bigger than in the Great Crisis of 1929–33, GDP decreased until 1993 (to 87 per cent of the 1989 level) followed by a decline in real wages (in 1993 to only 83 per cent of their 1989 level) and 1.5 million people (one quarter of the active population) lost their jobs and had to look for new employment. Disappointment was running high, there were severe tensions in all levels of society. Still, in Hungary there were no anomical ('disorderly') social movements; the extremist parties and political movements received less popular support than their counterparts in Western Europe. Privatization had already a turning point by 1994, with the private economy producing more than half of GDP, although the new private economy to some extent emerged in the degenerated form of the black or hidden economy. In the four years of the national-conservative regime there was some progress in democratization, privatization and marketization, but there were also many setbacks and distortions. Hungary has been modernized to a great extent, but the socio-economic and political price paid for this four-year excursion into the Glorious Past That Never Was has been too high.

THE PERIOD OF THE SOCIAL-LIBERAL GOVERNMENT

The first free and fair elections were 'foundational' in nature, providing both an entry-point and laying down the foundations for a new political system. In some sense, however, the second free elections have been more important, since they reconfirm the democratic character of the new system by giving a chance for the new, democratic opposition to take power through such free elections, that is, by a democratic alternation of power. Actually, this is what happened in Hungary in Spring 1994. It was a reconfirmation of democracy that after the full term of four years completed by the former government a new coalition was able to emerge from the centre-left opposition and the former centre-right governing parties have become the opposition. This was a smooth power transition, although it was preceded in the election campaign by a very tough party competition.

The new social-liberal government, with Horn as prime minister and Kuncze as the 'coalitional' deputy prime minister, has drastically changed both the political style and the policy agenda. Instead of the style of national romanticism a pragmatic political style has become dominant and, on the policy agenda, the issue of socio-economic crisis management has received the highest priority. The first eight months after inauguration of the new government on 15 July 1994 were, to some extent, 'lost' due to both hesitation and preparation. It was also a time for learning the techniques of political cooperation within the new coalition between the senior partner, the Hungarian Socialist Party, and the junior partner, the Alliance of Free Democrats, led respectively by Gyula Horn, the Minister of Foreign Affairs of the Nemeth government, who acquired international renown by opening the Hungarian–Austrian borders to the East Germans in 1989 and Ivan Peto, one of the most respected leaders of the former 'democratic opposition'. The HSP and AFD have, together, an overwhelming 72 per cent majority in the Second Parliament (1994 onwards), which is a solid political base for a tough period of crisis management.

New austerity measures were announced on 12 March 1995, called the 'Bokros Package' after the new minister of finance. These radical measures for reform of the state budget were the dominant political and policy issues – at least, until the end of 1995. The Bokros Package has provided the frame for all political debates between government and opposition in the Second Parliament, as well as for those between the governing coalition parties and among their emerging factions. By late 1995 the worst was already over, the economic crisis management having produced the first results in balancing the budget, and, parallel with Poland and the Czech Republic, in 1994–95 a solid, 2 to 3 per cent economic growth rate was evident in Hungary founded on the new, privatized market economy. Hungary has transformed first its micro-economic structure, that is the enterprise level, where there is about ten billion US dollars' worth of foreign investment and where both labour productivity and export capacity have improved rapidly in recent years thus providing a good opportunity to cope with macro-economic problems as well.[7]

Political developments also provide some basis for a cautious optimism. The democratic institutionalization process has come, more or less, to an end. A breakout has been made from the former vicious circle, in which the simultaneous tasks of democratization and marketization within a general framework of modernization have destabilized each other; from the mid-1990s we have entered the period of the virtuous circle, in which these processes rather reinforce each other, that is, a positive feedback has been developed between the new privatized market economy and the consolidated democratic polity. The economic and political Western orientation, already begun by the Nemeth government, resulted in Hungary becoming the first full member of the Council of Europe from the former state socialist countries, on 6 November 1990. Hungary concluded an association treaty with the EU on 16 December 1991 and applied for full membership on 1 April 1994. It has joined the Partnership for Peace programme of NATO and is preparing itself for both economic and military integration with the West to secure an international framework for comprehensive democratization. The year 1996 was relatively successful in both respects. In addition, according to the present government the whole privatization process is to be finished in 1998. Thus, around the year 2000, both democratization and marketization will be consolidated in Hungary.

NOTES

1. To be brief, I apply here the conceptual framework suggested by Huntington, distinguishing the long-term contextual (structural), the short-term transitional and the mid-term systemic problems, and adding the dimension of situational problems. See S. Huntington, *The Third Wave: Democratization in the Late Twentieth Century* (Norman and London: University of Oklahoma Press, 1991) pp. 209-10. For a more detailed analysis of political developments, see the Hungarian chapters in: A. Agh (ed.), *The Emergence of the East Central European Parliaments: The First Steps* (Budapest: Hungarian Centre for Democracy Studies [HCDS], 1994) and A. Agh and S. Kurtan (eds), *Democratization and*

Europeanization in Hungary: The First Parliament, 1990-1994 (Budapest: HCDS, 1995).

2. The HCDS has, since 1988, *The Political Yearbook of Hungary*, a comprehensive volume with data, documents, analyses and statistics. We have published, for example, a full set of public opinion data in S. Kurtan et al. (eds), *Political Yearbook of Hungary 1994*; see first of all the chapter by L. Bruszt and J. Simon, 'After Antall, before the elections – or "our democracy and our parties" through the eyes of citizens'.

3. The analysts of social systemic change underline that the most drastic change has happened not to the poorest, but to the lower middle strata with their relative impoverishment, see *Tarsadalmi Riport* (Social Report), (Budapest: TÅRKI, 1992) p. 62. The turning of the second economy partly into a black economy, along with tax evasion, has also had a strong polarizing effect on incomes. According to estimations, it contributed 15–20 per cent to GDP in the 1980s and 15–33 per cent in the 1990s.

4. 59 per cent of the Hungarian population was fully convinced and another 25 per cent partly, that the Antall government permanently discussed the great problems of the nation in order to turn public opinion away from the most important policy issues: those of the socio-economic crisis. Around 8 per cent supported extreme nationalist views, these being mostly uneducated elderly people. In general, the national issue was not high on the agenda of the population. See the public opinion survey by the Research Institute on Communication, published in *Nepszabadsag*, 20 March 1993.

5. In 1990 and 1991, the number of those employed in the private sector doubled. This meant a 10 per cent shift in these years from the state sector to the private sector. The state sector employed, in 1989, 31.6 per cent of the active population in administration and 38.1 per cent in industry; in 1991 the figures were only 28.4 and 31.1 per cent respectively. In the 1980s, three-quarters of the population were engaged in both sectors, and this has diminished only slightly. See *Tarsadalmi Riport*, pp. 48, 59.

6. We have dealt with the emergence of social actors, trade unions and business interest associations, in detail in A. Agh and Gabriella Ilonszki (eds), *Parliaments and Interest Associations in Central Europe: The Second Steps* (Budapest: Hungarian Centre for Democracy Studies, 1996).

7. Andras Inotai, in his paper, 'The Transforming Economies of Central and Eastern Europe' (*World Policy Journal*, Fall 1995) gives a comprehensive, comparative picture of the Hungarian economic transformation. He notes, *inter alia*, that in Hungary in 1993 the per capita foreign direct investment amounted to 231 USD, compared to 95 USD in

the less developed countries of Western Europe, and in 1995 that direct foreign investment in Hungary was still bigger than those in the other East-Central European countries combined.

10

Poland: an effective strategy of systemic change

Katarzyna Zukrowska

Systemic changes in each post-communist country have their own national preconditions and history, which lie beyond the 1989 threshold. The process commenced at that time (1989) embraces several spheres such as the economy, politics, social conditions, security issues, international environment and the linkages between them. Poland is no exception to this rule. The aim of this chapter is to point out how deep the roots of systemic transformation are and why, in Poland's case, the adopted strategy turned out to be a success.

POLISH LEADERSHIP IN REFORMS

The systemic transformation in Poland has turned out to be one of the most effective in the region. It indicates that the period of initial down-turn in production, a jump in prices of 600 per cent in 1989, and the opening of the market, brought about, in a relatively short time, a period of stabilization which can be measured by the rebirth of the economy and moves towards its restructuring. The whole process is heading towards adjustment of the national, formerly autonomous economy, to the world market with all its competitive demands. Moreover, it is creating conditions for the transformation of domestic companies into global industrial and service corporations. The Polish experience provides the best evidence that systemic changes in post-communist countries are part of a multidimensional process which is affected strongly by the international environment.

Since 1989, Poland has covered a major part of the distance towards the Western democratic state model. Systemic changes have consisted of two major developments: replacement of a single party system by a multi-party democratic system and a shift from a command economy towards a market model.

The strategy known as 'Balcerowicz's big bang' has succeeded, despite all the setbacks, difficulties and criticism that beset its realization. Success can be measured by the fact that Poland has experienced the highest rate of growth in the region since 1992. The rate of growth in gross national product (GNP) went from 2.6 per cent in 1992 to 6.5 per cent in 1995 and 6 per cent in 1996, while the rate of industrial production – after a deep fall of 24.2 per cent in 1990 and 11.9 per cent in 1991 – went up by 3.9 per cent in 1992, 11.9 per cent in 1994, 9.9 per cent in 1995 and 7.7 per cent in 1996. Moreover, the total collapse of production was the lowest in the region and the country was the first to reattain the level of GNP existing before 1989.[1]

The main difficulties in the systemic transformations in all the European post-communist countries stem from several factors, including the fact that the changes have embraced both the economic and political system, while normally, in the past, transformation has been confined to only one of these. Thus, there were no precedents for such vast changes which could function as a frame of reference or even simply a pattern to follow. The set-backs caused by the transformation often led to a rejection of liberalization and stabilization measures, which effectively limited the efficacy of the reforms, especially when there was insufficient determination to change structures. The negative impact of this latter factor was relatively strong when the role of international factors was limited and the politicians did not work out any special strategy that could help lengthen the period in which society would extend credit to its elected leadership.

POLISH SPECIFICS

The specificity of each country, Poland included, has to be viewed against some regional or group background. The regional progress of the reforms is illustrated in the table following.

Table 10.1 Division of post-communist countries into three groups according to the criterion of adopted therapy and progress achieved

Countries	Characteristics of the Reform
Poland, Czech Republic, Slovenia, Slovak Republic	All these countries are considered to be the most advanced in the transformation despite differences in their transformation strategies. Poland applied shock therapy. Hungary and Slovenia a gradualist strategy, and Czech and Slovak Republics a compound approach
Russia, Bulgaria, Croatia, Romania, Lithuania, Latvia, Estonia	These countries have followed a radical strategy, but their success in the economic field, as measured by economic growth, is smaller than in the countries grouped above. The Baltic states are more successful as they have kept strictly to the demands of economic transformation programmes, while the other countries were more hesitant, producing only minor effects in their economy.
Belarus, Ukraine, Moldova	The attitude of these countries was critical of employing a radical strategy, and this has resulted directly in the limited advancement of their transformations.

The Contents of the table enable us to reach several conclusions:

1. Post-communist countries can be divided into two groups, the first embracing those which have succeeded in the transformation and with their economies moving on to the path of development;

the second consists of countries which are still in transition depression;

2. Systemic transformation can not be conducted without meaningful costs. The burden of the transformation is borne mainly by society, which supports the transformation only for a limited period. This period is longer where there are trusted politicians in power (from the opposition) and shorter for politicians belonging to the former ruling elites;

3. A combination of two factors – a former opposition in power and shock therapy gives the best conditions for implementing reforms;

4. Parties based on post-communist elites can continue the reforms or accelerate them in cases of delay.

What are the specific features found in Poland that enabled the success of the economic shock therapy?[2]

In the political sphere, a widespread opposition, organized in the independent trade union 'Solidarity', facilitated the implementation of the reform. People in this union represented different political options from the left wing to the right, with social-democrats, liberals, conservatives, Christian-democrats and others also evident. Despite their political orientation, they were against the former system and in support of market democracy, even if they avoided specifying the nature of the future system.

The sweeping victory of the opposition forces in the 1989 elections enabled the introduction of shock therapy since the Polish population was in favour of reforms, and in the first period of the transformation were prepared to accept the burden of changes. Some of the initial steps towards the reforms were introduced in the former period (commercialization of the banking system, marketization of the agricultural market, or initiatory institutionalization of foreign ties). With the advancement of reform, the situation was changed both in the electorate and in the political structures, but political guidance was most important in the first stage of the reform. In the ensuing stages, the government's role changed from a locomotive of transition into an executor of international obligations, manager of the economy, and negotiator with trade unions.

Despite the outlined model of disengagement of the state in the transition, the government and its institutions cannot withdraw totally. In the field of the economy, the Central Bank controls the money supply, exchange rate and level of interest rate. This has to be done independently of political pressure, but in cooperation with the government. Other tasks are allotted to legislative reforms which endeavour to create a legal system compatible with the market economy and enabling further integration with Euroatlantic structures. New legislation envisages the preparation of a new Constitution as the state continues to operate within the framework formed by the temporary solution of the Little Constitution. The delay in this case should be evaluated positively, as it would be unwise to change the constitution along with implementing the political changes. Moreover, to continue the list of things to be done, it is clear that the reform also has to incorporate changes in the social-security system, decentralization of the administration, adjustments in agriculture and so on.

The Polish political system, despite or thanks to the rather quick changes of consecutive governments, was able to guide the reforms, introduce decisions in specific sequence, and finally take the correct steps despite limited and often obscure information. All the political turbulence and quick shifts of government policy did not stop the reforms although they had influence on the speed at which they were introduced. After a period of acceleration, Poland entered a stage of deceleration, which implies a following period of acceleration still ahead of us. One can expect that the source of the next acceleration can be ascribed to the political power of the ruling party or to impulses stemming from the international environment, for instance brought about by membership of the European Union. In specific conditions, both of these factors can work together, increasing the strength of the impulses.

In the economic sphere, there were some positive features, as well as negative, which were decisive for undertaking the shock therapy strategy. The Polish economy was characterized by a rather large private sector. At the beginning of the market-oriented reforms, the private sector accounted for 5 million jobs out of a working population of 17 million, or approximately 30 per cent. The economy was burdened by a high external debt, nearly $40 billion. Moreover, the so-called inflation overhang (the gap between demand and supply on the consumer market) was one of the highest in the region. The share of the external turnover in GNP was low as compared to other ECE countries. Most of its exports were concentrated in COMECON markets.

High debt, disequilibrium between demand and supply and limited ties with the world economy can be considered as crucial in determining the choice of radical solutions. Experience in the private sector helped in the rapid growth of individual entrepreneurship. Dissolution of COMECON and departure from ruble clearance forced a reorientation in foreign trade. Although the displacement effect was very costly for the Polish economy, it can be considered one of the tools that forced the economy into an accelerated restructuring process.

In the social sphere, Poles giving power to the opposition were ready to carry the burden of change for some, undefined time. This helped politicians to launch the 'big bang', enabling the 'jump' into a market economy, to use Jeffrey Sachs' term for the Polish reform.[3] Such support and high expectations of changes for the better were a unique precondition in the region for introducing the harsh IMF requirements of the economic stabilization programme. As practice shows, the support for changes vanishes with time as burdens continue to persist. The period of grace given to the opposition was, however, long enough to introduce market mechanisms into Polish economic institutions. The prolongation of this period was achieved by relatively quick shifts by the governments which, despite being subjected to criticism for their applied strategy, have continued the changes.

With regard to the international environment of the reforms, Poland generally received support. Poland has gained favourable reviews from international economic and financial institutions such as the IMF, World Bank, European Union, EFTA, and finally the

Paris and London Clubs. Moreover, Polish systemic transformations were supported by the governments of Western democracies. Without such external support it would have been impossible to implement the reforms in Poland. It should be stressed that reforms in Poland were also supported by experts of international institutions, foreign governments and independent scientific centres.

In the first stage of change, Poland was an island of transformation, surrounded by countries that were far removed from ideas of systemic transformation. The Hungary of that time can also be considered a precursor, along with Poland, on the road towards systemic changes. Perhaps the former Soviet Union can also be considered as one exception to the rule specified above. The last Soviet First Secretary, Mikhail Gorbachev, supported changes in his own country by launching *perestroika* and *glasnost*. Both of these notions were supposed to be implemented within the old system, reforming it, rather than undermining it. It should be stressed that Gorbachev was not against the changes commenced in Poland at that time.

The specified conditions can be divided into two groups: (1) the first group of factors were absorbed as part of the strategy of systemic transformation thus indicating that the transformation was planned before 1989; (2) the second group of factors existed independently of the political power centres in Poland. It is difficult to draw a sharp line between those two groups of factors. Despite this, from the beginning, it was clear that the social costs of transformation in Poland would be higher in comparison to the Czech Republic or Hungary since its economy was more destabilized. It should be noted, however, that its internal market was bigger – potentially, a significant advantage.

POLISH POLITICAL SYSTEM

The struggle for democracy began in Poland shortly after the Second World War.[4] For details on post-war history one should turn to a historian. Here, I shall omit all the well-known facts of open struggles in 1956, 1970, and 1981. Each of those upheavals resulted in an increase of sovereignty and political freedom. The last days of communism laid the ground for systemic changes in the economy and political life. The Round Table between the opposition and the representatives of the former political elites gave an initial impetus to a new political structure in Poland. The Round Table Talks began officially on 6 February 1989 and were finalized by the signing of an agreement on 5 April 1989. This agreement formulated the proportions of political forces in the Sejm (Polish Lower Chamber), and it also worked out the social security net that was supposed to cushion the inflationary rise of prices. Needless to say, only political settlements were kept. The Round Table was preceded by negotiations among the leaders of the last communist government and the opposition. The talks were held in Magdalenka, a village close to Warsaw. Along with the representative of the official elites, there were representatives of 'Solidarity' and the Episcopate.

It would be useful to refresh our memories with a few dates of events in our recent history:

4 June 1989: 'Solidarity' won the parliamentary elections;

19 July 1989: General Wojciech Jaruzelski was elected in indirect elections to the office of President;

17 August 1989: Lech Walesa initiated a coalition between the Communist successor parties, the Democratic Party (SD) and the Peasant Party (ZSL) and 'Solidarity';

24 August 1989: Tadeusz Mazowiecki was elected to the post of Prime Minister;

12 September 1989: A new government, headed by Tadeusz Mazowiecki, was formulated. The most crucial post, looking at it from the point of view of economic changes, was given to Leszek Balcerowicz, who became Minister of Finance. The Balcerowicz Plan was launched on 1 January 1990. The post of Foreign Minister was given to professor Krzysztof Skubiszewski, a widely known specialist on international relations, who was responsible for establishing relations with economic and financial institutions. Those three personalities in this government pushed the reform forward and guaranteed that all arrangements with the international institutions would be fulfilled. Some of the agreements contained conditional binding settlements, which regulate external relations irrespective of the political will to do so. This type of solution should be considered a safeguard for the continuation of systemic changes, separating them at the same time from political turmoils. In the first stages of the transformation, those arrangements were one of the preconditions of support from Western governments. Results of the reforms and references from the IMF helped Poland to reach an agreement with the Paris and London Clubs on writing-off more than 50 per cent of Polish external debt;

29 January 1990: The Polish Communist Party was dissolved and the Social-Democratic Union of the Polish Republic was born.

The Polish pluralist political system was reborn in a relatively short time in comparison with the period that was needed by Western democracies to establish such a system. This fact had its influence on the process of democratization. Parties were both disintegrating and integrating, seeking support in the electorate, articulating their programmes and ways of achieving strategic goals.[5]

The Round Table elections, in June 1989, were won by 'Solidarity'. This bloc gained 70 per cent of the popular vote with a 62 per cent turnout at the polls. The presidential elections, a year later, had a 60 per cent turnout on the first ballot. In the parliamentary elections of 1991, parties with a 'Solidarity' background won 55 per cent of the votes. Elections held on 19 September 1993 indicated a strong shift in the popularity of the leading political groupings on the Polish scene. The sympathies of the electorate were turning towards non-Solidarity groupings. A coalition, the Union of the Democratic Left – SLD – received 20.4 per cent of the votes, the Polish Peasant Party – PSL – 15.4 per cent, the Democratic Union – UD – 10.6 per cent, the Labour Union – UP – 7.3 per cent, the Confederation for an Independent Poland – KPN – 5.8 per cent, the Non-Party Bloc in Support of Reforms – BBWR – 5.4 per cent, the German Minority Party 0.7 per cent; and all gained representation in the Sejm. Electoral groups that did not overcome the threshold of 5 per cent for parties and 8 per cent for coalitions found themselves outside the Sejm. They include 'Solidarity' – NSZZ – with only 4.9 per cent, the Centre Agreement – PC – 4.4 per cent, the Catholic Election Committee 'Motherland' (a coalition), 6.4 per cent, and others a total of 18.7 per cent.

The 1995 presidential elections have stirred the left and right. Poland has still a long way to go before the political scene reflects the contemporary division in the West between those who opt for integration and liberalism and those who opt for more sovereignty, nationalism and protectionism. At the present time, the Polish political scene is somewhat reminiscent of the situation in Western Europe in the 1960s and 1970s, with the left-wing Social Democrats (SLD) – the former Communists – in power in Poland and the right wing divided and split among rival factions and integrating only with difficulty.

Parties in Poland can be characterized in many different ways. The last and most important in this study refers to economic programmes.

There are presently over 200 parties on the Polish political scene. The main divisions among Polish parties stem from their pedigree: the first group covers parties of 'Solidarity' background, the second of post-communist background (so-called transformed communists), the third consists of other groupings rooted in the inter-war period, and the fourth is comprised of parties organized *ad hoc* in contemporary times. The Left comprises the transformed communists, who are the heart of the ruling coalition, including the Social Democratic Party, and the Polish Socialist Party; the Centre includes the Polish Peasant Party, the Coalition of Democratic Left (SLD), and the Democratic Party (SD). The non-Solidarity parties include: Confederation of Independent Poland (KPN), Party-'X', Self-Defense and Union of Real Politics (UPR). The second division was introduced by the 'war at the top' that finally disintegrated the 'Solidarity bloc'. This division was also produced by pressures from below, as the electorate showed its preferences. The groups falling into this category consist of the left-wing Union of Labour (UP), the centrist Democratic Union (now Union of

Freedom – UW) and the Christian Democratic right embracing the Centre Agreement (PC) and Christian National Union (ZChN).

A third division has been brought about by the presidential elections in 1995. It divided political groupings into those that supported Lech Walesa for the Presidency and those against.

The fourth division concerns purely political issues such as the future shape of the state (division of power among government, parliament and president), administrative reform, and the place of the Church. The fifth division concerns purely economic issues, principally the question of measures for fighting inflation, economic openness, scale of inflow of foreign capital, role of state and level of taxes, redistributive role of the budget, issue of the trade deficit, policy over foreign reserves and so on.

It is possible to continue the list of other divisions and differences among the parties. The existence of such divisions can be considered proof of a specific process in which political parties learn to express their individual features, which were difficult to discern in the elections of 1989. This constitutes evidence that the political system in Poland is maturing. Now, the Polish party system is catching up with western-type democracies in an accelerated manner. This runs in parallel with the general systemic changes embracing institutions and the economy. As a result we can witness a process of gradual emancipation of the economy from political guidance, happening on both macro and micro levels.

The contemporary stage, with parties able to articulate their political and economic credos, indicates that although there are sharp differences among the economic programmes, there are also many features that form a common denominator. One can expect that the next stage should bring together those groupings that have some common elements in their programmes. This will be followed by further integration among parties on the Polish political scene. Others will be forced to terminate their activity, fading from the political arena.

This process is already reflected in the practice of political life. After the defeat in the 1993 elections, the smaller parties from the centre and right have organized coalitions. The small differences in their economic programmes provided a good foundation for unification. Those coalitions are closer together than the ruling SLD-PSL. This coalition represents different electorates, including peasants and land-owners as well as inhabitants of towns. Controversies within this coalition were reflected in the internal crises at the beginning of 1995, which led to the replacement of Waldemar Pawlak by Jozef Oleksy as Prime Minister. The next round of political problems occurred at the end of 1995, as a side-effect of the presidential campaign won by Aleksander Kwasniewski. New perturbations in the ruling coalition ended by changes in the Prime Minister's post, taken by Wlodzimierz Cimoszewicz.

REFORM: STILL REVERSIBLE OR FINALLY IRREVERSIBLE?

The economic reform in Poland is not reversible since it derives from the depth of the transformation processes, international linkages and several other leverages that are incorporated in the newly established institutional network. Looking at the economic programmes of different Polish parties one can say that none of them even thinks of going back to the former system. The main issue concerns the speed of transformation, the future shape of the state, the manner of concluding administrative reform and its scope, the division of functions between the centre and the municipalities, and the division of power between the president, government and the parliament. In the economic sphere, the main divisions arise while discussing the scale of trade liberalization, the scale of foreign capital inflows and conditions of EU membership and the place of the Church in the political arena. The programmes show a variety of options, some of which are far from economic realism. Fortunately, such options did not get much support from voters.

If we look more closely at the programmes, it becomes clear that the near future of Poland could see a coalition between the SLD and Union of Freedom (UW). The Union of Labour could also be considered as part of such a coalition. From the beginning of the transformation process, the SLD and UW were in opposition to each other, though the nature of that opposition underwent change. They could have cooperated together after the last elections to form a coalition, but they were not ready to do this. After the refusal of such an offer by UD, one might think that this was wise and that those two parties should stay in opposition to each other, forming two cores of opposing powers in the emerging party system. But in a longer perspective this seems to be impossible. The programmes of those parties are too close to each other and their life apart impedes the reforms. Working together, they could speed up the process. The possible coalition of these two parties is evidenced by some developments which, at first glance, could be read as enforcement of the coalition between SLD and PSL but which, in reality, lead towards an unavoidable divorce.

The recent decisions by Aleksander Kwasniewski and Wlodzimierz Cimoszewicz to pursue efforts to remove the obstacles to ratification of the agreement between the Vatican and the Polish government (the so-called Concordat) abolishes one of the crucial differences between SLD and UW. The possible rapprochement between SLD and UW can be considered as a reflection of changes in the Polish political system. The other scenario could be a return to a coalition that initiated the reforms in 1989.

Returning to the reversibility of the reforms, it should be stressed that according to the newest statistics released by GUS, 1996 can be considered a turning-point in the Polish economy since the private sector started to contribute more to GNP than the public sector. The share of the private sector in GNP in 1995 was 56.3 per cent (in 1992 it was 45.4 per cent) while the similar indicator for the public sector was 41.2 per cent (in 1992 it was 50.5 per cent).

Despite all the difficulties in estimating the accuracy of data, it is clear that the rapid growth in the number of small- and medium-sized enterprises is pushing Poland's environment closer to Western patterns.

These facts seem to be crucial for the further development of the Polish economy as they create the basis for accelerated economic development; formulate new challenges for the economy, where the main issue still remains the question of privatization; necessitate a revolution in people's mentalities.

What can be considered a danger to the further continuation of reform? Are such threats in the political or in the economic sphere, or perhaps at the point of junction between them? What are the most crucial problems that have to be solved in the Polish economy in the near future?

Starting with the second question, several steps have to be taken or simply continued:

1. Control over inflation. Speaking more precisely, there must be appropriate utilization of instruments of money supply control: a system of reserve assets, refinance credits, open market operations, control of interest and exchange rates as well as over the budget deficit.[6] In other words, Polish economic policy has to be oriented to the Maastricht criteria of convergence;

2. Continuation of privatization. There is a great discussion between supporters of privatization and those who are for commercialization of state industry. The superiority of privatization over commercialization is clear: first, the state needs the money from privatization, although they could be better used by the enterprises on their own; secondly, why should one seek artificial methods of increasing productivity when a tested and effective tool of privatizing the factory is within reach?

3. Less protectionism and more liberalism in foreign trade. Protection has a negative impact on competition, increases prices in the domestic market, and slows down the speed of adjustments;

4. Less paternalism and more free market. Polish economic subjects must learn how to react according to market rules and read the market signals. This can not be achieved under the government's protective umbrella;

5. Better utilization of foreign credits. This, too, can not be achieved under the protective umbrella of the government;

6. A more active policy aimed at attracting foreign capital. Although the results obtained in the Polish economy have positively influenced capital inflows, as can be seen by the increase in direct foreign capital investment from 2.8 billion in December 1993 to

12.027 billion in January 1997, nevertheless, such sums seem to be insufficient as compared to the size of the Polish market and the speed of restructuring in the economy. The Polish economy is capable of absorbing some $5–6 billion per year;

7. A more active policy to increase the competitiveness of the Polish economy, involving macrostabilization, attracting foreign direct investments, development of infrastructure, increasing flexibility of labour (education and branch restructuring);

8. Branch restructuring. Giving priority to development of services, down-sizing of heavy industry, transformation of agricultural production and so on.

The second question concerns threats to further reform: are they political or economic in nature? In answer to this question, I would say that the importance of political control over the economy is in decline, although there is always the possibility that political mistakes can result in economic problems. It has to be stressed clearly that none of the political parties is opting for return to the former system. The only difference among them as far as the reforms are concerned, is the speed of implementing them. Optimism is deeply rooted in the advancement of privatization in the Polish economy. It could be even said that the economy is living on its own and does not need any major guidance from the administrative centre: a push was necessary only at the starting-point. Now we can expect a reverse effect, as the development of the private sector influences changes in the political life of the country. However, pessimism is warranted by the fact that Poland still experiences high inflation rates and numerous legal regulations are awaiting their turn for amendment in accord with EU requirements.

There are still numerous issues that have to be solved by politicians, including the issues of privatization and reform of municipal government, not to mention the question of the future shape of the constitution. The municipal issue seems to be crucial for the future of the reform. Practice indicates that it is easier to solve most regional or local problems at such levels, not at the national level. This issue concerns the strategy of development, revenues, methods of using state funds and so on.

The dependence of the economy on the external support of international economic and financial institutions can be considered, in the long run, a sufficient guarantee of continuation of the reforms. In other words, not only is the international economy extending our national market but international institutions are also increasing their presence in our economic life. After a period of autonomous development, the increasing role of external factors in our economy can also be considered as a shock and revolution that has an impact not only on political decisions but also on the economy of our country. In other words, external factors are gaining in importance and, in many cases, they override the importance of internal factors.

In such circumstances, the role of the government changes slowly from position of leader towards that of a middleman between international institutions and the nation and, in the opposite direction, between the nation and the international institutions.

SUMMARY

The combination of shock therapy with gradual political changes has worked successfully in the case of Polish systemic changes. However, there are still several factors that create threats to Polish economic growth: (1) possibilities of return of high inflation; (2) slow-down in the economy; (3) destabilization in regions where the unemployment rate is relatively high (for Poland) and a generally higher unemployment rate than for other ECE countries.

Those threats can lead towards destabilization of the economy if their sources are not abolished. This fact indicates that political factors still matter despite the advancement of emancipation of the economy from political guidance. What are the optimistic features of the contemporary phase of transformation? The Polish transformation has arrived at the point of no return. The main issue now concerns the speed of further development: will Poland be able, once again, to accelerate the process of systemic changes or will it continue to slow down the reforms?

Acceleration of the reform means giving priorities to such areas as further decentralization, privatization and control over inflation. This can be achieved by the creation of conditions in which all enterprises in Poland will operate in an environment that supports entrepreneurship. There is no doubt that Poland is not yet able to restructure its economy, building competitive structures, by utilizing only its own internal capital resources.

We can expect that, after a temporary slow-down in reforms, Poland will face again a period of acceleration. This can be done either by internal forces (changes in the political structure of parliamentary representation or by changes in the ruling coalition) or by external factors (Polish membership in Euroatlantic institutions).

NOTES

1. P. Bozyk, 'Na tle sasiadow', *Przeglad Tygodniowy*, 8 May 1996.

2. This question is also presented in: L. Balcerowicz, 'Lessons from Economic Transition in Central and Eastern Europe', in: *Poland, International Economic Report 1993/1994* (Warsaw, 1994) pp. 193-201.

3. J. Sachs, *Poland's Jump to the Market Economy* (Cambridge, Massachusetts: The MIT Press, 1993).

4. K. Bolesta-Kukulka, *Gra o wladze a gospodarka: Polska 1944–1991* (Warszawa: PWE, 1992).

5. Polish political structures are discussed in: J. W. Golebiowski, 'Democratic Poland: Dilemmas of Stabilization', in: *Transforming the Polish Economy* (Warsaw, 1994) p. 22; J. W. Golebiowski, 'Political Changes in Poland and the Region', in: *Poland, International Economic Report* (Warsaw, 1994) p. 9; W. Lamentowicz, *New Political Elites in Poland*, manuscript (Warsaw: Warsaw University, 1993); M. Dehnel-Szyc, J. Stachura, *Gry polityczne, orientacje na dzis* (Warszawa, 1991); P. G. Lewis, 'Party Development in Post-communist Poland', *Europe-Asia Studies*, vol. 46, no. 5 (1994) pp. 779-800.

6. *OECD. Przeglad Gospodarczy. Polska 1994* (Warszawa, 1994) p. 38.

11

Romania: nationalism defines democracy

Tom Gallagher

INTRODUCTION

Romania is the former Warsaw Pact country that has enjoyed the greatest degree of continuity in personnel and policy since communism was overturned in Eastern Europe during 1989–91. In December 1989, within the space of ten days, ex-communists quickly filled the political vacuum that opened up when the national Stalinist dictatorship of Nicolae Ceausescu disintegrated in the face of popular uprisings in the cities of Timisoara and Bucharest.

Ion Iliescu, a 59-year-old former top-ranking member of the Romanian Communist Party became provisional President on 26 December. The backing of the vast party and state bureaucracy enabled him to consolidate his authority and a relaxation of the extreme austerity imposed on the population by his predecessor, won him early popularity. On 20 May 1990, Iliescu was elected President with 85.2 per cent of the vote and re-elected (for a four-year term) in 1992 with a much smaller victory margin. The pro-Iliescu National Salvation Front (NSF) was able to devise a new Constitution and revamp political institutions largely on its own narrow terms, thanks to the scale of its initial victory. The 1991 Constitution made Romania a liberal-democratic state with a parliamentary form of government in which the President enjoyed important discretionary powers. However, the promulgation of supposedly binding legal rights during the inter-war period had not prevented the state from behaving in an intolerant manner towards opponents and unpopular minorities. Despite a split in the NSF, the government has continued to be controlled by figures from the old party *nomenklatura* whose agenda for change is much more limited than in any other ex-communist state in the region (with the clear exception of Serbia).

Romania witnessed an imposed transition from communist rule directed by former office-holders who hastily tried and executed the former dictator on 25 December 1989 to show the world that a genuine break with the old order had occurred (and to remove an awkward witness likely to testify at his trial about their complicity with his regime). Opponents who had participated in the popular uprising branded Iliescu and other organizers of the internal party *putsch* as 'neo-communists' who had no commitment to meaningful democracy. 1990 witnessed a series of confrontations between two groups ill-matched in strength that claimed to carry the mantle of the 1989 revolution. The haste with which elections were organized (before the opposition could properly organize itself), the control of state resources (especially the media) exercised by the NSF, and the Front's recourse to strong-arm methods whenever its authority was effectively challenged, polarized the country. If the anti-communist opposition had managed to obtain power, it is likely that it too would have used authoritarian measures to stay in control. However, there was considerable evidence that Romania's rulers were reluctant democrats wedded to illiberal practices who expected citizens to offer automatic obedience regardless of how government conduct affected their welfare.

In the economic sphere, the core values of Marxism-Leninism had already been deeply eroded under the sultanistic rule of Ceausescu. Iliescu, while remaining committed to an active state presence in the economy, permitted privatization, especially in the agricultural and service sectors of the economy. But the prime beneficiaries were well-placed bureaucrats from the Ceausescu era. They recycled themselves as 'nomenklatura capitalists' by buying up state assets at low prices and preventing *bona fide* businessmen from competing against them. A new economic oligarchy dominated by speculators emerged in the first half of the 1990s which relied on the ruling party for freedom to operate in the black economy and enjoy untaxed profits.

THE ESSENCE OF CONFLICT

The clash between the NSF and anti-communists drawn from reconstituted 'historic' parties of pre-communist vintage, overshadowed Romania's halting political transition in 1990–91. At no time did the NSF ever look as though it was losing the initiative to its vocal but ill-organized opponents. Iliescu was operating in a terrain favourable to an enlightened brand of autocracy with some democratic mechanisms. Romanian society had been completely recast under communism.[1] Leaving aside nationalism, values from pre-communist times enjoyed little influence on political culture owing to the intensity of communist social engineering. The bourgeoisie had been liquidated, the professions recast, and small property-owners – including most peasants and skilled craftsmen – had been proletarianized. Most citizens had grown used to being centrally directed by the state. The prospect of electoral competition even proved unsettling to older voters and those in small towns and villages who viewed the arrival of pluralism – however attenuated – as a threat to their security.

The NSF benefited from the fact that large swathes of the population appeared to have a vested interest in the reconstruction of a modified version of communist Romanian society. Opinion polls after 1989 found that Romanian citizens continued to possess a strongly egalitarian outlook; between 70 and 74 per cent believed that income levels should be almost equal on a permanent basis. In a 1991 poll, simultaneously carried out by the Gallup Agency, on attitudes to the market economy, there was more opposition in Romania to sharply reducing the role of the state in the economy than in any of the other countries polled (which included Albania, Bulgaria and the former Soviet Union).[2]

Such disconcerting poll findings revealed how successful the communist state had been in transmitting its values across

Romanian society to a population which may have questioned particular policies or leadership styles but which never showed any sign of challenging the core beliefs underpinning the communist system. Understandably, the historic parties found it hard to obtain a hearing from social groups that remained strongly attached to egalitarianism and to state control of the economy. In the cities, all of the opposition forces found it difficult to establish any common ground with the ex-peasants who formed a numerically large social grouping in huge housing estates. The successive efforts to expand Romanian heavy industry from the 1950s to the 1980s had created a group variously described as 'worker-peasants' or 'neo-urbanites' who looked to the state for direction and who reacted with puzzlement or hostility to parties that urged them to stand on their own two feet and look for salvation outside large redundant industrial enterprises.

The results of the May 1990 elections showed that, with 66.71 per cent of the vote (on an 86 per cent turnout), the NSF was the clear choice of most voters. Opposition hopes that the NSF would be unable to withstand the outcome of the Cold War were replaced by the feeling that the West was once again abandoning Romania to local tyranny, the Yalta Treaty of 1944 frequently being invoked as a reference-point.

However, in June 1990, Western condemnation was quick and vigorous when the government enlisted the support of vigilante workers to crack down on the opposition in the capital. But, the balance of forces in the country was clear and would remain unchanged in the first half of the 1990s. The clear preference of most Romanians was for a leader and a party that offers paternalism and security rather than experimentation and unsettling choice. Social groups responsive to democratization, open to new ideas, willing to take risks, and not threatened by technological change existed, to be sure, but they were scattered and weak owing to the policy of social homogenization that had resulted in the dominance of a Romanian *homo sovieticus*.

Following the marginalization of anti-communist forces, the focus of political conflict switched to the area within the ruling party itself. A minority of reformers committed to a market-led economy had been placed in charge of key ministries to try and improve Romania's battered reputation. They were soon obstructed by old-guard conservatives favouring limited change who increasingly had the ear of the President. There was no dispute between the insiders over the level of democratization, Prime Minister Petre Roman sanctioning authoritarian measures (especially in local government), as well as appealing to hardline nationalists more than once. As factional struggles swept the NSF in 1991, Ion Iliescu rallied his supporters once it was clear that his former ally, Roman, might have presidential ambitions. In September, Roman was violently ejected from office when a mob of coal-miners, unimpeded by the security forces, seized Parliament. Roman accused the President of refusing to defend democratic institutions, and by the end of 1991, was describing Iliescu as 'a nostalgic communist'.[3] He also spoke of 'the survival of the mentality and methods of the Securitate' or former secret police. But if he had used his period in office to create an accessible democracy based on the rule of law, he might not have been overthrown in scenes which cast the infant Romanian democracy in such a poor light.

In 1992 the NSF split was formalized, the larger, pro-Iliescu wing becoming the Party of Romanian Social Democracy (PRSD) and Roman's wing renaming itself the Democratic Party. When in partnership, both leaders had used nationalism to fashion an electoral appeal for the NSF. This was a tactic Iliescu (but not Roman) would persist with as the failure of the PRSD to acquire a coherent political identity based on a programme or a set of philosophical ideas became obvious. But it was no longer possible for any one group to monopolize nationalism as had happened in the communist era. The governing party soon found itself in competition with groups that it had originally promoted to frustrate the anti-communist opposition in the province of Transylvania.

The Transylvanian elite was based on ethnic Romanians who had benefited from the crash industrialization programme of the 1970s and 1980s, which saw cities populated largely by ethnic Hungarians or Germans, 'Romanianized' in a fairly short period. This elite had its own particular agenda based on managing the transition on nationalist terms and preventing the Hungarian minority from recovering positions of influence, particularly in the economic and cultural spheres (most of the German speakers having emigrated by the early 1990s).[4] After 1992, the PRSD's reliance on the parliamentary votes of the Party of Romanian National Unity (PRNU) gave ultra-nationalists an important degree of autonomy in Transylvania. In the city of Cluj, its main stronghold, the PRNU has cracked down on the opposition far more stringently than the government elsewhere, opponents of ethnic intolerance suffering numerous penalties.

The conflict between advocates of a civil state and of an ethnic one has been an unequal affair. The PRSD and the nationalists regard foreign models of political and economic change with suspicion and see conflicts of interest regarded as normal occurrences elsewhere in Europe as inappropriate for Romania. The Romanian communist state greatly reduced social diversity and promoted a single unified stance on many issues, both large and insignificant. Chauvinists have used their local strength and their parliamentary presence to attempt to crack down on the press which has been far more successful than opposition politicians in defending freedom of speech. The cultural arena has also been fiercely contested between chauvinists and liberals, the former gaining the upper hand by 1992 with the appointment of hardline nationalists to senior ministerial positions. Domination of the cultural field gives nationalists important leverage in an area which has enjoyed marked visibility in the Balkans owing to the emphasis on the politics of identity during the state-building era following the end of Ottoman rule. A further important breakthrough for nationalists came in January 1995 when the three main nationalist parties signed a protocol with the ruling PRSD. This was a clear sign that the boundaries between the ruling party and ultra-nationalists were growing increasingly fluid and it brought an accusation from Adrian Severin, the chief economic reformer of 1990–91, that the alliance 'opened the path to fascism'.[5]

Despite the emphasis on uniformity and discipline in the Ceausescu era, the shortage of basic goods and services and the discretionary manner in which they were allocated generated a range of conflicts (urban–rural, generational, workers versus intellectuals, Romanians versus Hungarians). These combined with political disputes to make 1990 a socially disturbed year. The state's ability to curtail the rise of civil society and independent power centres has removed the possibility of social conflicts being articulated in a gradualist way by interest groups. However, deteriorating economic conditions for much of the population raises the possibility that social misery will lead to explosions of discontent that will be exploited by populist elements.

Already, in 1989, the poorest country in Eastern Europe after Albania, Romania experienced a 33 per cent drop in gross domestic product over the next four years with real wages only about 60 per cent of their 1989 level by the end of that period.[6] Social groups such as pensioners and working mothers that responded enthusiastically to Iliescu's promise of social protection, have suffered particularly badly in the recession. By 1993 over 60 per cent of pensioners lived below the officially-designated poverty line, women in factories were often the first to be dismissed when redundancies occurred, and the rates of infant mortality and tuberculosis had become the highest anywhere in Europe.

The most vociferous of the groups threatened by unfavourable economic trends has been the coal-miners of the Jiu Valley. In 1990–91 their discontent was exploited by conservative elements within the new power structure in order to crack down first on anti-communist protesters and then on economic reformers within the NSF itself. As for the Romanian opposition, it has been unable to effectively articulate the demands and interests of specific social groups. A party system, based more on personalities and slogans than on concrete ideas and issues, has emerged. Parties have been unable to interact effectively with sectors of the electorate which they claim to be defending. The failure of parties to respond meaningfully to the economic and social crisis that has brought ruin to perhaps millions of people raises the possibility that extra-parliamentary movements will supersede them. If this happens, it will be the continuation of a trend in Romanian politics noticeable during the previous engagement with democracy in the inter-war period.

Regional rivalries based on sharp cultural and economic disparities (especially between the rest of the country and the more developed province of Transylvania which only became part of Romania in 1918) have been hard to disguise. However, the state has gone to great lengths to suppress any overt regional conflicts. There is the fear that the articulation of regional grievances might lead to the break-up of the state given its weak performance in providing basic amenities to the population. It is worth recalling at this point that Romania is the only remaining state created or enlarged by the Versailles Treaty system whose borders correspond closely to the original decisions of the post-1918 'peace-makers'.

A party system has emerged in Transylvania different from the rest of the country where, excepting a few cities, the PRSD is electorally dominant. In the 1992 general election, the liberal opposition, the Hungarian minority, and the ultra-nationalists comprised three voting blocs roughly equal in size while the PRSD received only 12.5 per cent of the votes. But such electoral variations are unlikely to be a source of conflict as long as party politics remains largely irrelevant to large sections of the electorate.

THE CHALLENGES

Democratization

The elite formed around President Iliescu has retained a monopolistic attitude to power. The ruling party has husbanded state resources and sought to deny them to its mainstream opponents. This effectively rules out the prospect of a genuine contest for power. Other than having the opportunity to cast a periodic vote in national elections, voters have little or no contact with their elected representatives. Partly as a consequence, the level of political awareness is low. When asked to declare in a 1994 poll whether they belonged to the right, centre, or left of politics, 38 per cent of Bucharest respondents replied that they did not know where to align themselves within each of these political categories.[7]

Traditions of a politically-aware landowning peasantry were absent in Romania where, after their release from serfdom in the nineteenth century, the peasantry (especially in the South), became the tool of oligarchic forces. Political expectations have been historically low and a President like Ion Iliescu, with the aura of a benevolent autocrat, is widely regarded as a definite advance over a tyrant like Ceausescu. Liberty continues to be defined as an absence of foreign interference or control rather than in terms of individual freedoms, a definition which has shaped the relationship between state and society since independence in 1881.

The absence of political pressures from below means that it has been easy to block the reform of state institutions. In 1990, plans to ensure that civil service staff would be appointed on performance-oriented criteria rather than ideological ones were easily foiled. Simultaneously, reform-minded officers (pressing for senior-ranking ones implicated in repressive acts at the end of 1989 to be brought to justice) were purged. Also in 1990, the most controversial state body in Romania, the secret police, was given a new name (the Romanian Information Service) and a face-lift, but there have been persistent allegations that its operations are incompatible with a democratic society. Moreover, since 1994, the PRSD has been insisting that high-ranking state officials take out membership of the ruling party to bolster its size and its control over the national bureaucracy.

If, in 1992, the reformist parties aligned against President Iliescu had pushed their voting share up from 38 per cent to the low forties, this would have given them a narrow majority in Parliament. It is unlikely that they could have exercised effective control over the state bureaucracy, security services, and armed forces which had been communist-controlled until 1989 and which had not witnessed fundamental restructuring in the period since then. Currently, electoral rivals are seen as permanent enemies rather than as competitors with whom dialogue, and even compromise, are permissible. This means that the democratic arena becomes a battleground in which checks and balances have no meaning and in which political institutions like parliament are unable to act as integrative forces promoting co-operation across party boundaries.

Marketization

Privatization laws (advanced in comparison with other East European exemplars) were drawn up in 1990–91. However, after the removal of reformist ministers, progress towards dismantling the command economy slowed perceptibly. Such privatization measures as occurred were mainly the result of pressure from international financial organizations and it is mainly small and medium-sized state companies (particularly in the retail sector) that have been privatized. In 1993 the OECD identified slow structural change, delays in instituting key reforms, and the continuing power of bureaucratic vested interests as being responsible for Romania's economic malaise.[8] Particular concern has been expressed by foreign analysts about the subsidies that continued to be poured into loss-making industrial plants. In Brasov, the second largest industrial city, eleven thousand new private companies had been set up by 1993, but they accounted for only 2 per cent of the corporate capital of the city. The remaining 98 per cent, according to the chamber of commerce, was split among 243 state firms.[9]

Turning to agriculture, by 1994 less than 25 per cent of Romanian peasants had managed to take back their former property title deeds. Following a privatization law in 1990 much of the land is in an ambiguous position, being no longer state property and not yet formally private.[10] Since then President Iliescu has spoken up for previously landless peasants who are not poised to do well in any break-up of the collectives and he is clearly unhappy about the demise of state-controlled agriculture. As for the former owners of 250,000 residential properties confiscated after 1945, the state has passed a law that makes it virtually impossible for them to be restored, a position that puts Romania at variance with most other former communist countries.

The slowness of the privatization process may arise from a determination to block groups outside the old *nomenklatura* from acquiring economic power. Certainly, many members of the old party apparatus have recycled themselves as entrepreneurs as state assets have been sold off on a discretionary basis.

Early evidence suggests that the new wave of entrepreneurs will not act as pillars of democracy. Speculative, short-term business ventures that do not promote steady employment or encourage philanthropy and other forms of social responsibility are becoming the norm in Romania. Those capitalists drawn from the old *nomenklatura* look to the state for protection or immunity from the law. Consumer protection is minimal as shown in 1992–93 by the ability of the head of a pyramid-selling scheme to extract billions of dollars (in local currency) from small savers, money that Adrian Severin, the economic reformer, claimed may have fallen into the hands of ex-communist officials poised to organize a buy-out of the most profitable parts of the public sector.[11]

Nation-building

The disputed circumstances in which the NSF came to power means that the 1989 revolution has not proven to be an appropriate symbol for post-communist nation-building. Understandably, emphasis has been placed on the centralizing ethos that has been at the heart of state formation in Eastern Europe for over a century. The demand of the 1.8 million strong Hungarian minority for local autonomy, which would enable it to safeguard its cultural identity, has been firmly rejected.[12] Given the insecurity over borders and the degree of internal disunity which led to the collapse of several long-established East European states in 1991–92, the climate was not propitious for the adoption of a system of government that would break up the concentration of power in the capital city and allow minorities some control over their own affairs. The claim expressed by the leaders of the Transylvanian Hungarians that they were a 'co-inhabiting nation' living in the Romanian state who deserved special laws to safeguard their national personality, could not be accepted otherwise it dissolved the idea that Romania was a single national state.

Real differences of interest separate Romanians from Hungarians who comprise around 25 per cent of Transylvania's population. Easy solutions to questions such as a state-financed Hungarian university or the provision of Hungarian education in secondary schools will not exist as long as influential Romanians see concessions here as a diminution of state sovereignty. The moderate approach of the Budapest government of Gyula Horn and the reluctance of most ordinary Transylvanians to be manipulated by extremist politicians has prevented a dangerous polarization. However, the radicalization of a section of the Hungarian minority party in Transylvania and the perennial desire of ex-*nomenklatura* elements to make political capital by fanning Romanian fears about Hungarian intentions, could have unpredictable results. The best chance for resolving what is a low-level conflict lies in the adoption of pan-European measures, perhaps supervised by the Council of Europe, to adopt a common formula for dealing with minority issues in both Western and Eastern Europe.

Interestingly, Bucharest has been more flexible towards the independent state of Moldova, part of Romania between the wars until occupied by Stalin (and with a Romanian-speaking majority today). It adheres to the formula of 'one nation, two states', and irredentism has not been a noticeable feature of state policy. Fear of Russia's future intentions in the region breeds caution and relations between Bucharest and Moscow remain close (anti-communists claiming that it was pro-Russian elements in the pre-1989 leadership who were actually instrumental in toppling Ceausescu).

The new international environment

When viewed against the chaos in the former Yugoslavia and the chronic instability of the former Soviet Union, Romania begins to appear as a stabilizing factor in a zone of chronic insecurity. Since 1991 world opinion has not been scandalized by further overt abuses of presidential power and, besides, the warfare in ex-Yugoslavia has lowered the threshold of what the West regards as acceptable behaviour in Eastern Europe.

The accusation that Ion Iliescu is an archetypal Balkan tyrant is heard with less frequency and, in 1993, Romania was admitted to the Council of Europe, membership for new states being viewed as a badge of democratic respectability. In January 1994, Romania became a founding member of the Partnership for Peace and the US Senate restored most favoured nation status in bilateral economic ties during the same year. By now the World Bank and the International Monetary Fund were prepared to extend credits to Romania and, at the end of 1994, the prospect of eventual membership of the European Union (EU) even appeared to open up when Romania signed an association agreement that placed it on the same footing as countries like Poland and the Czech Republic.

Admission to European institutions, generous economic aid, official visits and cordial inter-state relations were regarded as goals which would maximise political stability and undermine opposition charges that Romania remained a pariah state under the successors of Ceausescu. But in 1995, visiting western officials, like Karsten Voigt, President of the North Atlantic Assembly, made it clear that the presence of an extremist force like the Greater Romania Party in the government would retard any prospects of further integration with western institutions. This party stormed out of government ranks after Iliescu compared its leader with the Russian extremist Zhirinovsky while on an official visit to the USA in October 1995.

The US's firm intervention in the Bosnia conflict may have persuaded Iliescu that the time was at hand to align more clearly with the USA and be less submissive to Russian concerns in the Balkans. Besides, poll findings showed that the Romanians were more committed to orientating their country to Western Europe than to any other Warsaw Pact state, so Iliescu's readjustment of foreign policy was in tune with the national mood.

Paradoxically, it is the reformist opposition which prided itself upon its civic outlook and orientation towards Europe that has begun to fish in the nationalist lake. Its advocacy of economic shock-therapy after 1989 limited its appeal and overtures have been made to the Orthodox Church, one of the chief symbols of

Romanian nationalism, in a bid to place it in a better position for the 1996 elections. There is a clear hope that distancing itself from the Hungarian minority party, which used to be part of the opposition electoral pact, will also win extra votes in Transylvania for the opposition. But this tactic is a sign of desperation that reveals the lack of a clear strategy on the part of Iliescu's opponents. Further schisms and infighting are likely to result following the death in November 1995 of Corneliu Coposu, the one opposition leader of real stature whose own National Peasant and Christian Democratic Party is now likely to split. So, despite widespread popular dissatisfaction with the economic and social policies of the government of Nicolae Vacaroiu, in office since 1992, the ruling party's grip on power has probably never been stronger.

Moral and psychological revolution

Romania has seen the return of basic rights such as freedom to travel and to express views at variance with those of the government, but the lifting of totalitarian restrictions has only had a clear-cut impact on the lives of those who live in the main populated centres. Many Romanians have been affected more by the negative effects of the dismantling of communist rule, such as economic insecurity and the sharp deterioration in public health standards which means that their commitment to political pluralism is inevitably uncertain; if it ever became clear that authoritarian political forces could bring a halt to declining living standards, then it is unlikely that their illiberal character would prevent them acquiring a huge following in Romania.

Anti-democratic forces already enjoy considerable influence over public opinion as well as in institutions like the military and the security services. The younger generation, who played the most active role in the struggle against tyranny at the end of 1989, have largely absented themselves from politics. It might have been different if the 1989 revolution had become an inspiration for political renewal rather than a bitterly-contested event. Many young people, possessing sharp political instincts, have gone into business, got involved with the media, or have tried to leave Romania, rather than link up with political parties. As for women, they arguably enjoy less political influence than they did in communist times, the percentage of women in Parliament practically being the lowest anywhere in Europe.

While the ruling party is dominated by old guard figures, the opposition parties are over-endowed with members of the intelligentsia whose capacity to influence the electoral preferences of the population is not great. There are compelling reasons why even politically-attuned citizens prefer to remain aloof from politics. Memories are still vivid of the repression of all opposition by the communists after 1945 (more systematic in Romania than practically anywhere else). Citizens are too absorbed in the battle for material existence to engage in an activity which offers few psychological rewards or practical incentives, outside the governing party. Political expectations remain low in Romania and people rely on the informal sector to survive, particularly the family, the local community, or ethnic and religious associations. The state is increasingly distrusted but there is no inclination to confront it directly despite strikes and demonstrations over the poor economic situation.

So the scale of Romania's contemporary problems and the destructive legacy of its totalitarian past makes politics a fringe activity. But, in 1996, a shift in political allegiances was noticeable as urban workers, previously loyal to Iliescu, deserted his camp in protest against the scale of economic mismanagement and corruption which had flourished under his rule. In parliamentary and presidential elections held in November 1996, Iliescu was voted out of office and a coalition of moderate reformist parties (including the Hungarian one) was able to obtain a clear parliamentary majority. The new government of Premier Victor Ciorbea had solid pro-western credentials. This gives a boost to Romania's ambitious bid to be accepted for NATO membership and it will strengthen the reconciliation process with Hungary that got underway with the signing of a long-delayed bilateral treaty in September 1996. But it will be far harder to relaunch the economic reform process or neutralize managers of unviable heavy industries whose political strength has enabled them to successfully block economic restructuring since 1989. The government will need to place competent and loyal officials in key ministries, state television, and the prefectures which control local government without incurring charges that a wholesale purge of political opponents is underway.

However, there are signs that Romanian political culture may be outgrowing the Balkan stereotype dominated by images of partisanship, collectivist values, and nationalism. The incident-free election campaign, the high turnout of 76 per cent, the ruling party's decision not to ring the vote and peacefully hand over power to its rivals, all suggest that a normalization of politics may be underway. Emil Constantinescu, the new President, does not conform to the Balkan strong-man image and has a background of activism in the civil society realm. He is seeking to redefine nationalism and separate it from utopian projects, individual career aims, and the manipulation of history.

But the biggest task will be to overhaul the state and create a new ethos of public service in which recruitment and promotion are based on meritocratic and performance-orientated criteria. To no small degree, the fate of the reform process will depend on the ability of the post-1996 regime to reform the civil service so as to narrow the gulf between state and society, a disastrous cleavage which has done great harm to Romania since even before the communist era.

NOTES

1. D. Chirot, 'Social Change in Communist Romania', *Social Forces*, vol. 57, no. 2 (1978).

2. I. Mihailescu, 'Mental Stereotypes in Post-Totalitarian Romania', *Government & Opposition*, vol. 28, no. 3 (1993) p. 318; details of the second poll were in the newspaper, *Adevarul de Cluj*, 14 February 1992.

3. M. Shafir, '"War of the Roses" in Romania's National Salvation Front', *RFE-RL Research Report*, vol. 1, no. 3 (24 January 1992).

4. For details, see chapters 3 and 6 of T. Gallagher, *Romania After Ceausescu: The Politics of Intolerance* (Edinburgh: Edinburgh University Press, 1995).

5. M. Shafir, 'Ruling Party Formalizes Relations with Extremists', *Transition*, vol. 1, no. 5 (14 April 1995) p. 43.

6. *Romania, Bulgaria, Albania: Quarterly Report*, 4th Quarter of 1993 (London: Economist Intelligence Unit, 1993) p. 20.

7. *Expres* (Bucharest), 18 October 1994.

8. M. Milner, 'A Sleeping Beauty Awaits Rich Prince', *The Guardian*, 24 July 1993.

9. Ibid.

10. A. Mungiu and A. Pippidi, 'Letter from Romania', *Government and Opposition*, vol. 29, no. 3 (1994) p. 360.

11. *22* (Bucharest), 31 August 1994.

12. The 1992 Romanian census claimed the size of the Hungarian minority was 1.8 million but Hungarian sources claim that the real figure is at least 2 million.

12

Former Yugoslavia: nations above all

Håkan Wiberg

YUGOSLAV SPECIFICITIES

Yugoslavia was a very particular post-communist case in several respects ('Yugoslavia' will refer to the old state or its geographical area, 'FRY' to the present federal republic). To show this, I will look at the four subsystems classical sociology counts with: *economic, political, social* and *cultural*.[1]

The post-war *economic* system of Yugoslavia initially copied the USSR, but after their rupture in 1948–49 there were large non-governmental sectors: predominantly privately owned agriculture, plus a big sector of self-managed enterprises.[2] There was an economic growth of Japanese dimensions until the mid-1960s. The economic reforms in 1965 abolished most of the central planning, consisting of much free market and little privatization. By 1990, Yugoslavia suffered from unemployment at a West European level, initiated by the 1965 reforms; a foreign debt of $20–25 billion; and permanent inflation, averaging some 30 per cent per year in 1965–90, and accelerating.

Yugoslav transformation is the oldest, but it is still controversial whether its economic miseries (and those of its successor states) were due to too much or too little transformation. Decision-makers knew that the 1965 reforms would create some short-term unemployment and counteracted it by permitting labour migration, with a beneficial effect on the balance of payments; they did not foresee that the unemployment would settle permanently at a high level. Without central planning and with economic decision-making increasingly decentralized, Yugoslavia was eventually unable to deal with the growing economic crisis. Remittances from migrant labour in Western Europe first served as a buffer, but dwindled after the 'oil crisis' in 1973, as many workers returned home and many others settled permanently abroad. The next short-term remedy was made possible by the lending spree in petrodollars during the second half of the seventies. It created the bulk of Yugoslavia's foreign debt and made long-term problems worse, being primarily used for consumption based on salary increases without coverage in increased productivity. The debt trap sprung when real interest and dollar rates sky-rocketed after 1980, forcing Yugoslavia to face tough IMF conditions, which doomed the political leadership to choose between accelerating inflation and making painful cuts in real incomes. The high decentralization and divergent economic republic interests prevented a choice, so Yugoslavia ended up with very much of both. This had political effects: Slovenia decided that the economic reform it wanted necessitated de-linking from the Yugoslavian economy, as *de facto* independent (with its own currency, and so on) in a confederation after radical constitutional change, or else by disregarding the constitution and proclaiming independence.[3] This made war largely inevitable: with Slovenia's departure the system of balances broke down.

The *political* system of Yugoslavia had become far more decentralized than in any other communist system by political and constitutional compromises during previous decades.[4] The theoretical one-party state in reality had eight regional Communist parties. Initially, this mattered little: a strong dose of 'democratic centralism' entailed purges of deviant party members, like supporters of the 1971 upsurge of Croatian nationalism. After the economic decentralisation in 1965 and the increased political decentralisation in 1974, the eight parties became 'ethnocracies' engaging in local protectionism and forming shifting alliances as in the nineteenth-century system of major European powers.[5] The latter decentralization made the federal government increasingly helpless to cure the deteriorating economic problems.

The *social* system was too weak to manage integration in the face of contradictions between different functional spheres of society and different regions. The anti-nationalist Tito regime first tried to transcend national cleavages by encouraging people to identify themselves as 'Yugoslavs', rather than Serbs, Croats, and so on. After 1964, these attempts were reduced to try to make Yugoslavian identity superordinate to ethnonational ones, rather than a substitute for them. The self-declared Yugoslavs, most of them from ethnically mixed families rather than 'ideological' Yugoslavs,[6] decreased from over 10 per cent to 6 per cent in the 1981 census and 3 per cent in the 1991 census. Many more combined identifying themselves in ethno-national terms with a *political* identification as Yugoslav citizens, even taking some pride in self-management and non-alignment as particular Yugoslav features. This combination, however, was very vulnerable to possible perceptions of contradiction between its elements.

Concerning the *cultural* system, no European state, except the USSR, was equally multifarious; Titoist Marxism-Leninism had many competitors. *Religion* seemed to be relatively neutralized: all religions were tolerated, having agreed to stay out of politics. The great majority of nominal Catholics, Orthodox and Muslims were secularized by the mid-eighties. Yet, as later developments showed, religions remained latent elements of ethnonational identification, resurging when the possibility arose. The position of the regime to *national identification* was also ambiguous. Expressions of national cultures were encouraged and supported. To the three traditional 'constituent nations' (Serbs, Croats, Slovenes) Macedonians and Montenegrins were added after 1945 and Muslims around 1970. The official languages of Yugoslavia were for a long time Slovenian, Macedonian and Serbo-Croat, which after 1953 had an 'Eastern' and a 'Western' recognized version; Croatian, different from Western Serbo-Croat, was recognized in 1974.[7] Hungarian was also official in Vojvodina and Albanian in Kosovo; schools were run in Italian, Romanian, Rusinian, Romani, Bulgarian and Turkish.

Still, anything like political nationalism, or even implying contradictions between nations, was heavily suppressed, from individual jail sentences to the crushing of the Albanian revolt in Kosovo in 1968 and the Croatian in 1971. The regime made concessions to both in the 1974 constitutional reforms, which eventually led to Serb allegations that *they* had been sold out and increasing Serb nationalism, in particular after the following Albanian revolt in 1981.

Yugoslav Marxism-Leninism was in a weaker position than most communist regimes to successfully claim a monopoly on defining *values* and *images of reality*. After 1965, people could travel freely, for example to work in Western Europe. By the late 1980s, millions of Yugoslavs had long experiences in the West or close relatives living there. Many spoke some Western language and had been part of civil society there: associations, unions, parties.

COMPETING SOCIAL CLEAVAGES

The specificity of Yugoslavia also concerned the relative importance of different social cleavages: classes, ideologies, regions, ethnonational groups and combinations. To see this clearly, we should first survey other post-communist states.

In several countries, ideology and class were soon the main bases for political organizations, even if the political rhetoric of the left wing had abandoned Marxist language. The first free elections brought centre-right-wing governments. Their economic programmes had painful short-term effects for large segments of the population and the following elections produced a centre-left-wing government, according to the well-known Western pattern: governments make more enemies than friends by governing. Ethnonational movements have acquired a social basis in some states, but rarely became separatist, Slovakia being the only clear case outside the former USSR and Yugoslavia. In most post-communist cases such movements tend rather to look across their state boundaries: at co-nationals in other states (irredentism as the strongest version), or by seeing neighbouring states as big and threatening, traditional threats, or both, in each case calling for internal national unity. Cleavages of regional type have sometimes played a role of their own, sometimes interacting or merging with ethnonationally defined ones.

Each country has its specificities, forbidding sweeping generalizations. Yet, we may find one crude basis for prediction (or postdiction) as to what cleavages would be strongest where, by looking at the ethnonational composition of the post-communist states in CSCE Europe and their successor states. We rank them from highest to lowest ethnonational heterogeneity.[8] 'DD' means that a state is dissolved, 'D' that it is divided, 'I' that one or more national groups demand some kind of sovereignty, and 'W' a war with at least several hundred people killed inside the state since 1990 or after its later independence (some 'I' may be missing for lack of information).

The simplest hypothesis on the relationship between heterogeneity and the balance of different cleavages is the following: 'The more ethnonationally heterogeneous a state is, the higher the likelihood that ethnonational cleavages, possibly also identified as regional cleavages, will predominate over class and class-related ideological cleavages'. This hypothesis is also strongly supported by an inspection of Table 12.1 below: the upper half contains far more dissolved states, internal political tensions and wars than the lower half.

CONFLICT PROGNOSES IN FORMER YUGOSLAVIA

From Table 12.1 below, Yugoslavia would be expected to run the highest risk of ethnonational cleavages dominating over others, side by side with Bosnia-Hercegovina; problems should also be anticipated in Macedonia, FRY and Croatia; Slovenia stands alone in having a low-risk figure. And ethnonational mobilization has indeed left little room for class mobilization in most of these states; in Slovenia only have we seen the more class-related changes in government composition and the relative failure of ethnonational mobilization that have been characteristic for several other post-communist countries in Europe.

Table 12.1 Ethnonational composition of countries

Country	Composition	Country	Composition
Yugoslavia (I, DD, W)	Serbs 36% Croats 20%	Bosnia-Herceg. (I, D, W)	Muslims 40% Serbs 32%
Kazakhstan	Russians 41% Kazakhs 36%	Kyrgyzistan	Kirgisians 49% Russians 26%
USSR (DD)	Russians 52% Ukrainians 16%	Latvia	Letts 54% Russians 33%
Tadzhikistan (W)	Tadzhiks 59% Uzbeks 23%	Moldova (I, D, W)	Moldovians 64% Ukr. 14% Russians 12%
Czechoslovakia (I, DD)	Czechs 64% Slovaks 32%	Estonia	Estonians 65% Russians 28%
Macedonia (I)	Macedonians 67% Albanians 22%	FRY (I)	Serbs/Montenegrins 67% Albanians 16%
Ukraine (I)	Ukrainians 74% Russians 21%	Croatia (I, D, W)	Croats 75% Serbs 12%
Azerbaijan (I, D, W)	Azeri 79% Russians 8% Armenians 8%	Belarus	Byelorussians 79% Russians 12%
Lithuania	Lithuanians 80% Russians 9% Poles 8%	Russia (I, W)	Russians 83% Ukrainians 4%
Bulgaria	Bulgarians 80–85% Turks 13%	Slovakia	Slovaks 80–85 % c. 10% Hungarians
Romania	Romanians 85–90% Hungarians 8–10%	Armenia	Armenians 90% then Azeri
Slovenia	Slovenes 91% several small groups	Albania	Albanians above 90% then Greeks
Czech Rep.	Czechs above 90% then Slovaks	Poland	Poles c.95% then Germans
Hungary	Hungarians 97%		

This element of prognosis tells us only that the likelihood that mobilization would be predominantly ethno-national was high in most parts of Yugoslavia. High mobilization, whether of ethnonational or other kinds, does not automatically mean armed conflict; there are often other ways of acting out conflicts and arriving at temporary or long-term decisions. In addition, however, Yugoslavia had a gloomy prognosis on the basis of several other dimensions that tend to be related to conflict (and most of them to conflict seen as ethno-national). First, no other state had been through as long and deep an economic crisis by 1990; the average Yugoslav lost about half his real income in the eighties. Second, it was difficult to find any other European state, except perhaps the USSR,[9] with such deep historical traumas between ethnonational groups, further nourished during World War II (Croatian genocide against Serbs and many other atrocities between groups) and after it (Serbian repression of Albanians). Third, Yugoslavia's history of disagreements over the Constitution since (actually even before) its creation in 1918 is hardly rivalled by any other state; from the very beginning, the Serbs wanted a 'French' state, the Croats and Slovenes a 'Swiss', and these conflicts had repeatedly brought the state to, or even over, the brink of collapse.[10] Fourth, very few of the other states have regional differences in economic development and GNP *per capita* that could be compared with those in Yugoslavia, where the gap in GNP *per capita* between the extremes, Slovenia and Kosovo, had grown from three times in the late forties to eight times by the late eighties. In addition, there was a strong, though far from perfect, relation between region and ethnonational composition. Fifth, there was for a long time the opposite of economic integration, the republics trading relatively less with each other while becoming more dependent on northern Italy and southern Germany. Sixth, very few other states had been as dependent for internal cohesion on the Cold War or were, for this reason, as negatively affected by its end. Given all this, it would have called for a miracle for Yugoslavia not to break up – and not to do so very violently.

No miracle occurred. Different nationalisms spiralled into each other, political leaders in several parts eager to use and manipulate the breeding ground provided by the factors above, blaming it all on crooks from the other side. In particular, the propaganda barrage in 1990–91 between Serbian and Croatian mass media contributed heavily to the actual explosion.[11] The blame game then quickly spread to the surrounding world, fairly closely related to religious boundaries: whom people see as the main crooks and victims depends heavily on whether they live in a Catholic, Orthodox or Islamic country.[12] From Christian or Islamic (but not, for example, Buddhist) perspectives, it is also important to pinpoint guilt at individual or collective actors in order to pass moral or legal judgment. There is a plethora of conspiracy theories about various actors, some of them possibly true; but it will take many years' patient work by historians to tell with some certainty which of them. Focusing on analysis, not blame, I shall concentrate on the complexity and multicausality of the conflicts. Let us begin with actors and issues.

For a long time, there were ten significant actors: the leaderships of the eight republics and the two autonomous provinces, plus the Yugoslav People's Army (YPA) and the Federal Council (with one representative each for the eight territorial units, and the YPA *de facto* secured veto power in national security issues). The curtailed autonomy in 1987–89 reduced the actors to eight, with Serbia having *de facto* taken over the votes of Kosovo and Vojvodina in the Federal Council. On the other hand, new *de facto* actors emerged in 1989–91: the Serb leadership in Krajina, the Serb, Croat and Muslim leaderships in Bosnia-Hercegovina, and the Albanian leadership in Kosovo; more marginal cases were the Albanian leadership in Macedonia and the Muslim leadership in the Sandzak Novipazar, straddling Serbia and Montenegro.

There was also a long list of major issues. A long-standing one was what to do about the economic crisis. The last attempt was the Markovic austerity plan in 1989–90, but that eventually broke down when it turned out that Serbia (and others) had created more money than agreed, to pay its pensioners and so on.

Another issue came to the fore in 1990: Croatian and Slovene demands for heavy cuts in the federal budget. Since main parts of that budget went to finance the YPA and the poorer republics, none of the other actors felt much sympathy, and the demand in fact moved the YPA leadership, with its strong 'Yugoslavist' orientation, closer to Milosevic, previously regarded by many of them as a dangerous (Serb) nationalist, but who could now present himself as a protagonist of the integrity of Yugoslavia.[13]

That issue spawned an even larger one: the Constitution. The Slovene leadership, backed up by the Croatian, called for very radical changes, making Slovenia and Croatia *de facto* independent states in a very loose confederation with the others. Slovenia also threatened in 1990 to unilaterally declare itself independent in 1991 if it did not get its way. Serbia and Montenegro would not agree to any radical changes in that direction; the (transethnic) leaderships of Macedonia and Bosnia-Hercegovina tried to find some formula of compromise, but neither side in this conflict would accept it.

Slovenia declared itself independent, having made sure that Croatia joined it, on 25/26 June 1991. This automatically made the main conflict a territorial one between Serbs and Croats, especially in Krajina. The apparent Croat–Slovene alliance soon disappeared when Ljubljana and Belgrade could agree, after a few days of mock war, on a common interest in Slovenia not becoming a forced ally of Croatia.[14]

The price for this was *de facto* acceptance of Slovenia's independence and withdrawal of YPA from Slovenia. This was acceptable for Belgrade, but it created new situations and great dilemmas for several other actors, since the division of Yugoslavia would entail a very high risk for most of its parts getting further divided. The potential 'second generation' secessionists were primarily Serbs in Croatia, Serbs and Croats in Bosnia-Hercegovina and Albanians in FRY, with Albanians in Macedonia and Muslims and Hungarians in FRY itself as further candidates. In each case, territorial conflicts would exacerbate the constitutional ones.

The Slovenian solution cemented the Zagreb dilemma: how to get the Croatian fist out of the Yugoslav bottle without first dropping the Krajina nut from the fist. It thereby undermined the possibility for compromise in Bosnia-Hercegovina, even if the three leaderships there continued to negotiate about that for many months after the outbreak of the Serb–Croat war in July 1991. The problem was great, their preferences being so difficult to reconcile. The Serb leadership preferred B-H to remain in Yugoslavia, with an independent Serb Republic as a fallback, the Croat leadership a confederation with Croatia, with an independent Croat Republic as second best. Under changing circumstances, the Muslim leadership eventually switched from remaining in Yugoslavia to getting an unitary independent B-H state, much preferred to the alternative: three independent republics. The first preference of each leadership was strongly unacceptable to the two others.

The Western invitation to declarations of independence cemented the Muslim dilemma: getting into a war with the Serbs by leaving Yugoslavia, or a war with the Croats by remaining in it. Now forced to choose, it opted for an alliance with the Croats against the Serbs, based on common interests in getting out of Yugoslavia and getting the YPA, or at least the minority in it that was from Serbia and Montenegro, out of B-H. These things taken care of by the Western recognition on 6 April, 1992,[15] the Muslim-Croat alliance quickly dissolved, succeeded for a long while by a *de facto* Serb-Croat alliance against the Muslims. The recognition gave them common defensive interests against the unitary state claimed by the Muslims, as well as common offensive interests in dividing B-H between them, if possible. The fragile cease-fire between Croats and Muslims in Spring 1994 – in the context of a (fictitious) federation – permitted the Muslims to concentrate on escalating the war with the Serbs, and the Croats to decide for themselves whether and when they would gain from cooperating with the Muslims or the Serbs. The predictable effect of the federation was more war, since the virtual convergence of expectations had again disappeared.[16] The stakes had also risen by the atrocities of war. By Western outsiders' counts, Serbs were the main perpetrators and Muslims the main victims; yet each group could point at many villages killed off and burnt by each of the two other groups, and memory is highly selective in each group.[17] The stalemate of the war was broken in August 1995 by a combination of NATO air strikes destroying the Serb infrastructure and a major land offensive from Croatia in extension of its expelling the Krajina Serbs. The ensuing Dayton agreement provided for a definite distribution of territory, where a Muslim Sarajevo was to compensate for the Muslims otherwise getting considerably less than they had rejected in early 1994 and the Croats correspondingly more. It also contained a set of military measures, monitoring the separation of Serb forces from the others (but not Croat from Muslim forces), withdrawals to barracks and a considerable degree of demobilization. It left all other problems unsolved, however, except on paper,[18] but as long as NATO remains, they are unlikely to erupt in a new war.

The worst may yet remain. While the Serb–Croat–Slovene and Serb–Croat–Muslim triangles have exploded, the Serb–Albanian–Macedonian triangle has not. If relations between Macedonians and Albanians break down completely in Macedonia, or if the spiral between repression and separatism in Kosovo spawns a war, there is a high risk that the southern triangle will explode even worse than in Bosnia. The military balance of power is more uneven, and there is, by contrast to the two others, a high risk that several neighbouring states will be drawn into the war, at least Albania, Greece, Bulgaria and Turkey.[19] The other side of this coin is that the awareness of these dangers may make all parties back down from risking a war, just as the three leaderships in B-H tried for many months to find a compromise.

TRANSFORMATION: CONDITIONS AND DIRECTIONS

Transformation in the parts of Yugoslavia has thus been very heavily affected by the perceptual primacy of ethno-national and regional cleavages over other dimensions. How popular sentiments and populist leaderships have interacted to bring about this primacy cannot be analysed here. It may matter for the issue of whom to blame for what, but matters little for prognoses, given the classical Thomas's theorem: 'What people define as real, becomes real in its consequences'. The horrible consequences will have made ethno-national cleavages even more predominant, no matter how 'false' these perceptions may be from a social science point of view. Let us now look at the transformations that have taken part under these adverse conditions.

The economic system

The successor states and entities of Yugoslavia have had, or still have, war economies; in Slovenia, this phase is largely over, and in Macedonia it is less prevalent than in Croatia, FRY and B-H. In addition, the UN economic sanctions have had catastrophic effects in concentric circles. Worst hit is of course FRY itself, with a GNP *per capita* at much less than a half of that before the war and about half of the labour force unemployed; the relative causal weight of sanctions, military efforts and economic mismanagement is a matter of dispute. The UN sanctions, with a Greek boycott added in early 1994, have also had very grave effects on Macedonia, where more than one-third of the labour force is unemployed. Other main losers from the sanctions are all other parts of Yugoslavia, plus Bulgaria, Greece, Romania and Albania, and to a lesser extent Hungary, Ukraine and a few others.[20]

The total effect consists in decreases everywhere in GNP *per capita* since 1990, ranging between relatively modest ones (10–20 per cent) in Slovenia and catastrophic ones in FRY. Rising unemployment ranges between modest figures in Slovenia and from one-third to one-half of the labour force in FRY and Macedonia (and even worse in Kosovo). Inflation was a long-standing problem in Yugoslavia, where the last monetary reform cut four zeros out of the banknotes in 1990. After the division, it was limited to a two-digit, and since mid-1992 one-digit, monthly inflation in Slovenia. A number of zeros were cut away from the currencies in other parts: two in Macedonia, three in Croatia, and in FRY first six in 1992, then seven in 1994: a hyperinflation with which only the Hungarian one in 1945–46 can compete in the history of money. Bosnia-Hercegovina has a currency in theory only: the Croatian kuna or the FRY dinar are used in most its territory, the Deutschemark everywhere. All these governments still face the same dilemma as Yugoslavia before the war: pressing inflation down at the expense of worse hardships for the population (like Croatia), or attempting to ameliorate these hardships in the short term by letting inflation start again (FRY).

The development of new economic institutions in different parts of Yugoslavia has thus taken place under very particular conditions, and governments everywhere have had a stronger interest than normal in keeping as much control as possible. 'Privatization' has indeed been on the agenda, laws on it have been passed in Slovenia, Croatia and Macedonia, and private enterprise has been encouraged in FRY. Still, the percentage of GDP deriving from private enterprise (30 to 40) lies at Bulgarian and Romanian levels, much below that of other European post-communist states (if employee-owned enterprises are included, the difference may be less). In several parts, much of the proclaimed privatization has been a *de facto* transfer of ownership from government or from the employees to supporters of the government parties, accompanied by large-scale corruption.

The political system

After decades of political monopoly, there were multi-party and (relatively) fair elections in all republics from April through December 1990. Rumours of widespread blatant cheating were not confirmed by reports from external observers. Other criticisms were made, especially against FRY and Croatia, where the opposition had scant possibilities of getting heard in the largely government-controlled mass media, and the election laws greatly over-represent the biggest party.

Ethno-nationalism of any kind had been kept down by strong repression until the late 1980s; once that lid was lifted, ethnonational mobilization became predominant and the party system became as ethnified as in the elections in the 1920s. The effect of this was amplified by the first multi-party elections in 1990 taking place over more than half the year, and in the separate republics, rather than at the same time in Yugoslavia as a whole. The new governments in Slovenia (with the centrist DEMOS leading) and Croatia, where the right-wing and highly nationalist

HDZ won, soon proclaimed their (initially ill-defined) sovereignty; in addition, Croatia deprived the Serbs there of their position as a constituent nation and started firing Serbs from public positions. The biggest party in Macedonia, the ultranationalist VMRO, was, however, kept out of government by a coalition of somewhat more pragmatic Macedonian and Albanian parties. The elections in Bosnia-Hercegovina followed ethnic lines fairly closely, almost four fifths voting for the three ethnic parties: the Serbian SDS, the Croatian HDZ and the Muslim SDA, and only a small minority for transethnic liberal or socialist parties. The Communist Party in Serbia, later transformed into the Socialist Party, had been the first (except Croatia in 1971) to embrace a nationalist platform in 1987; when Serbia was the last republic to hold elections after all the other events, it scored a clear victory, partly because the Albanians boycotted the election. All these new governments then spent the next half-year quarrelling about the future Constitution of Yugoslavia. Croatia and Slovenia called for radical changes, to make them independent states in a very loose confederation with the rest of Yugoslavia; Serbia and Montenegro stonewalled any radical changes; the ethnic coalition governments in Macedonia and Bosnia-Hercegovina worked hard, but in vain, at finding some constitutional compromise that all the others could accept. After that half-year, the first war broke out.

In spite of this, the political machineries in all parts of Yugoslavia have continued to operate. Parliaments have continued to function and almost everywhere there has been one or more new elections, against the *formal* carrying out of which external observers have had no serious criticism, except of the refusal of the governments of Croatia and FRY to accept their results. (Again, opposition access to mass media has been scant almost everywhere.) In these respects, Slovenia has behaved as a 'normal' post-communist state. In Croatia, the HDZ has a complete power monopoly due to its election laws, with hardly even token respect paid to the opposition. In Serbia and Montenegro, federated into FRY in April 1992, the Socialist Party has lost its parliamentary majority and is forced to make coalitions or political deals with different opposition parties, initially relying on support from the ultranationalist Radical Party and then seeking more centrist cooperation. The Albanians in Kosovo continue to boycott the Yugoslav political system, and have created their own Parliament and government in elections that were tolerated, but not recognized, by FRY authorities. In both Serbia and Croatia, however, the municipal elections in 1996 were a disappointment to the ruling parties. In Macedonia, the 1994 elections gave the previous Communist Party a majority of its own, as the ultranationalist Macedonian opposition was split; it nevertheless preferred to keep the main Albanian party in the governing coalition.

The exception is Bosnia-Hercegovina, where a referendum was held at the EU's request in February 1992. It was boycotted by the Serb majority areas, whereas the areas with a Croat/Muslim majority voted almost unanimously for independence, after which the Serb areas proclaimed *their* independence, eventually uniting to form the 'Republika Srpska' (RS). When the war broke out, the Serb party (SDS) was declared illegal by the others; its elected Parliament members then convened in Pale as the Parliament of RS. Soon afterwards, the 'Croatian Community Herceg-Bosna' set up its own (HDZ dominated) Parliament in Mostar. In May 1993, a referendum was held in the Serb-controlled areas, where a great majority rejected the Owen–Vance Plan; the large number of refugees from this area could not participate. The nine-person Presidential Council continued to exist until Autumn, 1993, when its majority (all six Serbs and Croats, plus the Muslim Fikret Abdic) called for negotiations on the basis of the further concessions made by Serbs and Croats after the first Owen–Stoltenberg Plan, but were disregarded by Izetbegovic. Abdic then proclaimed the Autonomous Province of Western Bosnia, which immediately led to two years of Muslim–Muslim war in the Bihac area. After the Croat–Muslim accord, the number of governments increased even further, to be reduced again by the military elimination of Abdic and the Dayton agreements. There is now one government in Sarajevo with theoretical sovereignty over the entirety of B-H, but virtually no powers; one for Republika Srpska; and one with theoretical sovereignty over the Croat–Muslim federation; while the Herceg-Bosna government is theoretically abolished, the Croats in B-H continue to *de facto* run their own affairs. The Serb, Croat and Muslim leaderships consolidated their positions in the parliamentary elections in 1996, majorities ranging between almost two-thirds (the Serb SDS) and seven-eighths (the Croat HDZ).

The social system

Speaking about 'society', Slovenia is the only case in which it is clear what it refers to. Even before the war, there was a perfect coincidence between a municipality having a Slovene majority and lying in Slovenia. The present government is in control of exactly the territory it claims, and is regarded as legitimate everywhere in that territory. Who does and does not belong to that society is no more problematic than for normal virtually monoethnic states, even if complaints have been made over restrictive citizenship laws and practice. The constitution also refers to the small Hungarian and Italian minorities (but not the larger, non-autochthonous minorities from other parts of Yugoslavia).

In all other parts of Yugoslavia, the very notion of society is problematic. There does not exist a B-H society and it is questionable whether one can ever be (re)created; Krajina Serbs clearly did not regard themselves as part of Croatian society, nor Kosovo Albanians as part of Serbian society; the position of Albanians in Macedonia seems less decided. In each case, the groups differ by both religion and (officially self-defined) language; outside Russia, it is only the Baltic states that have integration problems of a similar magnitude in Europe.

The cultural system

As we often see in intense conflict situations, cultural specificities are emphasised more than ever, by state policies as well as in social movements.[21] For most Yugoslav states, one central problem is to make a nation out of the state that the majority ethnonational group has cut out for itself. History is being rewritten to emphasise old heroes and martyrs. Religion is given an elevated role in defining national identity, with two main exceptions. The Albanians, like the Palestinians, are divided, rather than united, by religion, and the leadership therefore tries to keep it out of national identity. The Bosnian Muslim leadership is split: some want to make Islam the anchor of national (Bosniac) identity, there being little else to define Muslims (Bosniacs) as being different from Serbs and Croats; others want to deemphasize it and try to create a common non-confessional Bosnian identity that is anchored in territorial history, and so on, and shared by Serbs, Croats and Bosniacs. The number of officially different languages has multiplied even further, the latest addition being the creation of a Bosniac language in 1993; some local intellectuals are calling for a Montenegrin one. In most Yugoslav states, however, these were changes in the majority culture; but as they were accompanied by similar changes in the minority cultures, most of these states inherited the problems of Yugoslavia in even worse forms, notwithstanding their official proclamations to please the West. Their political systems then got working at them, discrimination and forced assimilation being the mildest instruments, harsh repression, mass expulsion and mass murder being further steps on an ascending scale.

FUTURE DEVELOPMENTS

In the Parsonsian tradition, history is primarily assumed to be governed from the cultural system downwards through the social system, the political system and the economic system. By this token, the prospects for virtually all parts of Yugoslavia are morose: what was a relatively modern system ten years ago has broken up into a number of much more traditionalist fragments. There is no chance of recreating that system within the foreseeable future, if ever, and the successor states – and groups within them – are likely to stimulate each other into even more traditional attitudes, with Slovenia as a possible (but by no means certain) exception. The bases for more modernist orientations have been greatly eroded by war, economic catastrophes and counter-productive external pressures – and large parts of the educated groups emigrating. In the social systems we may anticipate close linkages between the majority nation and state, with 'citizen states' as a distant prospect only, while the political systems are likely to remain authoritarian, even if in the forms of parliamentary democracy.

The perspectives do not become much brighter if we make the opposite assumption, along Marxist lines, about influences between systems. If economic developments are assumed to define the infrastructure that serves as a matrix for the political and ideological superstructure, the diagnosis is that even if war and economic sanctions do not reemerge, the effects of both are likely to continue to ravage the economies for many years, again with the likely exception of Slovenia. That in turn will lead to authoritarian regimes and reactionary nationalist ideologies to legitimate them, and again modernization will be a distant project.

Each part of the former Yugoslavia contains movements and intellectuals, like those represented in the study by Palau and Kumar,[22] trying to counteract these sombre prognoses. They are likely to have time on their side in the long run; but it is equally likely that the run will be measured in decades.

NOTES

1. I am using Parsonsian terms; their content in fact parallels Marxian infrastructure/superstructure language, although the the theories are quite different. Here, I presuppose neither.

2. For the economic development and sociopolitical effects, see Carl-Ulrik Schierup, *Migration, Socialism and the International Division of Labour: The Yugoslav Case* (Aldershot: Avebury, 1990).

3. Cf. Catalonia, North Italy, Flemish Belgium, Czechia and Baltic republics trying to cut economic links with less developed areas. The 'EU magnetism' contributed to the collapse of Czechoslovakia and the USSR as well as Yugoslavia.

4. For histories of Yugoslavia see, for example: Ivo Banac, *The National Question in Yugoslavia: Origins, History, Politics* (Ithaca, NY: Cornell Univ. Press, 1984) and Stefan Pawlowitch, *The Improbable Survivor: Yugoslavia and Its Problems, 1918–1988* (London: Hurst, 1988). More recent ones, such as Mark Almond, *Europe's Backyard War: The War in the Balkans* (London: Mandarin, 1994) and Noel Malcolm, *Bosnia: A*

Short History (London: Macmillan, 1994) are even more coloured by the political causes of their authors.

5. Sabrina P. Ramet, *Nationalism and Federalism in Yugoslavia 1962–1991* (Bloomington: Indiana University Press, 1992).

6. A nationality map of Yugoslavia shows clearly that Yugoslavs were most frequent in mixed areas, for example Vojvodina and parts of Bosnia-Hercegovina, but quite rare in more homogeneous ones.

7. A problem for Croatian national identity was that whereas the 'Eastern' version, *e-kavski što-kavski*, was spoken by Serbs in Serbia, the 'Western' version, *ije-kavski što-kavski*, was shared by most people in Croatia, Montenegrins, Bosnian Serbs and Muslims; the Zagreb area spoke another dialect group, *kaj-kavski*.

8. Demographic figures are from various issues of *Statesman's Yearbook* (London: Macmillan), especially 1990/91, supplemented by a few estimates; war data from recent years *SIPRI Yearbook* (Oxford: Oxford University Press), mainly 1992–94.

9. In the USSR, guilt was mostly placed on 'the Russians'. Russians stand relatively alone in placing it on 'Stalinism', with Russians as fellow victims.

10. Aleksa Djilas, *The Contested Country: Yugoslav Unity and Communist Revolution* (Cambridge, MA: Harvard Univ. Press, 1991).

11. Marjan Malesic (ed.), *The Role of Mass Media in the Serbian-Croatian Conflict* (Stockholm: Styrelsen för psykologiskt försvar, 1993) and Mark Thompson, *Forging War: The Media in Serbia, Croatia and Bosnia-Hercegovina* (London: Article 19, 1994).

12. For critical analyses of the biases in Western media, see Peter Brock, 'Dateline Yugoslavia: The Partisan Press', *Foreign Policy*, no. 93 (Winter 1993-94) and Jacques Merlino, *Les Vérités Yougoslaves ne sont pas toutes bonnes à dire* (Paris: Alboin Michel, 1993).

13. For the position and structure of the YPA, see Anton Bebler, *The Yugoslav Crisis and the Yugoslav People's Army*, Zürcher Beiträge zur Sicherheitspolitik und konfliktforschung, Heft Nr. 23 (1992) and James Gow, *Legitimacy and the Military: The Yugoslav Crisis* (London: Pinter, 1992).

14. The first book on the transition from crisis to war was a piece of good journalism, Misha Glenny, *The Fall of Yugoslavia: The Third Balkan War* (Harmondsworth: Penguin, 1992). The major work to date is Susan L. Woodward, *Balkan Tragedy: Chaos and Dissolution after the Cold War* (Washington, D.C.: The Brookings Institution, 1995). The end game around and after the break-up of Yugoslavia and the reasons why

external intervention tended to do more harm than good for conflict resolution are analysed in Håkan Wiberg, 'Third Party Intervention in Yugoslavia: problems and lessons', in Jaap de Wilde and Håkan Wiberg (eds.), *Organized Anarchy in Europe: The Role of Intergovernmental Institutions* (London: I.B. Tauris, 1996).

15. Hitler's attack on Yugoslavia started on 6 April, 1941, with a bombardment of Belgrade killing many thousand people in one night. EU's choice of date was probably due to ignorance and incompetence, but it is difficult to convince Serbs of that.

16. Owen and Stoltenberg had managed to get the disagreements over territory down to a fraction of 1 per cent. After the federation, they initially rose to some 20 per cent. Their frustrations are recounted in David Owen, *Balkan Odyssey* (London: Gollancz, 1995) and Thorvald Stoltenberg & Kai Eide, *De tusen dagene: Fredsmeklere på Balkan* (Oslo: Gyldendal, 1996).

17. Serb and Croat atrocities against Muslims are described in Ed Vulliamy, *Seasons in Hell. Understanding Bosnia's War* (London: Simon and Schuster, 1994), who refers to the Muslim massacre on Serb villages as 'a mistake' and omits Muslim massacres against Croats. Serbs as victims of Croats and Muslims are portrayed in Alan Sherman, *Perfidy in the Balkans: The Rape of Yugoslavia* (Athens: Psichogios, 1993), who has little to say concerning Serb atrocities. Croats as innocent victims of Serbs appear in Alain Finkielkraut, *Comment peut-on être croate?* (Paris: Gallimard, 1992).

18. Territory transfers and military measures were the only mandates of IFOR/SFOR. Other parts of the Dayton agreement depend on something new happening: great powers agree to make SFOR a long-term occupation force; the three ethnic leaderships have common interests; Serb and Croat and Muslim police are willing to go against their own people; the international community puts up much money. Neither appears likely to any large extent.

19. See John Zametica, *The Yugoslav Conflict*, Adelphi Paper no. 270 (London: International Institute for Strategic Studies, 1992) and Radovan Vukadinovic, *The Break-up of Yugoslavia: Threats and Challenges* (The Hague: Netherlands Institute of International Relations, 1992). Both are relatively balanced presentations of the neighbourhood complexities and do not differ much, in spite of the former author being Bosnian Serb and the latter Croat.

20. The extremely weak position of South Eastern Europe *vis-à-vis* the West is showed by the sanctions having cost those states some 30 billion

USD, many times more than they totally received in assistance and loans from the West. They were sternly discouraged from invoking Article 50 in the UN Charter (on compensations to states that suffer from participating in UN sanctions).

21. For the role of identity as another important conflict dimension in Yugoslavia beside politico-military security, see Håkan Wiberg, 'Societal Security and the Explosion of Yugoslavia', in Ole Wæver, Barry Buzan, Morten Kelstrup and Pierre Lemaitre, *Identity, Migration and the New Security Agenda in Europe* (London, Pinter, 1993), pp. 93–109.

22. Josep Palau and Radha Kumar (eds), *Ex-Yugoslavia: From War to Peace* (Madrid: Ecosimposio, 1993).

PART III

Democratic victory and the legacy of communism

13

Understanding post-communist transitions[1]

Leszek Balcerowicz

THE SPECIFICITY OF POST-COMMUNIST TRANSITION

The specific nature of the transition from communism in East-Central Europe (ECE) becomes clear when we compare it with other major shifts from one stable state of society to another potentially stable state. Other types of transition include (1) *classical transition*, meaning the extension of democracy in advanced capitalist countries between 1860 and 1920; (2) *neoclassical transition*, referring to democratizations in basically capitalist countries after the Second World War (West Germany, Italy, and Japan in the 1940s; Spain and Portugal in the 1970s; some Latin American countries in the 1970s and 1980s; South Korea and Taiwan in the 1980s); (3) *market-oriented reform* in non-communist countries (West Germany and other Western countries after the Second World War; South Korea and Taiwan in the early 1960s; Chile in the 1970s; Turkey and Mexico in the 1980s; Argentina in the 1990s); and (4) *Asian post-communist transition* (China since the late 1970s and Vietnam since the late 1980s). There is, of course, much internal variety, especially within the first two categories. We will, however, disregard it here in order to focus on the fundamental differences *between* rather than *within* the respective types of transition.

A number of features distinguish post-communist transition in ECE:

First, the scope of change is exceptionally large. Both physical and economic systems are affected, and changes in these systems in turn interact with changes in the social structure. All these internal changes in the respective countries came about due to, and within the framework of, the dissolution of the Soviet Empire. Most of the post-Soviet countries faced the additional transition problems of defining their territorial as well as social and cultural boundaries, and of building their institutional machineries.[2]

In all other cases of radical transition, there was either a focus on the political system while the economic system remained basically unchanged (as in classical and neoclassical transitions), or a focus on the economy while the political regime (usually non-democratic) was unaffected. The unprecedented scope of changes in East Central Europe means, among other things, an extreme information overload for top decision-makers. Errors and delays are hardly surprising, especially since decision-makers must work with a public administration largely inherited from the old regime. Massive administrative turnover proved possible only in the former East Germany after reunification, an option obviously not open to the other post-communist countries.

Second, although the changes in the political and economic systems *started* at about the same time, it is misleading to speak of 'simultaneous transitions' in post-communist Europe. It takes more time to privatize the bulk of the state-dominated economy than to organize free elections and at least some rudiments of political parties. Given the largely simultaneous beginnings of the political and economic transitions, this (or at least political pluralism, that is, some degree of legal political competition) develops first, and market capitalism later.[3]

Third, this sequence implies that market-oriented reforms, which must be exceptionally comprehensive because of the socialist economic legacy, have to be introduced under democratic, or at least pluralistic, political arrangements. Most of the other market-oriented reforms were introduced under non-democratic regimes (the third and fourth types of transition). Within this group, it is hard to find any case of economic transition that both approached the comprehensiveness of what occurred in post-communist Europe and was carried out under a democratic regime. Indeed, all the radical economic reforms elsewhere were introduced under clearly autocratic, oppressive regimes (Chile in the 1970s, China since the final years of that decade).[4] There were some economic reforms carried out under democracy in the 1980s, including privatization programmes in certain developed Western countries and stabilizations and structural adjustments in developing economies. Problems attributable to the democratic political environment did arise during these transitions, perhaps warning of similar hazards lurking in the much more comprehensive and complicated transitions of ECE.

These complications are, of course, far from being a sufficient argument for falling back on authoritarian solutions. This is not only because of democracy's intrinsic importance to human dignity, but also because authoritarian regimes do not invariably promote rapid economic development (as they have done in South Korea and Taiwan); many (such as Juan Peron's regime in Argentina) have disastrous effects on the economy.

A fourth exceptional feature of East-Central European economic and political transitions is their lack of violence. Other parts of the old communist-dominated east – in particular Yugoslavia, the Caucasus, and areas of what used to be Soviet Central Asia – have seen terrible bloodshed over the last few years even as ECE has undergone a peaceful revolution, with massive changes in political and economic institutions resulting from negotiations between the surviving communist elite and the leaders of the opposition. (The only case of violent transition in ECE took place in Romania, where there were no negotiations prior to the transfer of power.) Negotiations would never have taken place (or, had they taken place, would never have borne fruit) had not the Soviet threat been gradually eliminated by Gorbachev's *glasnost* and *perestroika*. These negotiated changes were not based on any explicit political pact and contained a large element of surprise for all the main actors. However, they would not have come about if the members of the old elite had felt physically threatened or even if they had not believed that they would be free to seek favourable positions in whatever new system would emerge. In this sense one can speak of a tacit political pact.

The non-violent nature of the transition in ECE related to such tacit political pacts has had important implications for other aspects of the transition. First, the old ruling elites are intact and stand ready to profit electorally from the dissatisfaction of that part of the population in proportion to the economic desolation that these old elites wrought while in power. Second, the newly emerging capitalist class is likely to include many of the former elites, a circumstance that tends to reduce the legitimacy of the whole capitalist transition and may fuel attacks by one part of the former opposition against the part currently in office. Such conflicts within the former opposition are good news for the forces of the old regime.

POST-COMMUNIST DEMOCRATIZATION COMPARED

Any consideration of the political transition in ECE should keep in mind that democracy means the institutionalized practice of peacefully choosing rules through regular, free and fair elections based on the principle of one person, one vote. This presupposes freedom of speech and association, which may also exist, however, under certain non-democratic regimes (for example, constitutional monarchies). In large societies, democracy cannot be direct, but has to be representative. Depending on what proportion of the adult population has the franchise, we can speak of *limited democracy*, in which only a fraction of the populace has the vote, or of *mass democracy*, in which practically all adults can vote. Stable and lasting mass democracy requires mass political parties.

We can isolate a number of peculiarities of the political transition in ECE by comparing it with the classical model of democratic transition. ECE's experience of a sudden shift from a clearly non-democratic regime to a mass democracy was quite distinct from the classical pattern of democratization, which features a gradual extension of suffrage under limited democracy until mass democracy becomes a new reality. Therefore, these two democratizations differed in both point of departure and speed. The new democracies of ECE are thus likely to require more learning-by-doing than earlier mass democracies of the West.[5]

This difference may be bolstered by the absence of competitive party systems prior to the post-communist democratization; the classical model involved the mobilization of previously established working-class organizations into electoral competition with other parties. The exclusive beneficiaries of the gradual extension of suffrage in the West were subordinate classes, especially the workers; thus, they were likely to feel a strong attachment to the democratic system.[6] This may be less true of the post-communist working classes, who share the suddenly gained mass democracy with all other groups. In post-communist countries, it is the intellectuals (whose standing in the society is much higher than it was in the West a century ago) who are most likely to esteem democracy. The intelligentsia, on average, benefits more than other groups from political opening, which means new-found access to information, foreign travel and the like.

Two other differences are also important. This classical model of democratization harks back to a time when the idea of using national budgets as engines of economic redistribution was fresh; there was much scope for the inauguration of social programmes whose beneficiaries could be enlisted as friends of democracy.[7] The situation today in post-communist lands is very different. They have inherited an extensive and increasingly inefficient 'socialist welfare state' characterized by high ratios of budgetary expenditure to GDP. Successful market-oriented reform, moreover, far from allowing any further increase in budgetary redistribution, actually demands the opposite.

A further difference concerns the role of the mass media, or more precisely the interaction of the mass media's role with developments in the economy and society at large. During the era of classical democratization there were a rather liberal press, no broadcasting media, and no fundamental change in the economy.

The post-communist transition, combining both political and economic openings begun under difficult economic conditions, came about in the age of powerful broadcast media (especially television). Under communism – especially before *glasnost* – the tightly controlled media did not report the negative aspects of the system. When political liberalization freed these media, they naturally focused on once-forbidden negative stories, a tendency strengthened by the generally low level of professionalism displayed by journalists trained under communism. As a result, there was a sudden increase in the public's exposure to negative mass-media coverage, and viewers often mistook the increased visibility of undesirable phenomena, such as crime and poverty, for their true growth. This 'visibility effect', absent in classical democratizations, was likely to encourage unfavourable assessments of the whole transition and, consequently, to influence electoral outcomes and subsequent direction or pace of the economic transition.[8]

If we compare the post-communist with the neoclassical transition, the visibility effect operates in both cases, but its dangers are smaller in the neoclassical case, which typically presupposes an already established capitalist economy. The economy at the start of the neoclassical transition was usually healthier than a post-communist economy, while the level of pre-existing redistribution in the former was usually much lower than in the latter.

SPECIAL FEATURES OF POST-COMMUNIST ECONOMIC TRANSITION

Let us try to disentangle the existing web of complex and dynamic interactions by focusing, first, on economic transition in ECE, and then on its interactions with political factors.

The post-1989 economic reforms in ECE are fundamentally different from those in the past in that they go beyond socialism, as defined by the overwhelming dominance of the state sector in the economy. (This fundamental change is best illustrated by the privatization process in Russia). The general direction of the present East-Central European transition is, therefore, basically in line with the economic reforms elsewhere: 'less state, more private enterprise and market'. But there are important differences between these two economic transitions. This can be best explained by pointing out that, in the context of market-oriented reform, there are three main types (fields) of economic policy:

1. macroeconomic stabilization, by means of macroeconomic policy;

2. microeconomic liberalization, that is enlarging the scope of economic freedom by removing various restrictions imposed by the state. This policy includes changing the general framework (for example, liberalizing the regime of property rights) and removing more specific regulations (for example, price controls, commands and rationing of goods);

3. fundamental institutional restructuring: making changes to existing institutions (privatizing state enterprises, reforming the tax system, and so on) and creating new ones (for example, the stock exchange). The two policies: institutional restructuring together with microeconomic liberalization may be called *systemic transformation.*

East-Central European economic reforms are different from other reforms in that the former require an unprecedented amount of institutional restructuring, if they are to reach market capitalism. This is due to the specificity of their initial economic conditions. Capitalism in ECE was *destroyed* and not merely *suspended* (as in Germany before 1948) or *distorted* (as in Latin America or India before their liberalizing reforms). Besides, East-Central European reforms have to contain an exceptional amount of microeconomic liberalization, as their economies were not only non-capitalist but also non-market, that is, coordinated by the command rationing mechanism – or in other words – the central plan.[9] The required scope of liberalization can be compared to dismantling the war economy mechanism in Western countries after the Second World War. It is much larger than the liberalization typical of recent-market oriented reforms in Latin America.

An unusually large scope of necessary systemic change is an invariant feature of all East-Central European reforms, due to the common elements of their initial conditions. Another common characteristic is the possibility of a relatively rapid implementation of that part of the systemic transformation which depends on quick spontaneous learning of specific new knowledge and skills (for example, marketing, finance). This possibility results from the high level of general education (human capital), one of the few positive legacies of the previous regime.

However, there were also some serious differences in initial states of the economy, which have had important implications for the economic transition:

Some socialist economies inherited extreme macroeconomic imbalance (open/or repressed inflation). This group included Poland in 1989, and the former Soviet Union and Albania in 1990–91. There was, by contrast, relatively little economic macroeconomic instability in Czechoslovakia and Hungary. Bulgaria and Romania were in an intermediate situation. Countries with extreme macroeconomic imbalance faced the double challenge of stabilizing and of changing the economic system at the same time. Countries with a much less serious stabilization problem had to tackle the issue of how to maintain and strengthen the macroeconomic stability while liberalizing prices and implementing other systemic reforms.

Every East-Central European economy was distorted by many years of import substitution, centralized investment decisions, dependence on the Soviet economy for exports and imports of oil and gas. This distortion can be expressed by the notion of *pure socialist output*, that part of the total output which could be maintained, if at all, only under a socialist economic order and the related existence of the CMEA. The economic structure in East-Central European countries was, on average, worse than that in China with respect to the difficulty and costs of economic transition. The former contained a very high share of distorted socialist industry, while the Chinese economy had a high share of technologically simple and, therefore, easily privatizable agriculture.[10] However, the share of pure socialist output differed across East-Central European countries. It was exceptionally high in Bulgaria and in most non-Russian countries of the former Soviet Union because of the very strong dependence of these economies on the Russian economy in exports. Within the former Czechoslovakia, it was much higher in Slovakia than in the Czech Republic.

Poland, Bulgaria and Hungary inherited much *foreign debt*, while Czechoslovakia and Romania were largely debt-free. Within the former USSR, Russia has taken over a sizeable Soviet debt.

THREE HELPFUL PROPOSITIONS

Here are three propositions to provide help in understanding both the challenges that post-communist ECE faces and the relative merits of various economic policy options:

1. *An extreme case of inherited macroeconomic instability calls for the rapid implementation of a tough stabilization* programme. Delay will only worsen the macroeconomic situation, and a gradual or mild stabilization programme will most likely fail to overcome inflationary inertia and expectations. A large macroeconomic imbalance, containing elements of hyperinflation, may be compared to a fire: it is very dangerous to delay putting it out, or to put it out slowly.

2. *There are important interlinkages and synergies within the package of market-oriented reforms.* Radical price liberalization is needed to eliminate massive shortages; the elimination of shortages is in turn necessary to ensure the more efficient operation of enterprises. Rapid price decontrol (including substantial adjustments of distorted administrative prices, for example, of energy) is also necessary in order to obtain more rational relative prices. Price liberalization, however, has to be linked to comprehensive foreign-trade liberalization so that increased enterprise autonomy is accompanied by an increase in competitive pressure on the newly freed enterprises. Widespread price controls and other forms of detailed state intervention will tempt enterprises to lobby for hidden or open subsidies, which may threaten macroeconomic stability. Thus, liberalization aids stabilization, which in turn is conducive to meaningful institutional change. This

is the link between stabilization-cum-liberalization on the one hand, and institutional restructuring on the other. Institutional changes including tax reform, social security reform, privatization, and enterprise restructuring are necessary not only in order to improve efficiency, but also to bolster macroeconomic stability. There is, therefore, a link between deep institutional restructuring and the longer-term sustainability of the macroeconomic balance.

3. *Different processes of economic reform have different maximum possible speeds.* Stabilization and liberalization policies, for instance, will bear fruit much more rapidly than institutional changes like reform of the tax system or privatization of a large public sector. Decision-makers should remain mindful that the third runs on a slower clock than the first two, and should be planned accordingly. Reformers face the choice between quickly stabilizing and liberalizing a still-socialist economy or implementing such changes at a slower pace in order to allow time for the institutional dismantling of socialism to 'catch up'.

Radical liberalization can be expected to spur a rise in the numbers of private firms that outstrips the ability to keep pace with the inherited tax system (designed to deal with just a handful of large state firms). A rise in tax evasion is thus an unavoidable by-product of sweeping liberalization. (There may be even more tax evasion if liberalization is limited and the tax system is full of various breaks and preferences). The danger is that increased tax evasion at a time of unavoidably growing budgetary expenditures will reduce the legitimacy of the capitalist transition and the governments and parties supporting it.

THE TIMING OF REFORM

Let us now look at economic policy as a variable that may differ along three dimensions: time of launching, phasing and pace. Time of launching refers to the interval between a political breakthrough and the start of the economic reform; phasing describes the relative timing of stabilization, liberalization and institutional-restructuring policies; pace describes the implementation rate for each of these main components of reform.

By applying criteria drawn from these three dimensions we may: identify many theoretical variants of economic policy, but for brevity's sake we will mention just two general types.[11] The first is a radical and comprehensive economic programme, in which stabilizing, liberalizing and restructuring measures are launched at the same time and implemented at close to the maximum possible speeds. Such programmes may be launched very quickly following political breakthrough or after some delay. The second type consists of non-radical economic programmes, defined here as those in which stabilization, liberalization and restructuring are not launched simultaneously, or are implemented at a slower pace than they might be, or are even interrupted (for example, stabilization in Russia in mid-1992).[12]

Under the economic conditions existing at that time of communism's demise in ECE, radical economic reforms, resolutely pursued, were the best choice for bringing about disinflation, structural change, and the takeoff into economic growth and market capitalism. Empirical analysis tends to confirm this hypothesis, as there is so far no example of a highly successful non-radical reform.

Given the naturally slower pace at which institutional restructuring (including privatization) must proceed, even the most energetically implemented transition to a market economy will require two stages. In the first stage, the economy undergoes liberalization and stabilization but remains more 'market socialist' than capitalist. In the second stage – assuming that it was successful – the gains of liberalization and stabilization are consolidated, and the transition to market capitalism is completed and institutionalized.

Given the challenging initial conditions and unfavourable external developments (especially the collapse of trade within the COMECON) that faced each country in ECE during the post-communist transition, each class of reform measures was bound to generate discontent in some section of the populace. Predictably, the intensity of these currents of discontent was directly proportional to the adversity of initial conditions and external developments. For example, the same set of economic policies produced four times more open unemployment in Slovakia than in Czech Republic in 1992 because 'pure socialist output' accounted for a much higher share of the Slovak economy.

In addition to turning disguised unemployment into open unemployment, radical economic reform also increases discontent simply by broadening the scope of general economic freedom. Since only some people can directly take advantage of the new opportunities, others may feel resentment, especially if they view the new winners as undeserving. Rapid shifts will occur in the relative pay and prestige of various occupations and professional groups as markets replace the planned socialist economy. Miners, heavy-industrial workers and other groups that see themselves as 'losers' – even if only in relative terms – are likely to be dissatisfied. There is an unavoidable trade-off, moreover, between opportunity and security. This hard truth may be poorly understood and bitterly disliked, especially by those who experience a much larger increase in insecurity than in perceived opportunities.

Given the same difficult initial and external conditions sketched above, non-radical reform will also produce discontent, though in different ways. If the initial macroeconomic situation is highly unstable, non-radical economic reform will find itself immediately bedevilled by high and growing inflation, which produces its own version of severe economic insecurity. Non-radical reform programmes do this by preferring hidden over open unemployment. Hidden unemployment is less psychologically painful to the persons concerned but it must be financed through fiscal or quasi-fiscal subsidies, which in turn spur inflation.[13] The result is inflation-bred insecurity and disaffection. Moreover, it must be kept in mind that any future attempts at macroeconomic stabilization will flush hidden unemployment out into the open.

Non-radical programmes, which typically feature less liberalization and correspondingly more state intervention, also give rise to new economic inequalities, with 'winners' being those who can successfully lobby the government. In practice, this means members of the old communist elite, who are more experienced, better organized, and better connected than others. The inequalities generated by their lobbying are less justified by economic performance than those that stem from radical reform programmes, and rankle the 'losers' even more. Finally, by channelling entrepreneurial and managerial energies into rent-seeking and corruption rather than the search for greater efficiency, non-radical programmes that avoid liberalization destroy the prospects for economic development. Anyone willing to take the longer view, then, should realize that the discontents and drawbacks associated with non-radical efforts at reform outweigh the problems brought by sustained and radical efforts at comprehensive liberalization, stabilization and institutional restructuring.

THE PERIOD OF 'EXTRAORDINARY POLITICS'

The key to understanding the interaction between the political and economic dimensions of post-communist transitions is to realize that any great political breakthrough in a country's history is followed by a period of 'extraordinary politics' that soon gives way to 'normal politics'. In simplified form it can be stated that the period in which radical reform is accepted and supported is limited. This finding is based on the assumption that liberation from foreign domination and domestic political liberalization produces a special state of mass psychology and corresponding political opportunities: the new political structures are fluid and the older political elite is discredited. Both leaders and ordinary citizens feel a stronger-than-normal tendency to think and act in terms of the common good.

Extraordinary politics, however, quickly gives way to the more mundane politics of contending parties and interest groups (as described, for instance by Nobel laureate James Buchanan and other theorists of the public-choice school). It is in this second period that certain features of political contention which are common in established democracies become much stronger (parties searching for an agenda and an ideological profile, the ensuing politicization of major issues, and so on). These features superimpose themselves on the developments typical of a new democracy – the visibility effect, the appearance of an inchoate party system, and the like – and then normal politics in the fledging democracy comes to seem unattractive, which is reflected in collapse of the social support for reforms.

Variations in sociopolitical characteristics from one country to another can be reflected in: (1) the initial level of acceptance and support; (2) the duration of 'extraordinary politics'; (3) the length of the downward slope after such a period; (4) finally, by the subsequent level of support persisting under 'normal' political conditions.

The brevity of the exceptional period means that a radical economic programme, launched as quickly as possible after the breakthrough, has a much greater chance of being accepted than either a delayed radical programme or a non-radical alternative that introduces difficult measures (for example, price increases) in piecemeal fashion. Bitter medicine is easier to take in one dose than in a prolonged series of doses.

Each of the clearly radical economic programmes in post-communist ECE was the handiwork of a government representing new political forces. This is true of Poland, the former Czechoslovakia, Bulgaria, Estonia and Latvia. Yet new political forces did not launch such programmes everywhere they were in control. Lithuania in 1992–93 was radical with regard to privatization but hesitant with regard to stabilization, while Hungary in 1990–94 pursued a 'gradualism' that was partly due to the weight of previously accumulated changes and partly deliberate.

By contrast, whenever the political system remained dominated in the first phase of transition by the forces of the past, only non-radical economic options were pursued. The clearest examples are Belarus and Ukraine, and to a lesser extent Romania. In each of the two former cases (as in Russia), the post-Soviet legislature erected formidable barriers to radical economic reform.

Countries that did not take advantage of the period of 'extraordinary politics' to launch a radical economic programme still face the challenge of making the transition to market capitalism, but now under more difficult political and economic conditions. From the point of view of economic development, the radical strategy is the best option regardless of when it is deployed. Yet countries that have missed the first period are in danger of going from one kind of non-market economy (central planning) to another, characterized by pervasive macroeconomic instability, detailed by chaotic state regulation, and related massive rent seeking. This is especially likely if the legislatures in these countries continue to be dominated by industrial and agricultural interest groups even after the second cycle of free elections.

Given the evanescence of 'extraordinary politics', time-consuming institutional reforms (for example, privatization, social security reform, health reform, and the like) are likely to meet more resistance than quickly implemented stabilizing and liberalizing measures. One must therefore expect delays in institutional restructuring, for reform of this nature is simply out of synchronization with the brevity of the 'extraordinary' interval.

If a country has been operating under difficult initial and external conditions, it is a mistake to blame social discontent on a particular type of economic programme. Attributing widespread dissatisfaction to 'shock therapy' for instance, is erroneous because under conditions grave enough to elicit such radical measures, *any* economic policy package will generate discontent. There is no *a priori* reason to expect that the dissatisfaction attendant upon radical reforms will be greater than that attendant upon non-radical ones.

Indeed, the reverse could well be the case. Even cursory examination of the East-Central European experience shows no clear link between intensity of displays of social discontent (strikes, demonstrations, and so on) and the type of economic programme pursued. Poland, Bulgaria and Romania have seen the worst displays of discontent, yet the former two countries pressed forward with radical reforms while Romania followed a stop-go gradualism. Hungary, Czechoslovakia (and later the Czech Republic and Slovakia), Estonia and Latvia have had few manifestations of discontent. Hungary never adopted a radical economic programme, while the others did.

THE IMPORTANCE OF INITIAL CONDITIONS

The foregoing suggests that one should seek to explain differences in social discontent and political instability from one country to another by first of all examining the conditions present as the transition got under way. A paucity of open unemployment during the transition is a great help, as officials in the Czech Republic can testify. The intensity of labour unrest seems to depend on the presence of militant workers like the miners of Poland and Romania, as well as on the existence of influential trade unions that played a large role in toppling communism only to turn increasingly populist ('Solidarity' in Poland, 'Podkrepa' in Bulgaria).

The character of the country's political class is also relevant. Demagogues presumably exist everywhere, but clearly they are not equally mobilized and vocal in all countries. The relative extent of their presence, along with the intensity of the visibility effect, may have serious impact upon popular attitudes and behaviour in different countries during the economic transition.

If it is erroneous to blame unrest on this or that type of economic reform, it is equally mistaken to attribute the electoral defeats of the political forces that ruled during the first stage of the post-communist transition to one sort of economic programme. Such defeats happened in 1993 in Poland – a radical reformer – but also in Lithuania, Russia and Hungary, where radical reform never came close to being adopted. Thus, causes other than the type of economic programme must underlie these outcomes. Among these causes are phenomena that are present everywhere but operate with varying force depending on circumstances.

The visibility effect is one such phenomenon; it strengthens the usual tendency of a part of the electorate to blame problems on whatever government is in power. In reality, the magnitude of these problems as well as the prospects for quickly solving them depend on a given post-communist country's initial situation, and this varied greatly across the region. Another important variable is the type and composition of the political class, especially the relative importance of its populist component. Also significant is the extent to which opposition to the government's economic policy becomes linked to the popular position on certain emotional issues such as a loss of empire in Russia, the status of the Hungarian minority in Romania, or the role of the Catholic Church in Poland.

Finally, the pre-election strategies adopted by the various political forces matter as well. For example, in Poland in 1993, the ruling parties of the moment committed the grave mistake of going through the elections separately even as their chief rivals, the ex-communists, were agreeing to run together under the banner of a single coalition. With help from a new electoral law, the ex-communists obtained about 21 per cent of the vote and 33 per cent of the seats in the Parliament, making them Poland's largest single political force.[14]

Even if, for some of the aforementioned reasons, the political forces that launched radical economic reform suffer an electoral defeat, the economy is likely to be in much better shape than would have been in the case had other approaches been adopted. Furthermore, radical reform tends to leave behind certain legacies – currency convertibility, an independent central bank, a large private sector – that even ostensible opponents are likely to respect.

From our analysis, a clear conclusion emerges. Given the typical initial conditions of a socialist economy, a country will be better off politically and economically in the medium-to-long run if it adopts a radical and comprehensive economic reform programme as quickly as possible during the brief period of extraordinary politics, and then stays the course of reform by implementing far-reaching institutional changes.

NOTES

1. Abridged version of chapter 9 in *Socialism, Capitalism, Transformation* (Budapest, London, New York: Central European University Press, 1995).

2. See P. C. Schmitter, 'Dangers and Dilemmas of Democracy', *Journal of Democracy* (March 1994).

3. V. Bunce and M. Csandi, 1993, 'Uncertainty in the Transition: Post-communism in Hungary', *East European Politics and Societies*, vol. 7, no. 2 (1993).

4. The case that comes relatively close to a comprehensive economic reform conducted under democracy is that of Argentina since 1989. Even there, however, the amount of necessary economic change was less than in the post-socialist economies, as capitalism in ECE had been destroyed, not merely distorted as in Argentina and other Latin American countries.

5. Exceptions to this hypothesis may be those countries that have strong traditions of well-functioning democracy dating back to before the Second World War. In ECE, only the Czech Republic meets this conditions.

6. This is pointed in D. Rueschmeyer, E. Huber and J. Stephens, *Capitalist Development and Democracy* (Chicago: University of Chicago Press, 1992).

7. For a summary article investigating to what extent the growth of public expenditure has been related to the expansion of suffrage and to what extent to other factors, see D. C. Mueller, 1987, 'The Growth of Government', *IMF Staff Papers* (March 1987) pp. 115-49.

8. The visibility effect may be conceptualized in economic terms as a mechanism introducing false utility information and thus likely to lead to wrong decisions. False utility information is also supplied by most economists in post-socialist countries, as official economics was heavily politicized and no better than the economy. Some Western experts and politicians are also engaged in producing false utility information.

9. Hungary and Poland had fewer commands and control in the economies before 1989, but were still controlled and distorted.

10. Besides, the Chinese economy at the start of the reforms, that is, in the late 1970s, displayed relatively little macroeconomic instability.

11. For a more comprehensive typology of economic policy options in the transition economies, see S. Gomulka, 'Economic and Political Constraints During Transition', *Europe-Asia Studies*, vol. 46, no. 1 (1994).

12. But the actual rate of implementation may differ between two countries because of differences in their initial conditions. For example, substantial previous price liberalization of an initially balanced macroeconomy may require only limited further price decontrol or macroeconomic tightening. This was the case in Hungary.

13. Another way to finance increased hidden unemployment is to accept reduced average productivity of labour, but this means a corresponding reduction in average real wages, and falling wages cut in buying power as surely as do rising prices.

14. On Poland's September 1993 elections, see: A. Smolar, M. Krol, 'A Communist Comeback?', *Journal of Democracy* (January 1994).

14

The waning spectre of neo-nationalism in East-Central Europe

Jozsef Bayer

The nationalistic tide emerging in the vogue for systemic changes in East-Central Europe (ECE) challenged the thesis that we were soon about to enter a post-national age. The revival of nationalism, however, has its limits, at least for those countries in ECE which are striving for membership in the European Union. The growing importance of regional integrations generally diminish the traditional sovereignty of national politics in many respects. In a much debated essay, Samuel Huntington rightly stated that we have entered a new age in which 'the great divisions among humankind and the dominating source of conflict will be cultural. Nation states will remain the most powerful actors in world affairs, but the principal conflicts of global politics will occur between nations and groups of different civilizations'. The nation-state should be a mere historical phenomenon with a transitory character. 'Westerners tend to think of nation states as the principal actors of global affairs. They have been, however, for only a few centuries' – he states. After the end of the Cold War, the clash of civilizations (in Toynbee's sense) will dominate global politics. 'For the relevant future, there will be no universal civilization, but instead a world of different civilizations, each of which will have to learn to coexist with the others.'[1]

We even ought to be happy with such a development if it leads away from the anarchy of rival nation-states that was so characteristic of our recent history. In the same number of the journal we learn about an alternative dark prospective from William Pfaff. He stressed that the nation-state, as a coextension of state and nation, was a dangerous mixture because of its underlying assertion of an ethnic state. However, 'the idea of the ethnic state is a permanent provocation to war'.[2] He demonstrated this in the context of the fate of the people of Bosnia, and in the new Balkan war, with its renewed danger of 'ethnic cleansing'.

In our region there are some specific reasons why the question of nations and nationalism has become so acute over the last few years. Jürgen Habermas lists three of them, as follows: first, the crumbling of East European communism, ending in German reunification and the dissolution not only of the Soviet bloc in general, but also of all the federal socialist states; second, the unification process in West Europe, with its new problem of the relation of nation-state with democracy on a European scale; third, the threat of a large scale migration from the East and the South, which makes the problem of the asylum and integration of immigrants and refugees a dominant political issue. It also raises the question of the relation between the universal values of a democratic *Rechtsstaat* and the particularistic aspirations of specific cultural life-forms.[3]

From all this I am concerned here only with the first issue and refer to the others only in so far as they become entangled in the outcomes of the new tide of nationalism in East, Central and South-East Europe.

The nation-state is certainly a historical phenomenon, not older then about two hundred years; this is a fact despite the legitimating stories about its organic nature being allegedly inscribed in people's souls and needs, as well as the tales about its genesis in the grey dawn of history. Why, then, has the nation-state become obsolete so soon? Or has it been anyway, as Peter Glotz put it, really only a mistaken road in modern history? It is true that with the development of a one-world economy and the trend towards ever greater political and economic integration, and a developing world-wide communication network, the nation-state loses its exclusiveness as a framework for organized political communities. Nevertheless, I doubt that it will lose importance in all respects and think that it will remain, for a long time, the focus of identity and the major form for social and political integration for most populations in the near future, even if it loses its centrality in international relations. Perhaps its boundaries will disappear at some time and a unified mankind will find another, possibly more appropriate structure for human society. In the meantime, however, it will surely maintain its importance during our lifetimes. Apart from saying this, I also agree with critics who stress that the view which regards the nation-state only as an irrational and demonic force in history is superficial and ignores the progressive side of its development; the latter went hand in hand with social and economic modernization and with secularization of politics.

Ralf Dahrendorf may be right when he stresses that the nation-state has, until now, been the only ground for a democratic polity, its central political institutions providing the sanctioning of power and the rule of law. It also provides the only guarantees for human and political rights.[4] In addition, with the development of the modern welfare state this political framework also guarantees the social rights and entitlements of its citizens. By nation-state I do not mean an ethnically homogenous state, however, because every state is to some degree multinational and multicultural. A *national* state, with its stress on ethnic homogeneity and with its policy of forced assimilation, is not the idea which is defended here. We must also be aware of the unavoidable ambivalence of every nationalism, even if the latter contains emancipatory elements (as in the national movements – those of *national awakening* – in nineteenth century Europe or the national liberation movements of colonized people in our century). This ambivalence is expressed plastically by Tom Nairn's notion of nationalism as 'the modern Janus'.[5]

However, peculiar to the new East European tide of nationalism is the fact that it hardly shows, at least it has not until now, any positive face. Thus it can be said that it is, on the whole, a rather regressive political phenomenon, even if the reasons for its emergence are all too understandable. How can we explain this?

There are different reasons for the emergence of nationalism in the region, and they deserve distinct analyses; the different combinations of causes and different clusters of historical and political circumstances led to nationalist tendencies of different types and intensities. In the following passage, I try to typify some reasons and analyse the special combinatory elements of nationalism.

In ECE, after a short period of joy and even euphoria about the blessings of liberal democracy – such as free speech and free political self-organization, along with development of political pluralism in all its institutional facets – the general mood swiftly changed. The enthusiastic hopes for a rapid return 'back to Europe' were very soon seen as idle hopes, as a positive change in welfare began to engender a wide and deep disillusionment. The rise and spread of nationalist feelings and re-emergence of ethnic tensions are partly the cause and partly the effect of the new political situation. It is unquestionable that the deep social crisis, the economic depression and political disappointment sharpened the ethnic and national conflicts; in the Yugoslav case, all these eventually exploded in a war of secession. Nevertheless, the process and the direction of causation is not so simple, such that one could ascribe this or that feature to any one specific cause. The dissolution of Yugoslavia, for example, is often ascribed to a 'natural' growth of nationalism; on the other hand, the other, even more plausible explanation – that the forces of disintegration caused the nationalism itself – has received much less attention.

The reemergence of nationalism and proliferation of new nation-states since 1989 contrast clearly with the general European perspective of former decades. From the very beginning of the process, historians and political scientists have tried to analyse why this new tide of nationalism has reemerged so forcibly in Europe. I have tried to make distinct four major variants of possible answers to this issue. They are not exclusive of each other, but shed light on

different aspects of the problem. I refer to them in the following
way:
1. The *refrigerator* hypothesis.
2. The *final step* in building of nation-states for nations whose
'natural' strivings for self-assertion were disrupted by hegemonic
power.
3. The *vacuum* hypothesis, involving a crisis of identity.
4. The *credibility gap* – referring to a crisis of legitimacy.

The refrigerator hypothesis holds that there were primordial or
national ties and solidarities as well as conflicts, which were only
deep-frozen by totalitarian communist rule and internationally by
the Cold War. Now they can develop their dynamics freely and
sweep away any 'unnatural', 'artificial' bounds and political
arrangements.

This view is plausible only if it refers to bad solutions in former
international arrangements and treaties imposed by great powers or
the hegemonic overpowering of strong and lasting national
aspirations; for example J. Rupnik's interpretation related to the
issue of the Trianon Treaty that dismantled the Hungarian
Kingdom, or the case of the Baltic states in the period immediately
before the Second World War. The hypothesis becomes, however, a
pure mystification if it is reduced to a 'comeback of demons' of
history – namely, it refers to nothing more than the alleged
irrational power of such primordial ties as national and ethnic
relations. Miroslav Hroch, one of the best historians of ECE
nationalism, therefore calls this 'deep-frozen' thesis a superficial
view which comes close to a fairy tale. The nation as such is not a
primordial entity, but a constituted political community. Ethnic
relations get politicized only at definite stages of social and
economic development, and under specific political circumstances
that break up the old structure of society and challenge its old
political form. There is no fatal logic of an outbreak of nationalist
turmoil and ethnic unrest; such historical events are only
understandable if reference is made to the specific context of social

and economic modernization, and the process of industrialization and urbanization.

Actually, the new outbreak of national fever is due not to an ever-present and suppressed power of primordial ties, but to the fact that the imperative of modernization was not fulfilled/performed by the communist experiment; the latter was in fact a mixture of modern and pre-modern elements. This is especially true of its monopolistic political form, which blocked the full development of a modern society. I would assert that under communist rule the East Europeans had to suffer all the known dark sides of modernity without enjoying its blessings.

Also, it was not the integration of formally sovereign nation-states into a socialist economic bloc, political community and military alliance itself that comprised the problem (which now appears to be the cause of a nationalist tide in the form of a repercussion). The problem was the command nature and administrative form of integration and the fact that behind 'proletarian' or 'socialist internationalism' there was a forced Soviet hegemony which left very little room for autonomous developments. This monolithic colossus could not be reformed without being destroyed first. This created chances for autonomous and free developments; however, it has also resulted in the disruption of economic ties, trade relations, the dissolution of former solidarity lines, and it has created numerous other signs of disarray. The sad picture of growing anarchy in the former Soviet bloc (with few exceptions) may be regarded as a fruitful chaos which will lead, sooner or later, to reorganization into more viable forms of integration in the long run; in the near future, however, it will be the negative effects that reactivate conflict-lines and intensive clashes that were formerly regarded as already having been overcome.

The *final step hypothesis* is related to the above explanation and may be regarded as its completion in one respect: namely, it refers to the creation of new nation-states, a process that in its significance goes far beyond the importance of emotionalized nationalism among nations and ethnic unrest in existing states. The dissolution of the Soviet Union today reminds us of the birth of nations in Central and South-Eastern Europe, when these emerged from the ruins of great multinational states such as the Ottoman or Habsburg Empires. The analogy has certain limits, but nevertheless it is striking. The formation of nations seems to be, in contrast to the political and organizational form of empires, a necessary step in entering modernity. With some hindsight, the process of semi-modernization in the Soviet Union can now be regarded as a preparatory phase, a kind of incubator for the birth of different nations from among a large mixture of peoples; but, at the same time, it was also an obstacle to their fully-fledged autonomous national life and sovereign political development. By creating and maintaining the administrative structure of ethnically based republics and territories, by promoting their native language and nurturing national culture (with the important exception of the newly attached Western territories – the Baltic states and Moldova – where a forced Russification in old imperialist style occurred), and by the recent conscious policy of proportional representation within basic political institutions, the federation actually helped to raise national consciousness and enabled the decentralized units of political administration to develop as nascent centres of future independent nation-states. At least politically and culturally they are now able to assert themselves, even if many other prerequisites of sovereignty – first of all economic viability and strong military force – are perhaps still lacking.

Here we come to a touchy subject: why have the other two federal socialist states also dissolved: first of all Yugoslavia, but also Czechoslovakia? Perhaps the problem lies in the form of federation and is connected with the multinational character of those countries? I think not, because there are other federal states that exist on a multinational basis, and these are rather stable: above all Switzerland.

Here again, I think the main reason for people's frustration involved the unresolved tasks of economic and political modernization, which led to the final failure of the state-socialist experiment (which was in fact a weak alternative to mainstream capitalism). This showed how weak social integration is without a stable economic foundation. The planned economies were integrated by central administration from above and not by a unified market from below. The centralization and reallocation of resources needed a strong political authority, and this explains many rigid features of the monolithic political system. This power-system lost its legitimacy during and after a long period of economic stagnation and depression. Central redistribution of economic gains is itself always a troublesome, but still manageable, task among regions and administrative sub-units of a country. Distribution of economic losses, however, brings unresolvable conflict, undermines solidarity among members of different regions and social groups, and leads very easily to the dissolution of the political framework as a whole. Such dissolution, as has been illustrated earlier in colonial territories, occurs mostly along borderlines of former administrative units, without respect to ethnic or national division lines. In such a situation, the creation of an independent nation on ethnic grounds necessarily involves – besides the usual conflicts of secession – an (at least symbolic) exclusion of large groups of formerly equal citizens and implies, in the last resort, the idea of 'ethnic cleansing'. This lies behind the slogan 'invitation to war', coined by William Pfaff. Revival of national aspirations have been, of course, supported also by other factors listed by Miroslav Hroch. He stressed the existence of 'relics of an earlier political autonomy', or even 'former independence and statehood', a long tradition of a distinct, written language and culture, or – we could add – distinct religious traditions.

Nevertheless, a secessionary war was not a necessary outcome and an unavoidable fate; and there is still hope that the Yugoslav case will not repeat itself in the territory of the ex-Soviet Union. There have been specific determinants of deterioration of the Yugoslav situation: a lasting hegemonistic striving by the forces of Serbian nationalism, the idle hope held by secessionists that there would be quick Western economic aid and a free path to integration (such hopes might have been also manipulated by certain Western powers); and hopes for security guarantees that were not, in the event, provided, except for an ineffective UN peacekeeping action. The main reason for the deteriorating situation remained, however, that all the unresolved problems were politicized not on their own terms, as political, economic and social conflicts capable of negotiation; rather, they were emotionalized and fought along national and ethnic lines, which has thus made them almost impossible to solve.

The *vacuum hypothesis* explains the emerging tide of neo-nationalism by referring to a crisis of identity after the implosion of the former political and ideological system. The change has been deep and all too rapid and many people lost their orientation.

Miroslav Hroch stressed the need for a new collective identity as follows: 'After the breakdown of Communist rule and central planning, familiar ties have crumbled, leaving a generalized anxiety and insecurity in which the national idea takes over the role of collective integration. In conditions of acute stress, people characteristically tend to over-value the protective comfort of their own national group.'[6] This need includes a rather personalized image of the nation. It makes plausible the perception of one national body, defined by the ethnic homogeneity of the population; this is often seen as a living historical territory, for it is assumed to have lived within the same traditional borders for thousands of years. Hroch calls this a kind of 'psycho-geography', perhaps as an inside analogy to the outside power-oriented notion of geopolitics. 'Leaders of the new national movements are once again inclined to declare state borders to be national boundaries and to treat ethnic minorities in their territory as outsiders.'[7] Why leaders are inclined to do this, will be explained in the next point.

In addition to the social reasons for this emotional side of nationalism, that is, the human need for inner security, Ernst Gellner also provides a political explanation: the lack of an organized civil society. He writes that nationalism is the best candidate for filling this emptiness.[8]

The notion of civil society is here used as an opposing term to a state-organized society which leaves little or no room for autonomous organizations independent of state and party licence. Now that the old forms of political and social organization have been discredited, and new ones are still lacking, the easiest way to satisfy the need for security is by belonging to a 'natural' community. Gellner stressed the important fact that liberal forces remained small intellectual circles, while the nationalist appeal of the populist movements gained large and massive support from the population.[9]

The strength of popular protest against the existing order depended on whether *national grievances* could be mobilized or not. As Miroslav Hroch underlines: 'there must be another weighty factor, besides social change and high levels of mobility and communication [...] a nationally relevant conflict of interests – in other words a social tension or collision that could be mapped onto linguistic (and sometimes also religious) divisions'.[10] In such cases the growing opposition could have been broken only by the use of massive force and terror against wide sections of the population. The communist elites, especially the better-educated, reform-minded new generation of communist leaders, were now – in contrast to earlier experiences – unwilling to go this way. They looked for other ways of getting out of this trap. In the more advanced societies they retreated into other fields of social activity: they gave up political power easily in exchange for career opportunities in the economic, cultural and other fields. In the least advanced societies, however, nationalism has gained an additional strength exactly due to the power-game of new and old elites; together they have used the manipulation of national sentiments as an instrument of power.

The *credibility gap* refers to a crisis of legitimacy of the old, but also new elites, in mastering an anarchic political situation of large-scale social and political change. The continuing economic crisis undermines the legitimacy, that is, the moral and political support of any regime in the long run. So it is no wonder if old and new elites resort to nationalist appeals in order to stabilize their power positions. The fact that members of the old communist *nomenklatura* tried to save their own power and status in this way is generally known and stressed in the cases of Milosevic, Tudjman, Iliescu, Meciar and other 'national populists'. Less attention has been paid to the intense use of the same strategy by the counter-elite, as demonstrated by the new conservative forces that formed governments in Central European countries.

Miroslav Hroch explains this phenomenon by referring to the functional imperative of self-legitimacy for the aspiring new elite whose status is still uncertain in the society. In this, the historian had a clearer insight into the power mechanisms of the new regimes than many enthusiastic political scientists who admired democratic institutions but disregarded this subjective factor of modern politics. Formerly, Hroch says, such ambitious elites had to contend with the established old ruling classes, while now they do not really have to compete for power. 'The vacuum at the top of society has created the possibility of very swift careers.' New strata reached the highest levels of wealth and power easily, often as a result of mere individual or nationalist egoisms. As he puts it, 'apprentice politicians', 'veteran bureaucrats' (the more skilful managers from the old command economy), and 'emergent entrepreneurs' fight among themselves for positions of privilege; 'and whenever different ethnic groups live on the same territory, it generates the leading tensions of a nationally relevant character today'. This also explains the curious revival of anti-Semitism, even in countries where only very few Jews have remained. If there are no enemies, they will be created. Also, while former periods of nation-building went hand in hand with economic growth, now economic depression and decline are being experienced, which leads to intensified conflicts. As Hroch says, this makes it 'difficult to speak of a single national programme'. However, with the means of high-tech communication the possibilities for manipulation are stronger as well. That is why 'control of mass media in ECE is a vital stake in the struggle of power'.

This self-interest of the new and old power elites was heavily responsible for the stirring-up of nationalist feelings and conflicts. Many politicians play irresponsibly with a fire they cannot stop at the right time. It is the low level of democratic political culture ('civic culture') which allows such a game, but it also reproduces the anti-democratic, authoritarian tradition of the political culture that has been usual in these countries. All this takes place in the name of democracy, pluralism and Europeanization of politics.

After this short review of the four main reasons for rising nationalists tides, we have to ask, how intensive and lasting a phenomenon it will be. Firstly, I think we can distinguish three different groups of post-communist countries according to the strategies they are following and the special problems of each.

The first group consists of those countries where systemic change is entangled with the territorial integrity of the state. This situation will keep the national issue in the forefront of politics for a long time to come, even if there are of course important differences between former Yugoslavia, certain territories of the ex-Soviet Union and the Czech and Slovak Republics as regards the intensity of the conflict.

The second group consists of countries in which the old elite has been partly able to hold onto its social status and power on the basis of the mobilization of nationalist feelings; for example, in Romania. These two groups partly overlap – for example, in the case of Serbia, Ukraine and some other countries – which only strengthens the probability of a long and intensive presence of nationalist politics in such countries.

The third group represents countries where nationalism has mainly been an issue for mobilization of the opposition against the regime, and after this it has been used as a manipulative force for legitimating and stabilizing the power of a new conservative elite. Hungary, Poland, and the Czech Republic certainly belong to this group. Here, nationalism can be regarded a mere transitional phenomenon which will be weakened and neutralized by every new turn of elections, and by the growing stabilization of the new political and economic order. Of course, in neither case is there a fatal logic involving a necessary sharpening of nationalist conflicts. With economic and political consolidation these conflicts might lose their political weight.

This hypothesis on the future dynamics and importance of nationalism in the region has been supported by a recent sociological survey carried out in seven ECE countries. The final report of the *Security for Europe Project* states that the people in these countries generally refuse nationalist policies.

The public throughout all seven countries studied is concerned about the rise in nationalist feelings throughout the region. To a surprisingly large extent, the public says this growth in nationalism does not spring naturally from people but comes from manipulation by politicians. This important conclusion was voiced strongly in all countries. Many among the public also want to distinguish between an aggressive or dangerous nationalism, and an honest pride in one's own nation and culture.[11]

The survey was aimed not only at members of the public, but also at experts on security issues and representatives of the intellectual elite. The above findings were in accord with the specialists' views on these issues. 'Except in Russia and Ukraine, national security specialists in ECE do not believe that the status of ethnic minorities should greatly detract from European security or [should] generate pressure for border changes in the years to come. This is true even of specialists in Hungary.' This is true even if specialists 'now regard the question of ethnic minorities to be one that is subject to manipulation by opportunistic politicians. They express dismay that the issue has lent itself to such abuse.' For example, in the opinion of Hungarian experts the new government has only worsened the situation of Hungarian minorities in the neighbouring countries. This means that not everything is well with their situation and that something should be done to improve it, in order to avoid explosion of the conflicts. However, specialists believe that 'in many cases minority rights problems can be handled by taking them to international adjudicative bodies'. They refer, as possible referees, to the EU, the UN or OSCE institutions.[12]

The outcome of the Hungarian elections in 1994 also proved the fading force of nationalism. While, in 1989, the concern about the fate of national minorities beyond the borders had a mobilizing effect in the promotion of systemic changes, the conservative attempt to reinforce nationalist feelings and the self-presentation of the governing party-bloc as the only national political force as against 'alien' and 'internationalist' parties was felt by the population as a provocation and a distraction from the real problems of economic and social consolidation. Such ideological politics was a total failure and led to the electoral defeat of the national-conservative forces, who have been replaced by a socialist-liberal coalition government. Since then, bilateral treaties with neighbouring countries, first of all Slovakia and Romania, have been negotiated. The tensions between these states has diminished, even if many problems will remain for the foreseeable future because of the much debated status of Hungarian minorities in the respective countries which have significant nationalist tendencies.

Do the above considerations provide a reason for being optimistic? The answer is not easy; the dynamics of nationalism has its own impetus that is difficult to control, especially when the social and economic crises drag on. Therefore, I follow the caveat of Miroslav Hroch, who states that the dynamics of nationalism depends on the

> existence of real deficits for full national life, and of significant tensions that could be articulated as national conflicts [...] once such national movements acquire a mass character [...] they cannot be stopped by governmental ban or use of force. At most, they can today be inflected by civic education in schools and media, perhaps today in a putative European direction, and by official measures to assure a reasonable ethnic balance in public employment.[13]

Knowing of the limits of such measures, he sees the remedy in terms of an almost utopian hope: 'a resolution of the economic crisis of the region, and advent of new prosperity'. If it is utopian, it is still a hope for the sake of the hopeless, in the sense that Walter Benjamin put this on the eve of the Second World War.

This leads back to the relation between West European integration and East European nationalization of politics. The process of West European integration, by its very existence, curbs the dynamics of nationalist politics in the Eastern part of Europe. It provides real options against nationalism for East European politicians – options that did not exist at the beginning of the century. Parties aiming for genuine European options have a chance to beat nationalist political forces in free elections, forcing them to be moderate and to change, albeit slowly. On the other hand, the debate on the character of the political form of the European Union – whether a post-national community of European citizens or rather a free confederation of nation-states that give up some, but not all, of their sovereign powers – will also be affected by the outcome of the East European crisis which has a clear expression in nationalist politics. Certainly, West Europeans are not as much in need of East Europeans as the other way around. A mindless and egoistic western policy towards the East, with its lack of solidarity and without the creative imagination for reconstruction and re-integration of the eastern part of Europe may, however, also result in serious repercussions for the future European Union.

NOTES

1. S. Huntington, 'The Clash of Civilizations', *Foreign Affairs*, vol. 72, no. 3 (Summer 1993) p. 22, 24, 49.

2. W. Pfaff, 'Invitation to War', *Foreign Affairs*, vol. 72, no. 3 (Summer 1993) p. 101.

3. J. Habermas, 'Staatsbürgerschaft und nationale Identität', in *Faktizität und Geltung* (Frankfurt am Main: Suhrkamp, 1992) pp. 632–60.

4. R. Dahrendorf, 'Die Sache mit der Nation', *Merkur, Deutsche Zeitschrift für europäisches Denken*, no. 44 (1990) pp. 823–30.

5. T. Nairn, 'Der moderne Janus', in Nairn-Hobshawm (ed.), *Nationalismus und Marxismus* (Berlin: Rotbuch Verlag, 1978) pp. 28–9.

6. M. Hroch, 'From National Movement to the Fully-formed Nation: the Nation-building Process in Europe', *New Left Review*, no. 198 (1993) p. 15.

7. In this sense, for example, Hroch points out that Hungarian nationalists see the Hungarian minorities as hostages of the Romanian authorities, since the new constitution of Romania is the state of the Romanian nation, beside which there are still some smaller national minorities (Hroch, ibid., p. 18). The same problem arose for the Serbs in the new constitution of Croatia in 1990.

8. E. Gellner, 'Homeland of the Unrevolution', *Daedalus* (Summer 1993) pp. 141–54. See also Kadritzke, who says: 'The only astonishing thing is that so many analyses are astonished by the rise of nationalism.' N. Kadritzke, 'Die überraschende Widerkehr der Nationalismus', *Prokla*, vol. 87, no 22 (Juni 1992).

9. E. Gellner, 'Nationalismus und Politik in Osteuropa', *Prokla*, ibid. I would stress, however, that Gellner's statement is valid only for certain countries with low political cultures. In Hungary, for example, the liberal parties are relative strong in organization and support.

10. Hroch, op. cit., p. 11.

11. *Security for Europe Project: Final Report.* A Project of the Center for Foreign Policy Development (Providence: Brown University, December 1993) p. 12, 13.

12. Ibid., p. 52, 53.

13. Hroch, op. cit., p. 18.

15

East-Central Europe: business unleashed

Katarzyna Zukrowska

Economic relations between the Czech and Slovak Republics, Hungary and Poland after 1989 can be divided into several phases which were influenced by both political and economic factors. Those phases cover: (1) external effects of economic transformation down-sizing; (2) institutional decoupling; (3) introduction of new institutional measures; (4) reestablishment of mutual relations on a new basis.

This chapter examines developments within this group of East-Central European countries and attempts to answer the following questions:

1. Why do those countries form a separate group and is it a closed formation?

2. Was the collapse of mutual trade unavoidable?

3. Are the contacts recovering, what stimulates them and what can be considered as constraints on them?

4. Is it possible to restore mutual relations to their former levels?

SPECIFICS OF THE CHOSEN GROUP OF COUNTRIES

There are several considerations behind the choice of the Czech Republic, Poland, Slovakia and Hungary as specific examples of study of changes in East-Central Europe after 1989. It will be sufficient to mention only some of the most meaningful.

Firstly, those countries in the former communist bloc can be regarded as most advanced in reforms. Such evaluation does not arise from the fact that they began their departure from the former system in the same period. Systemic changes were set going by Poland in 1989 and were followed by Hungary (1989/1990) and Czechoslovakia (1990). Despite that fact, the label of being the most advanced countries in the transformation is well founded on an estimation of the depth of the reforms, measured by advancement of the stabilization programme, achieved rate of growth, attracted amounts of foreign direct investments or level of foreign reserves.

Secondly, those countries are geographically situated in the same area, which forms a natural inducement for cooperation. After World War II, they represented a relatively higher level of development in comparison with the remaining countries of the Soviet bloc. Czechoslovakia, Hungary and Poland were able to be less dependent on the Soviet Union in comparison with the others. This is mainly evidenced by the limited economic dependence in mutual deliveries.[1]

Thirdly, the countries in question have established similar external links, done more or less at the same time and with similar sequencing. It is enough to mention: primarily trade, and afterwards European Agreements, with the EU, membership in the IMF, World Bank, GATT/WTO, IBRD, EBRD. The Czech Republic became a member of OECD in 1995. Hungary and Poland joined this organization in 1996. Moreover, all these countries aspire to EU membership,[2] as well as to NATO.

Fourthly, this group of countries has established mutual institutional links both in the political and economic spheres. By reason of those institutional establishments of a regional character this group of countries is often called the Visegrad-4, the Visegrad Group or CEFTA.

Those terms are often used as synonyms, although to be precise Visegrad should refer to the political cooperation between Poland, Czech and Slovak Republic and Hungary, while CEFTA is a free trade area covering them all. Moreover, CEFTA has recently been expanding, which cannot be said of the Visegrad Group. As economic issues prevail in contemporary international relations, I shall concentrate on them.

Despite all their similarities the group is not considered as homogeneous or a closed club with a fixed number of members. On the one hand, its membership is diversified from the point of view of economic performance, while on the other, membership has been opened after some modifications were introduced to the original regulations for acceptance of new members. The growing interest in achieving membership in such regional institutions can be illustrated by Slovenia (a new member since September 1995) and the progress of talks with the Baltic Republics, Romania, the Ukraine, Belarus, Turkey and Israel.[3] This list indicates that a free trade area of the four most advanced countries in the transformation is an attraction not only for other countries of the region but also beyond it.

PHASES OF MUTUAL RELATIONS

Generally, four characteristic phases of economic relations in the ECE region in the period 1989–95 can be discerned. Practice shows that it is often difficult to make sharp divisions among the consecutive phases as they often occurred in parallel or were mutually overlapping. 1996 can be considered as the beginning of a fifth phase, which will determine the nature of future cooperation within the region. Factors which have to be taken into account in all attempts to arrive at some prognoses on this issue have to include external and internal elements, which are difficult to predict precisely. It is sufficient to mention the expected length and results of the EU intergovernmental conference which commenced on 29 March 1996 in Turin and was expected to end in June 1997 or future political developments in Russia – to list the most important political events.

The first phase covers the years 1989–90 in which the level of mutual contacts was declining due to replacement of political factors which, in the past, had determined the parameters of trade by economic ones, followed by specific adjustments. This phase is closely tied up with the stabilization policy pursued in each country in question. It led towards a concentration on domestic issues in which realistic prices, defined by market forces, have clearly shown all the negative consequences of a closed and protected economy, which created artificial conditions for the national markets. This resulted in a market of deficits, using the famous notion introduced by Kornai.[4]

The former system created a phenomenon which was called by many economists 'falling competitiveness'. It was caused by opening up the economy to EEC (EU) trade.[5] In reality, it was a clear uncovering of the sad realities in which a lack of competition and closed economy had created artificial competitiveness limited almost completely to the national market, characterized by monopolistic structures, additionally controlled by state through centrally fixed prices. The fall of domestic production and mutual turnover indicates that the economies in question were linked artificially and had to reestablish their existing ties on an entirely new basis, reflecting market signals.

The results of macrostabilization policy, which formed the basic precondition for systemic transformation of the economy has influenced directly both: (1) level of domestic production; (2) foreign exchange reserves of the country. All ECE economies can serve as classical illustrations of replacement and creation effects in their foreign trade. The fall in mutual turnover was one of the main effects in regional economic relations. Its explanation is rather simple. The countries in question had similar economic structures. Foreign markets, mainly those of EEC/EU, turned out to be more attractive for them. In other words, ECE countries did not have much to offer each other in the way of trade as their national outputs were similar. Collapse of mutual turnover also resulted in lack of financial resources that could cover mutual turnover. The absence of a properly developed banking system was an additional obstacle in this process. Barter transactions, which occurred as temporary solutions in the transition period, were of marginal importance in the total regional turnover. Reestablishment of normal trade relations was necessary as barter has limited possibilities to shape the branch structure of the economy or to lead towards intra-branch cooperation. Moreover, barter transactions are usually concluded with different price levels in comparison with normal, traditionally concluded credit transactions.

The second phase covers the years 1990–91, when both COMECON and WTO were dismantled. Both of the organizations had formed institutionalized links among the former communist countries, which were based on political relations even in economics.

The third phase started in 1991 when representatives of the governments of some of the former communist countries started to talk together, trying to establish new institutional links within the region. Institutionalization of regional contacts was strongly encouraged by western partners as a precondition for normalization of European relations. Moreover, it became clear that the existing asymmetry in external institutionalization has a negative impact on foreign trade in the region. Increase in external turnover was on the one hand a precondition of increased competitiveness, while being on the other hand a result of enhanced competitiveness, which became a fact in 1994 and 1995.[6]

The fourth phase started in 1993 with the initiation of CEFTA but real effects in mutual turnover were seen in 1994, 1995 and 1996.

The fifth, contemporary phase of mutual cooperation within the region has to solve several problems: (1) How far should the enlargement of the organization go? (2) Should CEFTA countries think about some kind of coordination in their efforts to join the western structures or should they act individually? (3) Is the base of economic relations in Europe limited to a free trade area which will combine the markets of the EU, the remains of EFTA and CEFTA or it will go beyond this form of liberalization following the pattern of the EU's proposed monetary union? (4) What is the best solution for ECE countries from their strategic point of view: to try to join the core of integration or stay on the periphery, developing gradually?

Table 15.1 Consecutive steps towards establishing CEFTA and its further development

Date	Decisions taken
15.02.91	Leaders from Czechoslovakia, Hungary, Poland meet at Visegrad Summit, agree to begin negotiations on establishing a free trade area
21.12.92	The Central European Free Trade Association (CEFTA) agreement is finally signed in Cracow after numerous delays during negotiations. The members signed a joint declaration to start immediate negotiations on speeding liberalization.
1.03.93	CEFTA goes into effect eliminating duties on about 40 per cent of industrial goods. The remaining goods are divided into two groups – not so sensitive and sensitive – with duties being very gradually phased out by 1 January 2001 at the latest. The agreement also specifies that the four members negotiate bilateral concessions in agricultural products, and negotiate on bringing down non-tariff barriers.
29.04.94	Under the Protocols of Budapest, members agree to speed up liberalization schedules, bringing final abolition of duties on sensitive goods forward three years to 1998. In exchange, governments get to select a few favourite sensitive industries to protect – including the automotive, textile, paper and metallurgical industries, plus some chemical products – which will retain duties until 2001 (or 2002 in the case of Poland).
1.07.94	The first instalment of reductions under the new schedule goes into effect, bringing the proportion of duty-free goods to over 50 per cent. Bilateral free trade agreements between Slovenia and Hungary, the Czech Republic and Slovakia also come into effect, following the same structure as CEFTA agreement.

25.11.94	At a summit meeting in Poznan, CEFTA members decide to hold further negotiations on speeding up trade liberalization and to tackle the thorny question of systematically reducing agricultural duties, with the ultimate aim of total abolition.
17-18.07.95	At the Warsaw summit meeting, CEFTA members adopted a new schedule which went into effect in 1996. Under this timetable, tariffs on not-so-sensitive goods were abolished on 1 January 1996; on sensitive goods on 1 January 1997 and on very sensitive goods on 1 January 2000 (except for automotive duties in Poland which still remain until 2002). Members have signed an agreement on liberalization of agriculture trade, dropping duties by 50 per cent from 1 January 1996. Further liberalization will proceed step by step until zero is reached in 1998. Plans are made on enlargement of the agreement (Bulgaria, Lithuania, Romania, Turkey, Israel, Egypt) as well as deepening of the processes (including transfer of capital and labour).
11.09.95	Poland signed a free trade agreement with Slovenia, opening the path for negotiations on official accession to CEFTA. Slovenia became the fifth member of CEFTA.
1.01.96	Duties are due to be abolished (if the new schedule is in place) for a major portion of industrial products, and dropped a further 25 per cent and 15 per cent of base for sensitive and very sensitive goods respectively. Agricultural duties should be cut across-the-board by 50 per cent.
12.04.97	Romania signs agreement on trade liberalization with CEFTA.
1.07.97	Romania becomes sixth member of CEFTA.

Source: *Business Central Europe*, July/August 1995, and information from current dailies.

Answers to those questions can be mutually contradictory, especially when given by supporters of integration or opponents who follow national solutions in the economy. Further enlargement is possible under one condition – that newcomers are advanced in their stabilization programmes. Coordination of policies towards the EU is possible but one should not expect excessive results in achieved conditions of adjustment programmes as they will be negotiated individually by each member country. Future economic relations in Europe should not be halted on the stage of the free trade area as contemporary conditions bring into play a set of trade barriers which act similarly to tariffs.

Neutralization of those barriers is shown in the process of deepening the integration in the EU. Moreover, the best strategic solution for CEFTA would be to join the core of the EU in further stages of integration as this would: (1) accelerate both systemic, development and structural changes; (2) give access to development and restructuring founds of the EU if they will continue to exist, which seems problematic; (3) enforce stabilizing signals. Staying on the peripheries of integration processes would play an opposite role in the transformation process, constituting an impulse to stagnation. In such circumstances peripheral development should be considered as the last possible solution on which those countries should agree. A free trade area of 70 million is a temporary solution in light of the possibilities of reaching agreement on access to a market of 450 million consumers.[7]

New mechanisms of integration should give access to financial resources and reward international cooperation, based on flexible industrial structures. In such circumstances all ECE countries should adjust their ownership structures to the new requirements, enabling an increased inflow of foreign capital. Moreover, they should put stress on policies enhancing their competitiveness by: (1) increasing educational efforts; (2) changing the social security system; (3) introducing high environmental norms into their production.

In sum, the purpose of establishing a free trade area among ECE countries is fivefold:

First, it is designed to establish new economic contacts among ECE countries that were loosened after introduction of the systemic reforms in the region and dissolution of COMECON, a step unavoidable with withdrawal from payments in transferable roubles; second, it is aimed at initiating cooperation in production among the manufacturers of the region as a preliminary step towards deeper integration within the European Union; third, it is supposed to hamper some of the negative effects of the decline in industrial production in the first period of transformation; fourth, it creates prospects for utilization of advantages of scale and lowers the costs of technology imports, helping to close the technological and development gap between the West and East. Moreover, it attracts foreign direct investments; fifth, it forms a platform on which experiences on transformation can be exchanged and policy coordinated.

THE INEVITABILITY OF COLLAPSE IN MUTUAL TRADE

The collapse of mutual trade in the region was unavoidable as: (1) in the past it was based mainly on a political framework; (2) it reflected the downturn in national production of the countries in question; (3) the market system has shown that the countries in question have similar economic structures which offer similar goods for exchange; (4) intra-branch specialization was lacking.

The mechanism which was put in motion in most of the ECE countries was very simple. Liberalization of trade was part of the 'shock therapy' for enterprises. The ensuing brutal competition, coupled with price liberalization and the loss of state subsidies, gave companies no choice but to streamline. Suddenly incapable of surviving on domestic sales alone, it forced firms to find new markets. As exports to the ex-COMECON markets had all but become impossible, Western Europe was the only major alternative. Only of late have the governments begun to enact *ad hoc* protectionist measures for some of their strategic and infant industries, ironically often as a result of pressure from its powerful investor lobby. Other industrial 'communities' might take note and follow this practice.

Foreign trade is playing an important role as a factor stimulating growth and pushing towards structural changes. Traditionally it is considered a source of foreign currencies which can be used to cover the costs of foreign credits drawn by the governments. The truth is that the trade balance is not only structured by so-called visible exports, as invisibles also play an important role. Their share in the total turnover is increasing. The experience of all the post-communist countries shows that it is not only the export of goods that brings money into the economy. Services and intellectual property play a growing role in the balance of payments of developed countries. This is reflected in the GATT Uruguay Round, which ended in 1993. For the first time such fields of international turnover as regulations on transfer of intellectual property, capital, services and so on, were discussed in order to pursue three goals: (1) liberalize the international turnover in those specific categories, so very different from the traditional turnover in goods; (2) to protect exporters of those goods, by guaranteeing them fair payment; (3) approaching the problem of unification of regulations on those issues.

Table 15.2 Polish trade with CEFTA partners in million dollars

Year/ Country	CEF-TA Total	% of total trade	Value			% of CEFTA total		
			Cz	H	Slk	Cz	H	Slk
1994	919	4.3	502	221	196	54.6	24.0	21.4
1995	1625	5.6	892	252	381	54.9	21.7	23.4
1996/I	464	5.7	260	80	88	56.0	17.3	18.9

Source: CESTAT 1996, p. 66.

All CEFTA countries are approaching a stage of depreciation of their national currencies which is sometimes called 'appreciation' and which results in improving finances. This tendency is evidenced in the three consecutive stages of defining the national exchange rate which can be clearly seen, for instance, in Poland: first, at the start of the reforms, when exchange rates were fixed for a certain period of time; second, when fixed rates were replaced by gradual devaluation; third, when fluctuation was introduced: firstly by a certain rate each month, secondly the banking authorities started to diminish the monthly devaluation rate gradually.

Table 15.3 Polish foreign trade turnover by groups of countries (current prices) in per cent

	Total	Developed Countries	EU	EFTA	East & Central Europe	CEF-TA
Imports						
1981	100	37.3	21.1	4.3	49.6	-
1989	100	46.9	30.9	9.8	33.5	-
1990	100	63.8	43.9	10.2	23.2	-
1992	100	72.4	53.2	12.9	16.3	-
1993	100	76.2	57.2	11.2	13.5	3.6
1994	100	75.1	57.5	11.3	14.3	4.3
1995	100	74.3	64.7	10.6	15.4	5.6
Exports						
1981	100	34.5	22.4	6.5	46.3	-
1989	100	43.0	27.9	8.7	37.2	-
1990	100	58.6	44.3	9.3	23.2	-
1992	100	71.9	58.0	10.3	15.4	-
1993	100	75.1	63.2	7.9	13.3	4.8
1994	100	75.4	62.7	8.2	14.5	4.8
1995	100	75.0	63.8	1.6	17.3	5.4

Source: Rocznik statystyczny handlu zagranicznego 1996, [Statistical Yearbook on Foreign Trade], GUS, p. 5.

The exchange rate in all those three phases plays a stabilizing role in the economy. Most clearly it is seen in the first stabilizing phase of the transition but also fulfils this function during other phases of the transformation.

The exchange rate helps to import stabilizing tendencies from the world economy. It slims down false signals and induces acquisition of information on required structural changes to the economy. The strength of the signals depends on two things: (1) the width of openness; (2) the strength of the market sending the signals (internal and external, linked by different institutional solutions within the national economy of a country).

The width of the openness of the economy in all ECE countries is different, a fact conditioned by historical factors, the economic situation at the starting point of the reforms, as well as acquired strategies for change. Up to the end of the 1980s, the degree of centralization in external relations was not the same in ECE countries. The most liberal models were found in Poland and in Hungary, the most centralized in the former Soviet Union and former Czechoslovakia. It is worth stressing that centralization of foreign relations was not everywhere reflected by the relative scale of openness in the economy. In Poland, the economy was traditionally less open than in Hungary or in former Czechoslovakia.[8]

The state of openness of the economy in each case was a function of the scale of the internal market and the self-sufficiency of production. In turn, this has a further impact on at least two areas:

First, the level of competitiveness of the economy.[9] More open markets were able to compete more easily with partners from market economies. Their engagement in the international division of labour was higher. Moreover, the gap between the supply and the demand on the international market was relatively smaller, in other words it was easier to establish realistic prices, reflecting not only costs but also the relations between the supply and demand;

Second, the applied model of transformation of the economy. In relatively more closed economies full openness was required, while in formerly more open economies full liberalization was not considered a precondition of systemic changes in the economic sphere.

The results of the different strategies, concerning the width of openness, speak for themselves after five years of application. All CEFTA countries show positive economic indicators in 1994, 1995 and 1996. Poland achieved an increase in industrial production in May 1992, that is two years and five months after application of the 'shock therapy'.[10] The stabilization phase of the transformation is being replaced by a restructuring phase, in which external factors are gaining new weight and meaning in comparison with the former stage.

The openness of the Polish economy can be measured by liberalization of trade, decentralization of trade and introduction of internal currency convertibility. Moreover, in the first period of transformation the protection of the market by tariffs was temporarily suspended and the market was protected only by the undervalued exchange rate of the zloty. This instrument has increased the competitiveness of Polish goods, stimulating exports and halting imports. In the next stage of transformation, when a negative trade balance occurred, the market was protected by tariffs, which were reduced gradually according to the reduction of customs duties, which were agreed within regional arrangements (European Agreement, CEFTA and EFTA) as well as within GATT/WTO agreement.

At this stage, the mutual turnover of ECE countries is recovering. Although the process is slow, it indicates that regional cooperation is possible and makes sense under several conditions: (1) that the countries in question start to identify their mutual interests; (2) that they have goods which can be traded; (3) they develop infrastructure for mutual contacts; (4) that they do not become entrapped in barter exchange and forms of relations which increase mutual turnover but do not have any impact on the restructuring of the economy.

PROSPECTS OF RETURNING TO THE FORMER LEVEL OF TURNOVER

Return to the former level of turnover is possible but only in value terms, not in terms of share in the total turnover. This statement is based on the growing openness of the economy which is accompanied by accelerated development, measured by increase of GNP rate as well as by share of foreign trade turnover. The branch structure of the economies in ECE countries defines, in a way, the dynamics of future turnover. Prospects of some increase, but very modest in scale, can be seen in foreign direct investments, creating a new branch structure in the economies, coupled with a new competitiveness in products and production and increasing intra-branch division of labour. The ECE economies are gravitating naturally towards stronger economic centres, which are suppliers of advanced technologies and the goods produced by them. This natural tendency is reflected by fall in the share of the eastern markets and increase in the western ones.[11]

The limitations to increase the share of Eastern Europe in foreign trade are various and can be divided into several categories: (1) economic; (2) political; (3) historical; (4) external and internal.

Generally, the external relations of the ECE countries after World War II can be divided into several phases:

The 1950s. A period of reshaping external relations under influence of the USSR, a world super-power which, after Yalta, gained control in the region of East Central Europe. ECE countries gradually had to withdraw from all international economic and financial institutions, establishing some regional substitutes, which were based on political not economic concepts of cooperation;

The late 1960s. A time of slow return to or attempts to participate in some international economic institutions like GATT, later IMF and IBRD;

The late 1980s. The full establishment of foreign institutional linkages evidenced by membership in formerly forbidden organizations;

The 1990s. Suppression of regionally established institutions;

1990s. Establishment of new regional institutions, based on economic conditions.

We can expect that, in the longer run, common economic interests will create conditions which can bring the countries from the ECE region closer together. This assumption is based on three preconditions: (1) all those countries reshape their economies in close relations with the European Union and all want to become full members of this organization; (2) in a longer perspective, Europe will become a free trade area compressing all regional arrangements in free trade into one free market; (3) there are prospects for global liberalization of trade in the light of GATT/WTO arrangements, as well as taking into account the solutions of global governance in which the United Nations and its specialized institutions will play a new, coordinating role.

In such circumstances, a long-term horizon for our predictions shows that closer cooperation within the region is unavoidable. Its depth and speed of development depend heavily on the depth of systemic changes and process of adjustment. If we look at the post-communist countries today, it is difficult to estimate their degree of advancement in the transformation process, as they can be measured by different indicators, not all of which are precise. Such a claim sounds somewhat heretical, but it is indubitably true. The reason for the imprecision of instruments of measure lies in changes of the economy, difficulties in gathering statistics, processing them and the limited possibilities of making comparisons over a long period. Moreover, international comparisons enlarge the existing difficulties in this specific sphere. Traditionally, the rate of GNP growth is considered as an accumulative indicator of change.

Table 15.4 Changes of GNP in ECE countries

Country	1994	1995	1996	1997
Bulgaria	1.4	2.5	2.5	3.0
Czech Rep.	2.6	4.0	5.0	6.0
Hungary	2.5	1.0	3.0	4.0
Poland	5.2	6.5	5.5	5.0
Russia	-15.0	-4.0	2.0	4.0
Romania	3.4	3.0	4.0	4.0
Slovak Rep.	4.8	6.0	5.0	5.0
Slovenia	5.5	4.5	5.0	5.0

Source: OECD, quoted from *Zycie Gospodarcze* no. 2 (12 January 1996) p. 23.

This specific indicator can often be misleading, as lack of decline in industrial production is also one of the signs that the economic system has not been changed. Moreover, a fall in production by 50

Katarzyna Zukrowska

per cent which is accompanied by an increase of unemployment by 1–2 per cent is the best proof that market forces are not functioning.

The best way of making international comparisons is to use the same yardstick. The fulfilment of Maastricht criteria can best serve this purpose, as they indicate on the one hand the depth of systemic changes in ECE countries, while on the other hand, they show that those countries are using the same language (despite some differences in deduction of the indicators of convergence criteria between Poland and EU) in the field of economics, attempting to come closer towards the European Union.

Table 15.5 ECE countries and realization of the Maastricht criteria

Country	Rate of inflati- on 1995	Budge- tary balance	Date	Dis- count rate	Date
Bulgaria	51.9	-5.6	1994	34.0	1995
Czech Rep.	7.6	1.0	1994	9.5	1995
Estonia	28.4	0.0	1994	n.a.	-
Hungary	27.8	-6.8	1994	27.0	1995
Lithuania	35.7	-2.0	1994	29.7	1994
Latvia	26.5	2.0	1994	25.0	1995
Poland	22.3	-2.8	1994	25.0	1995
Romania	30.8	-3.5	1994	41.9	1995
Slovak Rep.	6.1	-4.2	1995	9.8	1995

Source: *Business Central Europe*, December 1995/January 1996, p. 65.

The ECE countries represent a lower level of development in comparison with the EU members. There is no doubt about that. If left to themselves, or located on the peripheries of EU integration processes, they will be condemned to vegetation and with very limited prospects of catching up with the standards of living in EU member states. This kind of solution cannot be considered acceptable. Acceleration in development of ECE countries is possible but there are certain conditions under which this can be achieved. Some of those conditions have to be implemented by the

ECE countries themselves, others with help of the international organizations and their constitutive country members. It is clear that such processes are underway and they have brought about spectacular results, which can be seen not only in the stabilization achievements but also in structural changes (ownership and branch) of economies in the post-communist region. Normalization of the conditions of cooperation within the region is also one of the signs that things are moving forward in the right direction.

In sum, it is clear that countries in ECE exhibit a similar level of development and face similar problems in their transformation, although their progress in the reforms differs much from case to case. This creates conditions for their keeping together, although the EU is the centre of their natural gravitation. All those common denominators form a basis for identifying the existence of interests, which can be used in the coordination of their foreign policies. All those common aspects of foreign policies are not only confined to economic factors but embrace other important matters which, until now, have yet to be resolved satisfactorily, such as the security and military aspects of pan-European cooperation.

CONCLUSIONS

Answering the question if integration in this region is possible and desirable, I have to say: *YES*. But this does not mean that it is an easy task that can be solved overnight. There is no doubt that any integration process is a time- and capital-consuming venture. The costs of such undertakings are always higher in an economically underdeveloped country than in a prospering nation. Any integration limited only to the region of post-communist countries would create only weak marketization impulses, and that is one of the reasons why ECE countries are gravitating towards the European hub in Brussels. Regional integration must be viewed in connection with pan-European processes. Those processes, despite their costs, are advantageous for Eastern and Western countries as they stimulate market impulses, forcing structural changes in both groups of countries. In both cases, those changes are stimulating development and an increase in living standards. The ECE region is recovering slowly from the transition depression and there are prospects that other ECE countries will follow. The Polish economy, which has been ascending the path of prosperity since Spring 1992 with a GNP increase of originally 2 per cent and recently 5 per cent, is thus a leader in transformation as far as stabilization measures are concerned. Moreover, this country was the first to reach the level of GNP of 1989, before the transformation depression.

The competitiveness which is a changing factor in the economy, is created by competition in an open market economy. In such circumstances, regional integration can play a twofold role: speeding up the processes of economic change and adjustments – creating a bigger and more effective field than any national consumer market, and can ease the tensions caused by external shocks brought about by signals from the stronger economies. All barriers and limiters of integration within the ECE region should be precisely identified, discussed and approached by politicians as challenges which have to be overcome. In parallel to some institutional arrangements introduced by the politicians, market forces are doing their job and creating wealth by finding niches in which enterprises can compete and find opportunities for further development.

Economic cooperation within CEFTA is a small segment of wider processes in the region, subregion and world-wide. All of them were set up by the end of the Cold War. Not all of them are proceeding without victims. They are accompanied by huge costs but in the long run their effects will override today's burdens and inconveniences. Creation of a free trade area in Europe is only a small step towards closer relations among European countries and part of a world-wide liberalization of trade.

NOTES

1. M. Dobroczynski, 'Istota integracji Europy Srodkowowschodniej', paper presented at *All-Polish Conference on CEFTA and Economic Integration in Europe*, Warsaw, 22–24 November 1995.

2. Hungary, Poland as well as Czech Republic and Slovak Republic had formally applied for the membership.

3. A. B. Kisiel-Lowczyc, 'CEFTA: Srodkowo-Europejskie Porozumienie o wolnym handlu', in E. Oziewicz (ed.), *Wybrane problemy procesow integracyjnych we wspolczesnej gospodarce swiatowej* (Gdansk: WUG, 1995) p. 87. See also A. B. Kisiel-Lowczyc, CEFTA: Srodkowo-Europejska Strefa Wolnego Handlu, (Gdañsk: WUG, 1996).

4. J. Kornai, *Droga do wolnej gospodarki* (Warsaw: Fundacja Polska Praca, 1991).

5. J. Misala, 'Competitiveness of Polish Products on market of the European Union Member Countries', paper presented at IRiSS conference *Towards Increased Competitiveness and Development*, Warsaw, 27 October 1995; D. Rosati, 'Zmiany w strukturze handlu towarami przetworzonymi miedzy Polska i Wspolnota Europejska', *Materialy No 49* (Warszawa: IKiCHZ, 1994).

6. B. Wyznikiewicz, 'Competitiveness of Polish Manufacturing Industry: 1986–1992', paper presented at the IRiSS conference, 27 October 1996.

7. E. Oziewicz (ed.), *Wybrane problemy...*, op. cit., p. 88.

8. P. Bozyk, *An Evolutionary Mode of Transformation of External Relations*, World Economic Institute, no. 114 (October 1994) p. 1.

9. 'Emerging Market Economies Report 1993', *The World Competitiveness Series 1993*, World Economic Forum, IMD, p. 23.

10. *Eastern Europe: Reforms Spur Recovery, Hearings of the Subcommittee on Technology and National Security of the Joint Economic Committee*, Congress of the United States, 15 July 1994.

11. W. Iskra, 'Rynki Wschodnie i ich znaczenie dla krajow Srodkowoeuropejskich', paper presented at *All-Polish Conference on CEFTA and Economic Integration in Europe*, Warsaw, 22–24 November 1995, p. 8.

CONCLUSION

16

The post-communist world: a conceptual framework

Bogdan Goralczyk

The collapse of the communist system in East-Central Europe (ECE) in 1989 and the Soviet Union two years later was an epoch-making event. A profound change has occurred, something to be mentioned in history textbooks as one of the major watersheds in the history of the twentieth century. Probably no one questions the enormous portent of this change. This kind of fundamental change, however, cannot be achieved only by one powerful blow, it must be a process; a highly complicated process of systemic transition from dictatorial system to democracy, as well as deep socio-political transformation of society.

POST-COMMUNIST TRANSITION

Collapse of the communist system brought with it a deep crisis of the theories of social systems, both in the East and the West. Visibly, there exist a lot of confusion and disorientation as far as the description of radical post-communist social change is concerned. One can agree with Edmund Wnuk-Lipinski, who wrote in answer to the question: Is a theory of post-communist transformation possible? – 'I am convinced that the complex and multi-faced character of transformations initiated by the collapse of the communist system cannot be placed within the framework of one theoretical system.'[1]

It is not this author's aim, in this study, to offer a theoretical framework of post-communist changes, either. It is rather a pragmatic attempt, based on practical observations, to clarify a few terms and systematize radical processes occurring in the post-communist territories.

The very subject of post-communist transition and transformation, multidimensional in nature and highly complicated by its character, encourages – to quote Edmund Wnuk-Lipinski again – 'utilization of theoretical eclecticism, which more elegantly can be labelled as the multidisciplinary approach and in the more ambitious version as the interdisciplinary approach'.[2] This is exactly the task of this volume – to provide comparisons for several post-communist states, undertaken by political scientists and economists mainly from ECE countries. The editors of the volume also had in mind a supplementary directive, that hypotheses need to be verified in more than one country undergoing systemic transformation of the same type.

Even from a current – therefore narrow – perspective, it is already evident that the new democracies in ECE require a lot of learning by doing, reactions for a quick process of radical socio-political change without a theoretical framework. Thus, this process of sudden shift from clearly non-democratic regimes to mass democracy is different from classical democratization processes in the nineteenth and early twentieth centuries. According to Leszek Balcerowicz, until the recent post-communist transitions, we had four types of systemic transitions:

1. *classical transition*, meaning the extension of democracy in advanced capitalist countries between 1860 and 1920;
2. *neoclassical transition*, referring to democratizations in basically capitalist countries after Second World War (West Germany, Japan, and Italy) and later (Spain and Portugal in 1970s);
3. *market-oriented reforms* in non-communist countries (mainly Far Eastern 'tigers' and some Latin American states);
4. *Asian post-communist transition* of China and Vietnam.[3]

Post-communist transition has a number of features distinguishing it from other previous transitions; for example, the unprecedented scope of changes, extreme information overload, massive administration turnover, and – first of all – simultaneous political and economic transitions which produce a historically new sequence, meaning that comprehensive economic reforms have to be introduced under democratic, or at least pluralistic, political arrangements. However, the requirements of the democratic system, the rule of law and observance of human rights – paradoxically – work against deep economic transformation and quick creation of private ownership.[4] In any event, the new democracies in ECE have produced a unique new sequence of events: mass democracy first, and market capitalism later. All four transitions in history, as described by Balcerowicz, had exactly the reverse sequence of events.

What exactly does transition in ECE mean? According to Robert M. Jenkins, four central elements of systemic transition can be identified, as follows: (1) a split within the regime between hard-liners, those wishing to perpetuate authoritarian rule, and soft-liners, those realizing that some freedoms must be introduced; (2) pact-making, or negotiated agreements among a select set of actors over changes in the rules governing the exercise of power; (3) popular mobilization, which occurs in response to liberalization and under certain circumstances creates pressures for expanding the limits of liberalization; and (4) founding elections, which bring parties to 'center stage in the political drama'.[5]

TRANSITION VERSUS TRANSFORMATION

From this perspective, the most classical form of post-communist transition has occurred in Poland and Hungary, where all four stages of it, as described above, are easy to specify. In other ECE countries those transitions were more or less the same.

According to the dictionary definition, transition is a movement or passage from one position, state, stage, subject, concept, to another. The term 'systemic transition' gives us the answer to a vital question: 'Transition from what to what?' – from 'real socialism' into an, as yet, unspecified post-communist category of state, under 'transformation'. 'Transition' brings a change in the system, 'transformation' is the process of change proper.

As such, the 'transition' in ECE is done, is over: no one here seriously takes into consideration any scenario of return to the previous, completely discredited, humiliated and defunct system. The system has been changed while the whole 'transformation' process has only just been initiated, and is at a different stage in each post-communist country or territory. 'Transformation', understood in this way, suggests that we do not know when, where and how this change will end. Transformation is the task for all post-communist states for years, maybe decades, to come.

COMMON CHALLENGE IN THE INTERNATIONAL ARENA

During this unprecedented process of radical change, post-communist societies, which moved from authoritarian 'real socialism' to multi-party democracies and transformed command to market economies, need to act simultaneously and as quickly as possible to achieve parliamentary democratic order, the rule of law, civil society, create a middle class and new strata of entrepreneurs. Those newly created 'open societies' (Karl Popper) must replace an over-centralized planned economy by an economy led by market mechanisms. They must also change directions of their trade and search for new economic partners, be ready to absorb foreign capital, and be able to cooperate with any international institutions. At the same time post-communist societies have to replace their prior security system, both internal and external. Moreover, there is a need to change social behaviour and the entire mentality of citizens. Individualistic activity, creativity, responsibility and risk, all of them almost destroyed by the previous system, must be encouraged in an effort to replace passive absorption of directions from above.

It is not surprising that while it is simply impossible to achieve all the above simultaneously, every maverick country of the former Soviet bloc is trying to find its own, individual path, searching independently, without blueprints, examples, efficient mechanisms, theoretical suggestions and frameworks or previous experiences. No one else in history has departed from communism to democracy. That is why this transformation is at the same time unprecedented, pioneer by nature, while also complicated – and dangerous. Only the final goal is obvious: to create a normal, efficient democracy in Western terms. The whole winding road to modernized, post-communist societies is – up to now – unknown. It was much easier to be done with the totalitarian system than to win through to democracy.

In such circumstances one has to add that ensuring the success of political and economic transformation of ECE countries constitutes one of the greatest challenges now confronting the international community, not only those countries undergoing transformation processes. This is the so-called 'Europeanization' challenge, which – up to now – has been highly disappointing from ECE's perspective. According to Attila Agh, the whole process makes the populations of ECE disillusioned: (1) because of the lack of interest on the part of Westerners; (2) because of the contrast between words and deeds; and (3) because of the short-term thinking versus a long-term perspective in the West's approach to the Central European Region.[6] Agh goes even further, writing elsewhere: 'It would be an illusion to believe that Western Europe could remain an island of wealth and peace while the young democracies of Central Europe face the danger of political defeat, economic backwardness, ethnic bloodbath. No wall can protect the democracies of Western Europe from the consequences of an unsuccessful reform movement in the East.'[7] The success of the ECE transformations must be a common goal for all Europe.

FROM ONE-PARTY SYSTEMS TO PARLIAMENTARY DEMOCRACY

Competitive multi-party systems emerged in all former Soviet bloc countries quickly and easily. Brief experience with their performance leads to the conclusion that it is much easier to establish a party than to create professional party politicians ready to lead the process of transformation. The political scene has crystallized in – more or less – Western terms, with clear division of the political scene into Christian-Democrats, Social-Democrats, Liberals, Nationalists and Populists. Still, that does not mean that those political parties are crystallized, or easy to define. Most of them are in the process of creation, self-discovery and self-definition.

In every post-communist country a clear distinction between 'parties of reform' and 'parties of frustration' have emerged. The former have democratic and Western-oriented attitudes and programmes, the latter are trying to achieve their goals by exploiting wide-spread social frustration, dissatisfaction, and even disgust at the heavy social cost of transformation (the previous, even if not perfect, social security net has been dismantled and not replaced by any new version). The former are trying to act and behave according to democratic rules, whilst the latter have more charismatic leaders (V. Zhirinovsky in Russia, J. Torgyan in Hungary, L. Moczulski in Poland, to mention but a few) and many traces of the previous system in their activity (black-and-white Manichean scenarios and explanations of events, readiness to search for scapegoats to blame for the heavy social costs of transformation, and so on).

The same division – 'reformers' versus 'the frustrated' – explains to a certain extent why some 'post-communist' politicians prefer nationalistic, authoritarian and ideological solutions (prevalent – until now – in the territories of former Yugoslavia and the USSR), while the others are trying to establish real multiparty systems (especially in ECE).

Most of the post-communist states, probably with the exception of the Czech Republic, had long-term authoritarian traditions in both institutional and political culture.[8] That was confirmed and prolonged by four (in ECE) or seven (most of the former Soviet Union, except the Baltic states) decades of 'real socialism'. As a result, it has been extremely difficult to democratize the political macro-sphere. The previous reflexes led to 'overpoliticization' of the whole transformation process.

Memories and reflections of 'real socialism', its social habits, nostalgia for the previous social security net, led to a revival and return of the former 'communists' to power, after a few years of interposing rule by the former anti-communist opposition. This has happened even in Poland, a country which justly boasts of a long history of anti-communist revolts in 1956, 1970, 1976, 1980–81. Post-communist forces emerged from former communist parties, renamed themselves as Socialists, or Social-Democrats, and then democratically won multiparty parliamentary elections. However, even the 17 December 1995 elections to the Russian Duma won by open Communists were described by the American State Department as 'an encouraging and positive development', because – according to this assessment – the elections were conducted in a 'free and independent manner' and represented a 'strong indication of growing pluralism'.[9]

The 'return of the communists' was the price of the enormous transformational burdens, and the lack of political experience of the new post-1989 political elites. According to Aleksander Smolar, analysing the success of post-communist Aleksander Kwasniewski over legendary leader of Solidarity, Lech Walesa, in the presidential elections of November 1995, the 'people are searching for some familiar points of reference. The feeling of nostalgia begins to be shared not just by those who had been privileged under the old regime, but also those who have suffered the most recently: be it because of unemployment, a fall in living standards, the loss of a sense of security or of their social status.'[10] No one had ready answers for the new, emerging challenges of the post-communist era, while the requirements of the democratic system are completely different to the challenges faced by the opposition elites during 'real socialism'. Now, creation and construction, not destruction, are at the top of the new agenda.

ESTABLISHMENT OF THE RULE OF LAW

With the exception of some territories of the former Soviet Union, and – as a politically different category – the former Yugoslavia, which 'went to war', there was no major problem in establishing the pillars of a modern institutional framework for democracy: the highest officials of government came to depend, directly or indirectly, on popular elections; elections were on the whole free and fair; freedom of expression was relatively well protected, as well as the right to form independent organizations, including political parties; citizens had access to alternative sources of information not under control of the government or otherwise monopolized; there is a visible growth in the role of the judicial system and, especially, constitutional Courts.

On the other hand, one can readily identify some major current problems in these spheres:

1. The problem of how to consolidate those achievements.
2. The need for Parliaments to devote a comparatively larger amount of their time for supervision of government activities.
3. While most of the parties in ECE are immature, there also exists a kind of institutional deficit. Some internal parliamentary institutions, including structures and procedures are missing or have been only partially created.

Here one can find an important source of diversification of the post-communist countries. There can be no question that transformation towards the rule of law will be a long-term process. However, at least among the leaders of transformation, that is, the Visegrad Group states (the Czech Republic, Hungary, Poland and Slovakia), Slovenia or even the Baltic States, there is one very positive 'accelerator', a requirement of legal system harmonization as a first step towards full membership of the EU.

Most of the post-communist ECE countries have established 'checks and balances' in practical terms; they have a bill of rights but still need to work out modern constitutions, as a pre-requisite of a new, democratic order. As such, they are not yet modern Western democracies.

EMERGENCE OF CIVIL SOCIETIES

State control over society was a paramount feature of the communist system, thus communication between ruled and rulers always had an enormous meaning. Slowly, as the utopian Marxist-Leninist experiment started to fail, and party-state control began to wane, some dissident counter-movements began to play a role in shaping the reality of the Eastern bloc. The question: 'What came first – the decline of the communist system, or grass-roots activism against predominance of the party-state?' is still vital and unresolved, with one exception. The pressures to yield ground to opposition behaviour led to a re-emergence of embryonic civil societies, which were the catalyst for change in 1989–91 and proved to be stronger than the communist leadership's capacities to resist them. In consequence, as Adolf Bibic rightly observed: 'Recent theoretical reflections on civil society and democracy have strongly stressed the crucial importance of civil society for democracy, democratization and democratic theory, especially with regard to the transition from authoritarian rule to democracy.'[11]

The very existence of 'civil society' was a problem identified in ECE countries at least from the late 1970s and in the Soviet Union after the inauguration of Gorbachev's *perestroika* and *glasnost* strategy in the mid-1980s. In the Eastern bloc there were the Polish and Albanian extremes. In the Soviet Union, the fundamental change as far as civil rights were concerned began only with the Gorbachev era. One of the major differences between dissident movements trying to fill the gap between state and society in former Soviet Bloc countries and the Soviet Union proper (as well as in former Yugoslavia) was that the former were mainly political, religious or social movements, while the latter were also to a large extent ethnically motivated. The whole 'internationalistic' theory of Leninism led finally to ethnic tensions and some grass-roots counter-reactions, and later – after the collapse of the system – led directly to a search for scapegoats outside their own ranks, and to facile black-and-white explanations of former and current problems. The result has been a new wave of nationalism, that is, a continuation of former anti-democratic behaviour and way of life.

There is no doubt that minorities (as well as migrants) have become a major social and security problem on post-communist territories. Probably the only wise attitude towards this highly complicated – and growing – problem is to treat the demands of minorities and ethnic groups to organize, administer and govern themselves not as a destabilizing factor, but as a way of reducing tensions and preventing further explosions. Another, important method of resolving this question is the entire, so-called Europeanization process.

In many regions (the Balkans, Caucasus, Central Asia, even the Baltic states and Hungary) national minority questions have once again become the centre of gravity of new democracies. Here and there, the process of 'nation building' re-emerged as the crucial task of the early-post-communist era. Without resolution of minority and ethnic questions, the ghost of authoritarianism may reappear in nationalist form, as has already happened in the territories of former Yugoslavia and the Caucasus.

TOWARDS THE MARKET ECONOMY

Politicization of every area of life under the communist system was almost proverbial. In every walk of life one could easily find political connotations. The party-state was 'Big Brother' in all domains. As Valerie Bunce has correctly observed, original 'Stalinism redistributed power from the Soviet Union to Eastern Europe and from the party to society.'[12] As such, the system was slowly liberalized, while the redistribution of power thus created led directly to its being undermined and finally rejected.

Further liberalization after change of the system produced tremendous social costs in the post-communist economic transformation, a fact less well-known in the West and even difficult to imagine there. Just one example. According to Janos Kornai, the economic crisis of post-1989 in Hungary was deeper and wider than the great crisis of 1929–33; if one takes the level of 1929 as 100, in 1932 it diminished to 96.2 per cent of GDP and to 81.9 per cent in industrial production, while the level of 1989 taken as 100 was diminished in 1992 to 80.9 per cent (GDP) and 63.8 per cent (industrial production).[13]

After the change of the system, there were some radical economic reform attempts made especially in Yugoslavia and Poland in 1989, Russia in 1992, the Czech Republic and Slovenia in 1993. Some of them collapsed, some of them (Poland, the Czech Republic, Slovenia, and later the Baltic states) proved very successful, confirming the correctness of radical rather than gradualist approaches to reforms. *In any event, economic results, measured by all major indicators in the years 1990–95 everywhere confirmed that shock or gradual approaches notwithstanding deep recession, budget deficits and macroeconomic decline, are strongly linked with post-communist market experiments and transformations.*

It is absolutely certain that everyone must pay for the previous monstrous economic mismanagement of 'real socialism'. Rejection of the whole former economic system, both in institutional and managerial terms, has proved not to be identical with immediate economic growth, and has created, instead, a much larger than expected recession. This has led to social disillusionment, and later – in the majority of cases – to the return of 'communist forces' to power. This unexpected return does not mean, however, that they want to reestablish the former system. Rather, 'post-communists' want to reduce the social costs of transformation. Whether this aim is achievable and, if so, how to do so, still remain open questions.

In some aspects it may be easier now than immediately after the change of the system. According to comparable statistical data for 1995 in ECE countries which apply similar methods for producing statistical statements, one can already observe not only negative (high inflation and unemployment rates, high budget deficit to GDP) but also very positive phenomena, such as – at least in some ECE countries, if not all the approximately 25 countries under post-communist transformation – rather impressive economic growth or very rapid development of the private sector.

THE CREATION OF THE MIDDLE CLASS OR NEW STRATA OF ENTREPRENEURS

So called 'embourgeoisement' had already started under the previous system. The Hungarian experience in this domain was especially rich. Later, the same kind of attitude towards wealth creation without implying the restoration of capitalism has been found in the mainstream of market reforms in the communist China of Deng Xiaoping. Poland, with its mainly private agriculture of family entrepreneurs, was also carrying out this 'silent revolution' in everyday practice over decades.

'Embourgeoisement' in Hungary, Poland, Yugoslavia and China was more or less an attempt to find their own models, a 'third way' with mixed economies. As one of the theoreticians of the 'third road', Ivan Szelenyi wrote in mid-1980s: 'Hungary is moving towards a mixed economy and dual system of social stratification which is distinguishable from both Western capitalism and Soviet-style socialism.'[14] These were the reforms *within* the previous system in which directives from above met with some kind of 'revolution from below', at least in economic life. When 'real socialism' collapsed, those attempts lost their previous vital meaning (with the exception of China and Vietnam), but the experience gathered this way was not in vain. Many new real capitalist entrepreneurs emerged directly from the 'socialist entrepreneurs' of the previous decade. As one can observe, those countries which first allowed the creation of a middle class, so crucial for the market economy, emerged as the leaders of post-communist market reforms.

CREATION OF OPEN ECONOMIC SOCIETIES

Under the COMECON order, 'trade' was predominantly of a radial nature; that is, each country of the bloc was heavily dependent on the dominant partner, the Soviet Union, which served as raw-material and energy supplier for its satellites. The Soviet Union also served as a receptive market for low-quality manufactured goods from ECE. This kind of 'integration' collapsed due to the disintegration and economic collapse of the Soviet Union itself. Institutional, systemic reforms reoriented most of the former Soviet bloc countries towards the Western community, which was also an absolutely necessary step towards modernization.

Since the implementation of the economic transformations, it has been obvious that the internal forces of any post-communist economy are insufficient to achieve the goals of transformation. Large-scale and well thought-out strategic assistance from external sources was – and still is – absolutely vital.

Most ECE countries have already signed Association Treaties with EU, but the queue is still a long one. Not everyone applying can count on eventual free-trade zones with the EU, even in the distant future, while everyone would like to participate and share Western well-being as soon as possible. This is one of the most dangerous fault-lines on the European continent in the post-Cold War period. Instead of the 'Iron Curtain' and the Berlin Wall, the spectre of a 'prosperity Wall' has emerged on the horizon.

Immediate liberalization of some ECE economies and their extensive opening to Western trade, market and capital at the outset has led to rapidly shrinking GDPs and demand for domestic sources and goods. Those economies were not competitive and hardly prepared for an immediate opening. As Zita Maria Petschnig has rightly observed: 'The state has already no capital, the new private sector is still too weak, while foreign capital – due to integrational constraints – refrains from deeper involvement [in ECE].'[15]

Post-communist countries initiated reforms in 'distorted' capitalist circumstances, that is, their economic transformation process, to quote Leszek Balcerowicz:

> consists of many interrelated transitions: from public ownership toward private, from industry toward services, from an economy dominated by large enterprises to one with many small firms, from seller's markets to buyer's markets (including the labour market, where open unemployment replaces hidden unemployment), and from CMEA product standards toward world market standards. Another fundamental change is to

transform the financial sector from a passive player to an active one and to desocialize risk-bearing.[16]

Most crucial of all is the process of privatization during which the behaviour of governments, domestic entrepreneurs less well supplied with capital, and Western investors are very important. To some extent, a new *Catch-22* situation has appeared: reorientation of economies and trade to the West can be made only at the cost of some domestic interests. Most of the elites and societies in ECE countries (as the results of public opinion polls confirm) are pro- rather than anti- strong cooperation with the West. They know well that when trying alone, prospects for modernization and 'Europeanization' are not bright. However, the Eastern transformations should not be a one-way street. As Andras Inotai and Magdolna Sass argue in a study on economic integration of the Visegrad Group with the EU:

> The future of intra-regional contacts among the Visegrad countries predominantly depends on two, certainly interrelated issues: the success (or failure) of the transformation process and the type of relations with the EU, as the main modernization pole for the region [...], development of intra-regional trade among the Visegrad countries will be the consequence of successful integration into the world economy (particularly the economy of Western Europe) and not the precondition for it.[17]

A NEW SECURITY SYSTEM

The 'defence mentality' of the West is also clearly expressed in Western security concerns. The collapse of the Soviet-dominated system has abolished the old European security system. Many former Soviet bloc countries are openly applying for NATO membership, while – from their perspective – NATO seems not to be ready to meet the completely new challenges of the post-Cold War era. First of all, NATO itself must be redefined and find its own place in completely new circumstances, a fact confirmed by an authoritative source: 'Since these events [the end of the Cold War –

B. G.], which have transformed the political situation in Europe, the security requirements of the members of the Alliance have fundamentally changed. However, as events have proved, dangers to peace and stability remain.'[18]

Some ECE countries after the change of the system have found themselves in a 'security vacuum', with no guarantees of their external security, while the number of new challenges is increasing. Organized crime and mafia activity, weapons and arms trade, the spread of environmental pollution, local conflicts, and even danger of nuclear fall-out, represent just a few of the new problems faced by these countries. While previously the dangers and threats were mainly external and military, now internal security and non-military threats are predominant in post-communist states.[19]

A visible lack of strategic thinking in the West[20] has met with some unpredictable, even chaotic, events in the East. Only close cooperation supported by an efficient, clear-cut and reliable Western assistance programme for the modernization of ECE is going to produce more mutual benefits. The 'Partnership for Peace', launched at the NATO Summit in Brussels in January 1994 is a proper initiative to enhance stability and security on the whole European continent. From the perspective of ECE countries, the PfP Programme has a strategic meaning as a chance to expand NATO eastward. Of course, this must be an evolutionary process with the new NATO memberships at the end, rather than at its beginning. Happily, what is important, the process of the creation of a new security system in Europe, has already begun.

The NATO connection and the whole idea of expanding the Treaty is crucial for ECE countries when viewed from yet another perspective. As many specialists in post-communist countries argue, the current security environment is even more dangerous in some ways than in the days of the Cold War, when at least the former Soviet military threat was largely localized, predictable and controlled. Now the situation is fragile and easily reversible. All of Europe has entered into a turbulent transition period, characterized by increased tension and instability, while instability as such is a major security problem in its own right. What should be done? According to Adam Daniel Rotfeld:

> In the former security system, based on military alliances that mobilized states against a clearly defined opponent, enemies were known and menaces recognized. The security systems now sought are intended to organize states not against anything or anyone but rather in defence of common values. The new system cannot be founded on a balance of power and fear but must be based on prevention of conflicts, the nature and sources of which are different from those in the past and not yet fully understood.[21]

Currently, until a new security architecture in Europe has been established, NATO seems to be the only security institution with capabilities for dealing with ethnic conflicts or other urgent missions (as in Bosnia-Hercegovina). This is why most of the post-communist states are again standing in line, applying for NATO membership.

CONCLUSION

One of the reasons why the closed societies of ECE and the former Soviet Union were opened was the growing gap between the oversimplified and distorted image of reality promoted by the totalitarian (later, authoritarian) state and the genuine complexity of society. It was too wide to be tolerable. At the same time, a huge 'modernization vacuum' was growing. From the late 1970s, high-tech products and services strongly started to reshape international relations. All this led to a major crisis, which, at least in ECE (and up to now) assumed the form of implosions ('velvet revolutions'), instead of real, bloody revolutions. In any event, the whole process of change is unquestionably revolutionary and still far from over. This is a radical change of social systems.

Immediately after the 1989–91 changes came the sobering reality confirming the existence of several 'vacuums': ideological, modernization, political, economic, security, but, first of all, mental and psychological, which is obviously an umbrella for all the other 'vacuums' and challenges. The mentality of the people has a crucial meaning in every domain of post-communist transition and transformation. It was precisely the mentality of citizens (if they were citizens in Western terms) that was extensively destroyed by the previous system. One can argue whether *Homo sovieticus* still exists, but some psychological results of long-term indoctrination have remained in the behaviour of every individual citizen. Thus, absolutely crucial is freedom from previous constraints; people in post-communist countries need to change their behaviour from passive absorption of directions from above into individualistic activity, responsibility and risk.

Having that in mind, as a conclusion to this study one can propose that the whole post-communist transformation is in effect a 'quintuple revolution' of five, strictly interconnected and simultaneous processes, namely:

1. *Democratization*, which, to use Adam Michnik's term, is an 'institutionalization of freedom' process, consisting of the creation of a multi-party parliamentary democracy, the rule of law, civil society and proper institutions for them.

2. *Marketization*, together with modernization and opening to the world, which – in the case of ECE – means especially the EU.

3. *Nation-building*, which means creation of an open society internally and a secure country externally; in some cases, such as the former Soviet Union, Yugoslavia or Czechoslovakia, new independent states emerged with a priority goal of being included in the international community.

4. *New international environment*. A crucial matter for newly independent states (prior to that they were part of a unified bloc) is to avoid finding themselves in a security vacuum, while dealing with a completely new neighbourhood. Reorientation of foreign policy to the West, symbolized by the term 'Europeanization', comes together with the necessity of 'modernization'; that is, catching up on the modern world and the new high-tech revolutions, which evolved mainly outside the Soviet bloc.

5. *A mentality revolution*, which is absolutely crucial for the success of the first four programmes. Without a change of mentality

of the people the whole post-communist transformation cannot be successful.

All of the challenges, specified above, are equally important. What complicates the case is that those efforts must be made as quickly as possible and simultaneously. Neglect in one dimension can directly lead to distortions in others. The events of 1990–96 in ECE confirm that, enormous difficulties notwithstanding, there is already a visible progress. Those are the countries on the right track, while continuing the 'Valley of Tears Journey', as Ralph Dahrendorf once termed the process. Transformations are far from over, but many positive changes already observed leads us to the final conclusion that one can be cautiously optimistic as far the future of the ECE region is concerned (which is not exactly the case for the whole post-communist world).

This volume is devoted to the subject, of how transition, transformation and deep socio-political changes in the post-communist world, and especially ECE, during the years 1989–96 can be evaluated. To a certain extent a scheme of 'quintuple revolution' has been adopted by some co-authors.

NOTES

1. E. Wnuk-Lipinski, 'Is a Theory of Post-Communist Transformation Possible?', in E. Wnuk-Lipinski (ed.), *After Communism: A Multidisciplinary Approach to Radical Social Change* (Warsaw: Institute of Political Studies, Polish Academy of Sciences, 1995) p. 6.

2. Ibid., p. 15.

3. L. Balcerowicz, *Socialism, Capitalism, Transformation* (Budapest–London–New York: Central European University, 1995) p. 145.

4. I. Szelenyi, D. Treiman, E. Wnuk-Lipinski (eds), *Elity w Polsce, Rosji i na Wegrzech: Wymiana czy reprodukcja?* [Elites in Poland, Russia, and Hungary: Exchange or reproduction?] (Warsaw: Institute of Political Studies, Polish Academy of Science, 1995) p. 189.

5. R. M. Jenkins, 'Society and Regime Transition in East-Central Europe', in Gy. Szoboszlai, *Flying Blind: Emerging Democracies in East-Central Europe* (Budapest: Hungarian Political Science Association, 1992) p. 115.

6. A. Agh, 'The Europeanization of the ECE Polities and the Emergence of the New Parliaments', in Attila Agh (ed.), *The Emergence of East-Central European Parliaments: The First Steps* (Budapest: Hungarian Centre of Democracy Studies, 1994) p. 10.

7. A. Agh, 'From Competition to Cooperation: The Europeanization and Regionalization of Central Europe', in *Integration and Disintegration in Contemporary Europe* (Budapest: Institute for Political Studies, Hungarian Academy of Sciences, 1995) p. 58.

8. G. Schöplflin, *Politics in Eastern Europe* (Blackwell, Oxford [UK]–Cambridge [USA] 1993) pp. 5–37.

9. J. Collins, a senior coordinator for the New Independent States. *Wireless File: A Bulletin of the Embassy of the United States in Budapest*, 20 Dec. 1995.

10. A. Smolar, 'Polish Elections' in *Institute for Human Science (IWM) Newsletter*, Vienna (September–November 1995) p. 23.

11. A. Bibic, 'Democracy and Civil Society', in A. Bibic, G. Graziano (eds), *Civil Society, Political Society, Democracy* (Lubljana: Slovenian Political Science Association, 1994) p. 53.

12. V. Bunce, 'Democracy, Stalinism and Management of Uncertainty', in Gy. Szoboszlai (ed.), *Democracy and Political Transformation (Theories and East-Central Europe Realities)* (Budapest: Hungarian Political Science Association, 1991) p. 143.

13. As quoted by J. Ladanyi and I. Szelenyi, 'Egy posztkommunista "New Deal" eselyei' [Chances of post-communist New Deal], *Kritika* (December 1995) p. 32.

14. I. Szelenyi, *Socialist Entrepreneurs. Embourgeoisement in Rural Hungary* (The University of Wisconsin Press, 1988) p. 17.

15. M. Z. Petschnig, *Oröksegtöl öröksegig: A Magyar gazdasag 1990–1994* [From heritage to heritage: Hungarian economy 1990–1994] (Budapest: Szazadveg, 1994) p. 11.

16. L. Balcerowicz, *Socialism, Capitalism...*, op. cit., p. 220.

17. A. Inotai, M. Sass, 'Economic Integration of the Visegrad Countries. Facts and Scenarios', *Working Paper*, no. 33 (Budapest: Institute for World Economics, Hungarian Academy of Sciences, 1994) p. 27.

18. *NATO. A Handbook* (Brussels: NATO Office of Information and Press, 1995) p. 21.

19. J. Stefanowicz, 'Central Europe between Germany and Russia: A View from Poland', *Security Dialogue*, vol. 26, no. 3 (March 1995) p. 60 and following.

20. As Ch. Bertram writes in the above issue of *Security Dialogue*: 'NATO is not on track for the 21st century. Instead it is in deep, enduring crisis and may not even reach the end of the decade', ibid., p. 65.

21. A. D. Rotfeld, 'The Fundamental Changes and the New Security Agenda', in *SIPRI Yearbook 1992* (Oxford University Press, 1992) p. 2.

Index